THROWIN FREE

SIMON & SCHUSTER

HOW THE EAST GERMAN SPORTS MACHINE

MOLDED, TRAINED, AND BROKE AN

OLYMPIC HERO AND HOW

HE WON HIS FIGHT

FOR FREEDOM

William Oscar Johnson and Anita Verschoth with Wolfgang Schmidt

New York   London   Toronto   Sydney   Tokyo   Singapore

Simon & Schuster
Simon & Schuster Building
Rockefeller Center
1230 Avenue of the Americas
New York, New York 10020

SIMON & SCHUSTER and colophon are registered
trademarks of Simon & Schuster

Designed by Caroline Cunningham
Manufactured in the United States of America

1 2 3 4 5 6 7 8 9 10

Library of Congress Cataloging in Publication Data
Johnson, William Oscar.
Thrown free : how the East German sports machine molded, trained, and
broke an Olympic hero and how he won his fight for freedom / William
Oscar Johnson and Anita Verschoth with Wolfgang Schmidt.
p.   cm.
1. Schmidt, Wolfgang, date.   2. Track and field athletes—Germany,
East—Biography.   3. Discus throwing.   4. Sports and state—Germany,
East.   I. Verschoth, Anita.   II. Schmidt, Wolfgang, date.   III. Title.
GV1094.S36J65   1991
796.4'35'092—dc20
90-22884
CIP
ISBN 0-671-68094-3

[B]

PART 1

THE BERLIN WALL CAME DOWN IN THE AUTUMN of 1989, and the people of the German Democratic Republic began a life in which all things were possible: free elections, free speech, free markets, free men.

But at the time of which we are writing—the summer of 1982—the GDR was still a totalitarian country ruled by cruel and paranoid men. Ever since the formal division of Germany in 1949, citizens of the GDR had remained cowed and docile inside their police-state cocoon.

Yet, at the same time, the leaders of the German Democratic Republic had remained fearful and insecure. They trusted no one. Not their Cold War enemies to the west. Not their comrade communist states to the east. And least of all, their own citizens.

They built The Wall through the heart of Berlin in 1961 and turned their country into a vast penal colony. They created a capricious system of criminal law that could be manipulated to make the most whimsical political criticism punishable by a prison sentence. Merely mentioning that one wished to go to the west was a constitutional crime. The East German writer Monika Maron once wrote, "They criminalize your dreams."

Much as they hated the West, the leaders of the GDR were starved for recognition from the outside world. Since neither their industry nor their culture offered anything worthwhile to people not already mired in socialism, they decided in the early 1950s that the best way to attract attention was through sports. They set out to develop an army of world and Olympic champions. It turned into an athletic blitzkrieg. In the past thirty-five years, the GDR, with a population of just 16.7 million people, has won more Olympic medals (572) than any other countries in the world except the two superpowers—the US (872) and the Soviet Union (1,133). Their hated brothers in West Germany, with three times more people and infinitely more money, have won only 335.

But after the leaders of the GDR perfected their assembly line of athletes, they couldn't bring themselves to trust the champions they had created. The exposure of these athletes to the free world frightened them. Ultimately, their sports system became a by-product of their paranoia. They melded together the national sports machine, known as the DTSB (short for Deutscher Turn- und Sport-Bund), and the national secret police, known as the Stasi (short for Staatssicherheitsdienst), which were a latter-day version of the gestapo. Sooner or later the Stasi touched the lives of just about everyone in East Germany. But because of the regime's sinister amalgamation of sports and spooks, the elite athletes of the GDR were more harassed by the secret police than the average citizen was—more than the average criminal for that matter. There were always informers around—teammates, coaches, doctors, trainers, sports club officials, even ostensibly adoring fans. Athletes' sex lives were routinely investigated. Their mail was monitored. Whenever they left the country to compete, they were trailed by Stasi watchdogs.

Most of East Germany's superstars accepted these violations of freedom and privacy without complaint. No one wanted to risk losing the special privileges that sports stardom guaranteed in the GDR. No one wanted to test the limits of Stasi wrath.

Well, almost no one.

This is the story of the man who did—Wolfgang Schmidt, a 6'6¾", 253-pound blond giant who held the world record in the discus throw at the time of which we are writing.

S CHMIDT AWOKE LATE FROM UNEASY DREAMS
and arose, not knowing that his life was about to be transformed
in a terrible way. It was July 2, 1982, a glistening summery Friday
in East Berlin.

He was alone in his family's apartment. His parents had earlier
left for their summer house on the edge of the city. Schmidt had
been restless in the night and his sheets were twisted and damp.
He felt tired, utterly uninterested in the day that lay ahead. He
had spent the previous night, until three A.M., at a discotheque
called Mocca-Eck. Long hours at the disco had become a nightly
habit in recent weeks. The Mocca-Eck was a deadfall for Schmidt,
a place he used to kill hours, numbing his brain with loud music
and repetitious conversation with the same two male friends every
night. He didn't have a girlfriend at this time. His life had fallen
into a profound state of inertia.

He brushed his teeth slowly and he shaved slowly. He dressed
slowly, pulling on a plain white T-shirt, a pair of Levi's jeans,
and a pair of Adidas athletic shoes. He slowly packed his training
bag with clean socks, a clean T-shirt, and the wide leather girdle-

belt he wore around his waist when he threw the discus. That
was about all he did in the apartment that morning. He did not
read a newspaper, he did not listen to the radio, and he did not
eat breakfast.

Somehow—Schmidt could not remember exactly how—he
consumed more than two hours from the time he got up until
he was prepared to exit the apartment at precisely 1:15 P.M. He
was caught in a limbo that sapped his energy and preoccupied
his mind:

My life had no point that year. I had been disqualified from my
sport for no good reason I could understand. I was always wondering, What the hell will become of me? I was still in very good
condition, but what good was a strong body without a sport to use
it? Sometimes I felt like a ghost with no hope and no energy.

Yet beneath his lethargy, Schmidt was seething.

He was only twenty-eight and still capable of finishing first in
any world-class event he entered. Yet he had been forbidden to
compete. He had even been forbidden to train seriously. He had
committed no serious political gaffes, flunked no drug tests, suffered no injury to warrant his removal from sport.

Late in March, they had suddenly given me *Sportverbot*. This is a
word that existed only in East Germany. It meant that they had
banished me from practicing high-performance sport for the state.
They had told me that I no longer fit into the system. *Sportverbot?*
For the world-record holder? I didn't take them seriously. Yes, I had
broken rules. Yes, I had a big mouth. Yes, I had lost the national
championship in 1981 by a few inches to a lucky lummox who got
off the throw of his life. Yes, it was no secret that I had a few friends
in the West. But I was the best in the world.

The dirty pigs, the assholes, the bastards! They had given me
permission to continue light training at my old club—the Sports

Club Dynamo Berlin—but it was to be only for the purpose of "warming down," to allow me to bring my body back to normal from extremely high performance sport. They let me keep a room at the club where I put my clothes. They let me eat my lunch there.

Each day I slept late, drove to the club for lunch, did my bit of training, had coffee and cake at a café, then walked around town with my friends. I spent my time with Steffen Müller, a world-class walker, and Ulf Leischner, a discus thrower who trained with me. We went walking in the vicinity of The Wall almost every day. Sometimes we would go to one of the high rises on Leipziger Strasse. We'd take the lift to the twentieth floor. From there we could look across The Wall into West Berlin. We would talk about how easy it would be to fly over there with a hang glider.

In principle, my life was like being on leave or vacation, but it was not that. I hated every minute of it.

Even as he moped about the apartment that morning, the trappings of his fame were everywhere. Glassed cases were filled with trophies, medals, and crystal baubles given to him for victories over the years. There was a photograph framed in silver on the wall showing him shaking hands with the First Secretary of the GDR, Erich Honecker. Other photos showed Schmidt in action at competitions throughout Europe and the world. The apartment was a little like a shrine to his athletic achievements.

Outside, parked at the curb, was another trophy, a sporty, white, Russian-made Lada 1600. It had been a gift to Schmidt only seven months before from none other than Erich Mielke, the minister of State Security, the nation's number one Stasi, who also happened to be the president of Sports Club Dynamo since it was sponsored and funded by the nation's police.

How could I take them seriously? They wanted medals, I gave them medals. I really believed that *Sportverbot* was only a ploy, that they were trying to break my spirit, to make me a sheep like all the others in their damned pen. I really believed it was only a trick.

At quarter past one on the dot, he left the apartment as he always did. SC Dynamo stopped serving lunch at one-thirty and he liked to arrive at the last minute.

He descended one floor to the street. His parents' apartment house was located at Stahlheimer Strasse 4 in a comfortable residential section of East Berlin called Prenzlauer Berg. Many of the buildings dated back to the 1920s and 1930s. They had escaped the rain of bombs that had leveled much of the city at the end of the war.

There were leafy vines climbing the front walls of most of the apartment houses, and an occasional small tree grew along the sidewalk. Schmidt knew every building, every tree, every crack in the sidewalk. He had lived here from the day he was born, romped beneath the laundry hanging in the backyards, and hooked rides on the trolleys that rumbled on tracks along the street.

The day was clear and bright. He strode a few yards to the Lada, climbed in, and pulled away for the familiar trip to SC Dynamo. He drove slowly for two blocks down Stahlheimer Strasse, then swung right into Wisbyer Strasse, a slightly busier thoroughfare. East Berlin traffic moved at a turgid pace with ample room between cars on even the busiest thoroughfares. Still, there were traffic policemen standing on almost every corner. They wore white caps and shiny white coats that fell to their ankles. They were called *weisse Mäuse,* white mice, and since the flow of cars rarely caused a problem, their sole duty seemed to be to bark threats at the occasional pedestrian who tried to cross against the light.

On Wisbyer Strasse, Schmidt passed the *weisse Mäuse* and entered the thin stream of traffic. He glanced into his rearview mirror and was startled.

Not two meters from my rear bumper, I saw a dark red Volkswagen Golf. Two men were in it, and immediately I thought, Are they following me? I had seen cars following close for unusually long distances two or three times soon after I had been categorized "not fit for the system." I never knew if they meant to be there or not. I thought maybe I was imagining things. This time I decided to find out for sure if they were after me.

I didn't take my normal route to the club, but continued on Wisbyer Strasse. The light was green and I crossed Prenzlauer Allee, the main thoroughfare, and then I quickly turned right on Sültstrasse, a tiny, narrow street, only one lane wide with cars parked on both sides. No one would follow me at that corner unless they were chasing me.

The red Golf turned with him and stayed glued to Schmidt's rear bumper as he sped along for two blocks on tiny Sültstrasse. Schmidt slowed for a stop sign at a larger thoroughfare, Erich-Weinert-Strasse, and the Golf pulled up close behind him. He could see the driver glaring at him. Schmidt floored the gas pedal and swung left on Erich-Weinert-Strasse, his tires screeching. The Golf followed, also screeching.

A block later, Schmidt zigged right onto Gubitzstrasse, a fairly busy street, then zagged left onto Grellstrasse, a major thoroughfare. Schmidt watched anxiously in his rearview mirror. The Golf stayed close behind.

I stomped on the gas and raced along Grellstrasse at a hundred and twenty kilometers per hour. And still they followed. I hit heavier traffic. I had to slow down, and every so often I had to stop at a red light. It was easy for them to stay on my tail. I drove four blocks on Grellstrasse, and when I got to Greifswalder Strasse, I quickly turned left. Now I was on my normal way again to SC Dynamo.

I looked in my mirror. I saw a motorcyclist behind me, but I didn't see the red Golf at that moment, and I thought maybe I had lost them. I stepped on the gas again to put some distance between them and me. But then I realized that the motorcyclist was part of the chase, too. He was wearing black, all black leather, with a black helmet and big dark goggles, and he was riding a small, fast machine, very fast. He pulled up until he was riding next to me, very close to my car door on my left side. He hung right there maybe a meter away. He looked at me furiously.

Schmidt was pretty sure he couldn't outrun the motorcycle, but he stepped on the gas again anyway and watched his speedometer touch a hundred kilometers per hour. The bike easily stayed at his side. Greifswalder Strasse was a big street with double lanes on each side of a wide center boulevard where the trolley lines ran. The buildings were no more than four stories tall and not thickly built. The street name changed to Klement-Gottwald-Allee after several blocks. Schmidt sped ahead, weaving past cars here and there, holding a treacherous speed of one hundred kph. The motorcyclist didn't fall back an inch. Schmidt kept watching in his mirror for the red Golf, but it was no longer there. Then, suddenly, he spotted a welcome sight in the mirror.

I saw that a green-and-white police car was speeding up behind me. It had no flashing lights on it, but I knew that it was from the police because of the colors. The motorcycle was still exactly at my side. I thought to myself, Well, now you must slow down, old boy. You can't drive so fast anymore with the police here. I eased my foot on the gas pedal and soon the police car was only a meter or so from my back bumper.

The presence of the squad car changed the nature of the chase for Schmidt. Things were no longer quite so sinister. At least he knew who they were. Schmidt, after all, was a salaried officer in the Volkspolizei, the People's Police known as the VP. Because SC Dynamo was the sports organization of the nation's police, Schmidt had been inducted into the VP at nineteen, issued a uniform, and put on full salary. Schmidt had started with the rank of patrolman and was now a second lieutenant. He had worn his uniform exactly three times in his life—each time he got a promotion. He never worked a minute as an actual policeman.

Unfortunately, being a VP under these conditions was not necessarily an advantage when dealing with real police officers. Many of them resented having their service used as a front to pay off pampered athletes.

We continued to drive along Klement-Gottwald-Allee. The police car remained very close and the motorcycle hugged my side. I turned right into Indira Gandhi Strasse. Now the club was only a kilometer or so down the road on the left. I thought maybe they would simply stay with me as an escort until I arrived at Dynamo Berlin, but then the police car suddenly swung out wide, speeded up to pass me, then cut sharply in across my front bumper. I slammed on my brakes. The motorcyclist stopped sharply next to my door. The police car blocked my way. I started to get out, but first I took another look in my rearview mirror. Coming up behind me, I saw more cars, two, maybe three. The red Golf was leading them.

The caravan had come to a halt on Indira-Gandhi-Strasse, a major thoroughfare with trolley tracks down the center, where it intersected with Bizet-Strasse, a smaller residential street. No sooner had they all pulled over than Schmidt saw two other cars move slowly out of Bizet-Strasse to block the corner. Obviously, this spot had been preselected by Schmidt's pursuers as the point to pull him over. But it seemed an oddly impractical choice. Indira-Gandhi-Strasse curved here, and traffic tended to bunch up. Also, there was a trolley stop in the center of the thoroughfare at exactly that point. There was a pub on each side of Bizet-Strasse not ten meters from Schmidt's car. Across the main thoroughfare was a brick wall, beyond which lay a hospital and a cemetery. All in all, it was a busy, visible spot to take a wanted man into custody.

Three policemen in green uniforms jumped out of the squad car and hurried to Schmidt's car. Other car doors flew open and more men poured out until the street corner was quite crowded.

Schmidt counted no fewer than thirteen men waiting for him when he stepped out of his car.

He drew up to his full height, expanded to his full width, and gazed down at them. The impact of his physique produced a brief tick of hesitation in the movements of the smaller men before they gathered around him, forming a cordon.

Schmidt said lightly, "All this for me? I must be incredibly important."

A uniformed VP was neither cowed nor amused. He said sharply, "You will come with us!"

Schmidt said, "Where to?"

The policeman snapped, "No questions! Just come along!"

Schmidt said, "I am not coming along anywhere."

The policeman spoke more tentatively, "Don't make trouble."

Except for the three officers in uniform, all of Schmidt's captors were in plain clothes, all Stasi, he assumed. A small group of people at the trolley stop across the street were watching curiously, but they were careful not to seem too inquisitive. They knew who the grim men in the plain suits were as well as Schmidt did.

None of the Stasis spoke during the sidewalk confrontation, only the uniformed police officer. He said again, "Don't make trouble. Come with us! Now!"

They had never asked for my papers and they never did call me by name, but I knew this was definitely not a case of mistaken identity. They wanted me, and even though they were wary, I knew they had come prepared to fight with me if necessary because there were so many of them. They had planned to take me any way they could—trussed up and unconscious or upright on my own two feet. I could see a rubber truncheon lying between the front seats of the police car.

Then a VP reached out and gripped my arm. It startled me and I yelled, "Don't touch me! Let go!" I tore my arm free, and he leaped back as if I had fired a pistol.

When I have thought about the situation since, I sometimes wonder what would have happened if I had fought them and fled. Maybe I could have gotten away for a time, but I knew that if the Stasi wanted me, they would get me. Sooner or later, if not today at the corner of Indira Gandhi and Bizet, then some other time, at some other street corner.

So I relaxed and told them, "Okay. Where are we going?" They told me to park my car on Bizet-Strasse. I drove it around the corner. I took out my gym bag and locked the car. Then I got into the police car with the three policemen. I was sitting in the rear. The truncheon still lay between the front seats.

Schmidt's shoulders filled two-thirds of the backseat, crowding the frowning young police officer who sat next to him. Schmidt's long legs were sharply bent and cramped against the front seat. The officer in the passenger seat stared straight ahead. His hand lay close to the truncheon, but he did not touch it. The driver maneuvered the car quickly through the city streets, heading toward the southern districts of East Berlin. Schmidt turned once and looked out the rear window to see if the other cars were following. The red Golf was close behind. The rest of the escort was strung out behind it.

They reached the autobahn after driving through an industrial section close to The Wall, then rolled on out the open, level highway for perhaps twenty minutes through wooded countryside dotted with farms. The fields were bright green in the summer sun.

Schmidt was not frightened. He was irritated at the delay in his training. He asked his captors if they would have him back in Berlin in time for him to train that afternoon. They did not reply. He tried to relax, but the cramped conditions in the backseat made it difficult. He looked at his watch. It was not yet two-thirty in the afternoon. Just over an hour ago he had left his parents' apartment with no thought in his mind except to drive to the Sportforum at SC Dynamo for his boring little workout. Now he was squeezed into this rolling sardine can with three policemen. He felt a slight claustrophobia rising, and he turned to study the sun-drenched landscape along the autobahn.

The squad car swung off the highway and cruised on a two-lane road through the medieval villages of Mittenwalde and Gallun. Schmidt turned again and saw that the red Golf was still gone, although two cars still followed. They continued along the narrow road, which was lined with a majestic row of tall trees. After a few miles, a woods appeared on one side of the road, and Schmidt caught glimpses of a body of water shining through the trees. This, he knew, was the Motzener See, a lovely three-mile-long lake whose gently wooded shores were dotted with the dachas and villas of Berliners seeking a little peace and beauty outside the city.

The police car moved sedately along past fenced-in lots lined with plots of flowers and many pretty little villas decorated with window boxes full of geraniums. Some of the villas were not so little. There were some large, white Italian-style structures with perhaps ten rooms that might have belonged to government ministers. On the sides of the road vacationers ambled along barefoot, wearing bathing suits and summer frocks. Bicyclists pedaled along at a leisurely pace. Through the trees and beyond the villas, Schmidt could see boats on the lake and people picnicking here and there along the shore.

At last the caravan slowed and turned off the narrow concrete road onto a gravel driveway leading into a heavier section of woods. Within a short distance, they came to two sentries standing in the road. They stopped so the guards could scrutinize the occupants of the squad car as well as the two behind, then they rolled on. A moment later, they came to a gate set in a ten-foot fence made of crisscrossed barbed wire. There were two sentries here, too, who let them through the fence after the proper identifications were made.

Not far beyond the barbed-wire fence Schmidt saw what looked to be another modest two-story villa on the shore of the lake. It seemed to have recently been constructed, but looked much like the others he had seen. The squad car stopped. The three officers got out quickly and gathered at the back door as Schmidt was let out. The other two cars pulled up, and the four Stasis in them also gathered menacingly around him to cut off any attempt to escape. They escorted him quickly toward the villa.

Now Schmidt took a closer look at the building and realized that it bore only a superficial resemblance to the other recreational retreats on the lake. This one was made of concrete blocks, and all the windows were equipped with steel bars. Clearly it was a prison.

Once inside, Schmidt was surprised again. The first-floor rooms were furnished like a summer home, with overstuffed furniture, plastic lamps, curtains, carpets, and a television set. He was even more surprised when the three policemen ushered him upstairs to a room that was to be his cell. It contained a bed made up with a flowery bedspread, a large built-in closet, a table, four chairs, and another television set.

It was like an average citizen's bedroom except the windows were barred. When I looked out through the bars, I could see trees, and beyond them the blue water of the lake. It was strange. I could see people swimming out there, frolicking in the water. It was a beautiful day.

Two men in civilian clothes joined Schmidt and the three policemen in the second-floor room. They were staff guards. They looked like low-level Stasi should, neutered and nondescript, the kind of faceless losers Schmidt thought of as *Null Acht Fünfzehn*. The term, which means "oh eight-fifteen," was the title of a trilogy by Hans Helmut Kirst about an army private's battle with the absurdities of the German military system in World War II. The term had long been a popular term for nonentities. The *Null Acht Fünfzehn* stared at him with brazen curiosity. One of them held a ring of keys in his hand. After a few moments, the Stasis and the policemen left the room. The door closed with a sharp click. Schmidt heard a key turn once, then he heard another door click shut and another key turning in another lock. The room had double doors, double-locked.

Schmidt stood silently, gazing at the inner door for a minute or so. Then he called out, "I will have to call my parents to tell them what's happening."

A voice sounded through the doors, "There is no phone here."

"But I must call if I am to be here more than a very short time."

"No phone."

He tried again. This time there was no answer. He pounded on the door and shouted, but there was only silence outside.

Schmidt went to the window. He lay on the bed. He got up immediately. He paced the small room. He tried the television. It didn't work. He was outraged, confused, angry, frightened; then he began to be hopeful. It had been a mistake. Or a joke. Or a lesson to teach him humility. Or perhaps it was more practical. A week later, there was to be in Karl-Marx-Stadt the first dual meet ever between the GDR and the United States. Perhaps the Stasi were holding him until that was over so that he wouldn't attend as a spectator and spill his story of *Sportverbot* and banishment to American athletes and journalists he knew.

He pondered all this. After a time, he convinced himself that he would soon hear keys turning in the doors as they came to let him out. He listened closely. He put his ear to the keyhole. No one came, so he pounded on the door. There was no sound out there, but he could clearly hear the cheerful shouts of swimmers and picnickers on the lake. He looked out the barred window again at the robin's-egg sky and the bright green leaves and the happy people in the shimmering water. He fought down a wave of panic, then a wave of grief.

The time was passing very slowly. I had a cracking sensation in my head, as if gunfire were going on in there. I experienced a great melancholy that seemed about to drag me down beneath the earth. And I wondered, *Why? Why? Why?* None of this could be true. I felt I was watching a movie about someone else.

IF THERE WAS ANY MOVIE PLAYING ON THIS DAY, it was the story of Schmidt's life, and it was running backward. It was as if all the discuses he had ever thrown were flying in reverse, leaping up off the stadium turf and rising airborne backward to the apex of the curve, then drifting down until they snapped back into the clutch of his hand as he rotated backward in the throwing circle, slower and slower until he came to a stop, and strode backward away from the throwing cage, away from all the competitions he had ever entered, away from all the medals he had ever won, until he disappeared backward through a door under the stadium and none of his heroics had ever happened.

Schmidt had been a certified national hero of the German Democratic Republic for virtually all of his adult life. He had won his first national discus throwing championship for youths in 1969 when he was fifteen and the junior championship in 1972 when he was eighteen. He had won the senior national championship and the Europa Cup in 1975 when he was twenty-one. He had won the silver medal at the Olympics in Montreal in 1976 when he was twenty-two. He had won the Europa Cup twice more (1977 and 1979), and the World Cup twice (also 1977 and 1979). He was the European champion in 1978 and set the world record that same year when he was twenty-four.

During the surreal decades of the Cold War when no war could be fought among major powers for fear of blowing up the world with nuclear weapons, winning at sports had become a substitute for winning in battle. By those standards, Schmidt was a heavily decorated soldier of the German Democratic Republic.

He was recognized everywhere. Despite his great size, he moved with the grace that God gives only to jungle cats and natural athletes. His eyes were gray-green, and his features could have been taken from the statue of a Greek god. He possessed a big radiant smile that often lighted his face without warning and made him look carefree as a boy. He wore his blond hair long. The West German press had long ago dubbed him "Sunny Boy," and a few reporters from the GDR used the sobriquet, too.

Men envied his size and his indomitable masculinity. Women found a subtler quality that men didn't know about: tenderness. A woman who knew Schmidt as a friend explained, "For a man so muscular, he was very gentle. He never gave you a bruising hug, only a sort of warm cuddling that was so sweet it made you want to stay inside those big arms for a long time."

When he wasn't numbed by the lethargy of *Sportverbot,* he was a passionate, rampaging fellow who was quick—very quick—to share with the world whatever mood happened to strike him. He tended to raise his voice in public. His outbursts—of either anger or happiness—were often embarrassing to friends and strangers alike. He was a practical joker with a high hooting laugh. Model sports heroes in the eyes of the East German state were sober, stoic, obedient. No matter which side of his personality was on view—the sunny or the stormy—Wolfgang Schmidt never exhibited the sycophantic style preferred for socialist athletes.

I was proud of our system when I won, but I didn't get myself psyched up for a competition by memorizing Marxist-Leninist slogans. I never thought before a meet, I've got to go out there and win for communism. I liked winning for the GDR, yes, because I was proud of how powerful we were in sports. But first I wanted to win for myself, second for my family, and maybe third for the GDR. Maybe not third. If I had ever sat down and really thought seriously about whom I was winning for, I doubt that Marxism-Leninism would have been fourth or even tenth on the list. I would have won for a girlfriend or a friendly competitor or maybe even for some rock group like the Rolling Stones before I'd have dedicated a victory to communism.

Even when East Germany's very hard-line communist leaders put Schmidt on a pedestal, he refused to play the sycophant.

At the end of every year, the best of us were honored in a big ceremony in Berlin. When we received these awards from some high potentate, we were supposed to say, *"Ich diene der Deutschen Demokratischen Republik,"* which means, "I serve the German Democratic Republic." However, I always said only, *"Danke schön."* Twice I was given the Vaterländische Verdienstorden, the Fatherland's Order of Merit, our highest prize, and four times I got the Verdienter Meister des Sports, Master of Outstanding Merit in Sports. Always I said, *"Danke schön."*

He knew that his attitude had always irritated the authorities. He assumed that he had been given black marks over the years for this and that it was very likely one of the reasons he was in this predicament. But certainly, a big mouth and a maverick personality were not reason alone to throw a man into a cell. As he watched the swimmers through the bars, he began to consider other crimes and misdemeanors that the DTSB and the Stasi might have used as grounds for his arrest.

1) The Crime of Making Friends in the West:
Americans particularly had always intrigued him. He had first

committed this crime against the state in 1974, when he was barely twenty and making only his third trip abroad. He had met Dwight Stones, the world-record high jumper, John Powell, one of the world's best discus throwers, and Al Feuerbach, the world's record holder in the shot put, at a meet in Siena, Italy. Though there was a Stasi watchdog with him, Schmidt couldn't resist using his schoolboy English to engage these fascinating aliens in conversations about the cars they owned.

The following year at the World Games in Helsinki he broke the rules again by making friends with Mac Wilkins, a discus thrower from California—a shaggy-bearded free spirit who looked like a hippy and held strong antiestablishment views about just about any and all establishments. After the first meeting, they became arch-rivals on the field and warm friends off. At the 1976 Olympics in Montreal, their competition had provided one of the highlights of those games.

Wilkins had been leading the competition and John Powell was in second place. Both had completed their throws. Schmidt was in third place and down to his last attempt. He had been performing poorly. Then, suddenly on the final throw everything felt exactly right, and he stood watching with growing excitement as the discus flew into the distance. It landed twenty inches ahead of Powell's best mark and it won the silver medal for Schmidt.

I was so happy. I lifted my arms to the crowd. And then, suddenly, out of the corner of my eye, I saw Mac coming toward me, a big grin shining through his beard. He was happy I hadn't beat him and he was maybe even happier that I had beat John Powell, whom Mac particularly didn't like because he was a professional cop in real life. Without warning, he embraced me and raised me up high off my feet and held me there. After what seemed a lifetime, he let me down and I thought, Good God, what are the watchdogs thinking? I congratulated him rather quickly and walked away in order not to prolong the situation.

It made for a dramatic Cold War tableau—the black-bearded American radical hugging Sunny Boy, one of the greatest living symbols of socialist supremacy in sports. But if it was unforgettable to the billion or so spectators who saw it on TV, it was unforgivable to the gimlet-eyed Stasi looking on—and certainly his friendship with Mac Wilkins became an entry on any list of his crimes against the state along with each of the dozens of other Western athletes he befriended over the years. And he knew of another that was on that list, too.

2) The Crime of Falling in Love with Unapproved Women:

In the winter of 1977, he had taken up with a married woman named Uschi. She was twenty-six, three years older than he, the mother of an eighteen-month-old boy. Though Uschi and her husband still shared an apartment, their marriage was on the rocks and divorce proceedings had begun. Thus, neither Schmidt nor Uschi had seen any need to keep their romance a secret. They met in public and used Uschi's apartment when her husband was not there.

Word reached officials of the SC Dynamo Berlin that their star discus thrower had been seen with an unknown young woman and a small boy. An investigation was ordered. Soon the chief of the track-and-field section of the club, one Rudi Ortmann, summoned Schmidt to his office and delivered a sharp lecture about the disruptive effects of affairs with married women. He then informed Schmidt that he would have to sign a formal contract promising to sever all relations with Uschi until her divorce was final. The contract lay on the desk and he handed Schmidt a pen.

I knew Uschi's divorce was only a few weeks away. I also knew that I was going to continue to see her secretly whether I had signed this piece of paper or not. So I signed it.

The Stasi must have put a watchdog on me to see if I kept my word. One night—it was February 11, 1977, I remember it well— I had visited Uschi at her apartment and I was starting to drive home. I was in my father's car—I had only got my driver's license a few months earlier and I did not yet have a car of my own. It was a bad night, snowing and raining at the same time, and there was a lot of slush on the road. Suddenly, I noticed that I was being followed by a car. The headlights, very bright, were a few meters behind my car. I was alarmed. Why the hell would anyone shadow me on a night like that?

I became panicky. I swung into a one-way street going the wrong way. The other car followed close behind, its headlights blinding me. Now I was really frightened, and panic took over completely. I stomped hard on the gas—a stupid reaction because I was going too fast. The car went into a skid on the ice and slush. It scraped by one tree, kept sliding in the slush, and crashed into another tree. I must have banged my head. The steering wheel came off between my legs. I had no idea what had happened or where I was.

I was in shock. When the police came, I couldn't remember anything at all. I couldn't remember that I was being chased when I crashed. I was taken to a hospital, a police hospital. From there, I telephoned my mother three times, telling her that I had had a car accident. I told her the same thing all three times I called.

Schmidt threw a tantrum in the emergency room, rampaging about and shouting at the head nurse that he wouldn't stay in the hospital no matter what was wrong with him. Orderlies calmed him down, but the ferocity of his behavior combined with his great size frightened the nurse. She had him transferred to an asylum for the mentally disturbed the next morning.

He stayed there ten days and it turned out to be a good thing. He had not been injured physically except for a twisted back, a bruised sternum, and a broken molar. But his memory was impaired. He could not remember anything about the accident. Doctors gave him a brain scan, which didn't show any damage, and put him on tranquilizing medication. Eventually, he improved and remembered some details of the accident. However, months passed before it slowly dawned on him that he had been fleeing from someone when he crashed into that tree. But whom?

Schmidt sought out the policeman who had filed the accident

report and asked him if he had seen another car at the scene. The officer told him that there had indeed been another car, driven by a man in civilian clothes. The man had claimed that he was a member of the police and that he had been following Schmidt because his driving had been so erratic. However, the so-called policeman was never identified by name in the accident report.

Was the man a Stasi? Could something like that be coincidental? That someone would go the same way I was driving—against the one-way street? I doubt that. Someone was following me, no question. A Stasi? Also no question, I would say.

So *l'affaire* Uschi had gone into his dossier of crime. Three years later he was sure that it had been joined by his most sensational violation of them all.

3) The Crime of Insulting Socialist Comrades in the Mecca of Communism:

This had occurred on July 28, 1980, in Moscow at Lenin Stadium before 100,000 spectators during the XXII Olympic Summer Games. These were the first Olympics ever held in a socialist country, and the Russians desperately wished them to be a triumphant celebration of their system. Unfortunately, all hope of that vanished long before the games began. The Russians had invaded Afghanistan to put down an anticommunist rebellion against a Soviet-backed regime late in 1979. In January 1980, American president Jimmy Carter called for a boycott of the Moscow Olympics in retaliation for the invasion. Sixty-five countries stayed away from the Soviets' games, and the Russians stayed in Afghanistan for nine years, ultimately suffering a defeat every bit as humiliating as the US had experienced in Vietnam. The boycott accomplished nothing except a reduction of the quality of competition at the games by preventing hundreds of the world's best athletes from competing.

Schmidt was the reigning world-record holder and was the favorite to win the gold medal. The boycott dampened his enthusiasm, too.

With so many good men missing, I could never make myself believe the Olympics in Moscow were really the Olympics. So even if I had won the gold medal in Moscow, I would never have considered myself a true Olympic champion.

The Russians tried to pretend the boycott hadn't happened. The opening ceremonies were lavish and colorful with armies of costumed folk dancers and children dressed like cartoon bears. But it was hopelessly star-crossed. Teams from sixteen of the eighty-one nations that did attend refused to carry their flags into the stadium in the opening parade of nations. A skeleton team of five athletes from New Zealand marched behind a black flag with the Olympic rings and an olive branch superimposed in white. Great Britain's team refused to march and sent a single official carrying the Olympic flag instead of the Union Jack. A Soviet TV commentator remarked angrily as the Englishman strode past, "There is the clumsy plot that you all can see, against the traditions of the Olympic movement."

After this bleak beginning, things got worse. The games were played out in an atmosphere of Soviet hooliganism and bad sportsmanship that shocked the world. The Soviets had somehow convinced the International Amateur Athletic Federation (IAAF) that it should not assign its usual teams of neutral observers to monitor Russian umpires during track-and-field competitions. It would look as if the IAAF were "suspicious" of them, said the Soviets. What followed was an appalling display of favoritism and cheating by the Russians.

When the Russian javelin throwers prepared for a critical throw, Soviet officials opened the stadium gates to allow a favoring breeze to blow on the infield. The Russian won a gold medal. The Soviets disqualified an Australian for a triple jump that was obviously a legal attempt and would have won him a gold medal. They cheated a Cuban out of a gold medal in the discus throw by marking his effort more than a full meter short. And during a marvelously dramatic pole vault competition that featured a Russian, two Poles, and two Frenchmen, ferociously partisan Soviet spectators became so raucous that the Soviet public address announcer had to plead for quiet. When one of the Poles, Wladyslaw Kozakiewicz, won the gold medal with a world-record vault, the whistles rose in earsplitting dissonance. Flashing a fierce grin, Kozakiewicz gave the whole stadium a mighty obscene gesture with his arm.

When Schmidt entered the stadium for his competition, he was not prepared for the meanness of the crowd.

I felt very good when I began warming up on the infield of the stadium that day. My practice throws were all right and the weather was beautiful. There was a bit of wind and I knew that if I could manage to throw to the left of the landing sector, the discus could catch the wind and fly maybe as much as one or two meters farther. I was feeling in very good shape, for sure.

Then I stepped into the ring for my first throw, and all of a sudden I heard spectators whistling. I was absolutely startled. Were they whistling at *me?* No, I thought, they must be doing this to someone else. But at that moment, there were no other events going on, only the discus. My God, they had to mean *me!*

Now this I could not fathom. I had thought of the Soviet Union as a brother country. Why are they disturbing me? Why are they trying to ruin my concentration? It made no sense, but they kept whistling, then booing. More and more. I felt like an animal being tormented in a cage.

The crowd kept up the din. Schmidt found it very difficult to concentrate.

Every throw I made was followed by sneering laughter. I felt as if I were throwing into a solid wall of noise. Still, my first throw was very good. It would have been the gold medal throw. It caught the wind and flew 67.50 meters [221' 5½"]. However, it drifted a bit too far to the left and landed half a meter outside the legal sector. I had made a technical error and swung the discus too far to the left. After this foul, I knew I had to land a safe throw, and I did on my second turn, but it was too short. Now on my third throw I had to land safely and yet cover enough distance so I could stay in the final. [After the initial three throws, the field was cut to eight competitors who were allowed to compete in the final three throws.] I managed 65.64 meters [215' 4"]. This put me in the final, and even briefly into the lead as well.

Yet every time I entered the ring, the public was whistling. After my fourth throw, I fell back to second place. The crowd roared. They loved that. It made me mad. Just as I got into the final moves on my fifth throw, I twisted my right ankle badly in the throwing ring. The throw fell short. The crowd went crazy with joy. The ankle swelled up immediately and I couldn't move it normally at all.

Before my last throw, I stood in the cage and looked up at that mob of maniacs—thousands of them in tiers of seats that went up, up, up, all around me in every direction I turned. My ankle hurt. I felt as if I were in hell. I was trying to think, trying to visualize the throw I wanted to make. I couldn't concentrate at all. I threw my last throw. I failed completely. The throw went about forty meters [just over 130']. It was feeble, girlish. From a standing position, I can throw fifty-seven meters. I purposely made it a foul by stepping out of the ring before it landed. The crowd was shrieking with pleasure at my pathetic effort. It was then I committed socialist heresy.

Infuriated, Schmidt charged limping across the field, shaking his fist at the jeering multitude. He bellowed into the bedlam, "You stupid pigs! You assholes!" The stadium exploded with hoots and whistles. Laughter rebounded across the infield.

A few minutes later, the place exploded again when a twenty-nine-year-old Russian, Viktor Rashchupkin, an also-ran who was not even ranked in the top twenty discus throwers worldwide, uncorked the best throw of his life—66.64 meters (218′ 8″)—and won the gold medal. A Czech, Imrich Bugar, was second, and the cheated Cuban, Luis Delis, was third.

Schmidt was fourth, out of the medals but a respectable place. His tantrum had lasted for only a few seconds. If it had occurred anywhere but in Moscow, it might have been overlooked. But the cloud that fell over him that day never lifted again.

At the Olympic Village a couple of hours after the fiasco, Schmidt ran into Manfred Ewald, president of the DTSB, a shrewd and powerful bureaucrat who had been the czar of the East German sports empire since its genesis almost thirty years before.

Ewald was pretty angry that I had failed so miserably. I said to him, "I hurt myself."

He shrugged. "Oh, that. You should have won anyway."

But he didn't say anything about my gesture. Nobody did. That was their way—never chastise an offender until we are safely back inside our own country. Also, I think maybe they realized the true impact of what I did only after they heard it reported on Western TV and in the press. It was thoroughly discussed on Werner Höfer's "Frühschoppen" on West German TV [a long-running and highly intelligent political talk show hosted by a well-respected journalist]. Höfer said I had been the victim of very shabby treatment but that I was the only athlete who had the courage to shake his fist at the rotten sportsmanship of the Russians. Of course, Wladyslaw Kozakiewicz did, too, but he had won and I had lost.

Nothing was ever said openly to me about it. No GDR journalist wrote about it. It appeared on GDR TV, but the commentator said I was waving to the Soviet public.

An Olympic tantrum, an affair with an unapproved woman, an affinity for friends in the West—were these grounds for snuffing out a superstar of Schmidt's magnitude? Maybe. But he was pretty sure that none of these crimes would have led to Sportverbot and a prison cell if he had not committed one other.

4) The Crime of Wanting to Leave the GDR:

The crime of wanting to leave, of course, was not actually punishable as long as a man kept thoughts of defection to himself. Only when he spoke of it did he put himself in jeopardy. Unfortunately, the garrulous Schmidt spoke of it way too often and to way too many people. He told his close friends, Ulf Leischner and Steffen Müller, about it. He told acquaintances at the Mocca-Eck disco about it. He told some of his teammates. He told friends in the West. He talked about it by telephone with a friend in West Berlin even though the phone was certainly bugged. And he put it in writing on a postcard to Mac Wilkins and Al Feuerbach in California. The Americans had invited him in the spring of '82 to an informal competition in California called "2 Big Guys' Mountain Games." The invitation included a return-mail card, and Schmidt sent his back with the "Yes, I will compete" box checked. But he had scribbled next to it, "But I can not. I can never start all over! No more sport for me in DDR. Never. Please help me!"

Schmidt had also confided his desire to leave the GDR to a mild-looking, middle-aged man named Jochen Brüggmann. They had first met when Brüggmann asked for an autograph during a meet in Cottbus in the spring of '81. Eventually he had become such a close friend and confidant that he was often a guest at the Schmidts' apartment. As we shall soon see, none of Schmidt's loose talk was quite as damaging as the remarks he made to Brüggmann—except perhaps for what he said during endless arguments with his own father in the privacy of their home. It is possible they may have hurt him most of all.

Ernst Schmidt was an imperious man, a dedicated Communist Party member who had been one of the leading coaches in the DTSB for more than thirty years. He was sixty-two in the summer of '82, a brawny, white-haired lion of a man who had been the decathlon champion of Germany in the early 1940s under Hitler's Third Reich. Most East German athletes and coaches had long assumed that because of Ernst's position in the sports hierarchy, Wolfgang basked in an aura of extra protection and special favors. That was quite true. Nevertheless, Ernst was a firm believer in the harsh discipline and rigid rules laid down by the East German machine, and he greatly disapproved of much of Wolfgang's maverick behavior. Indeed, father and son had fought a private war for many years over politics and oppression in East Germany.

Father made life difficult for me because of his blind belief in the DDR. I began to argue with him about it after I had begun to travel to the West and saw what lies they were telling us back home. I told him there were too many contradictions in socialism. I told him that the freedom I got as an athlete wasn't real freedom because they treated all of us like misbehaving children.

Our arguments were particularly fierce after I got *Sportverbot*. I would shout at him, "See? I told you there was no freedom here. I want out! I want to go West!"

And he shouted back, "Well, you're out of sports! You can't compete! You can't go West anymore. You can go to work, you can take a job!"

And I would scream back, "So I will compete somewhere else. I will break out of this barbed-wire box!"

And father would give me one of his goddamn huge supply of slogans: *"Jeder ist seines Glückes Schmied*—Life is what you make it."

And I yelled, "Do you know what my slogan is? 'Better dead than Red!' And do you know what DDR really means? 'Der Dumme Rest!' The stupid ones who are left behind! Just give me a hole, and I am gone!"

Berating his father with such dangerous sentiments was no risk in itself, for loyal as he was to the German Democratic Republic, Ernst Schmidt ultimately loved his son more than he loved his politics. It would never have occurred to him to turn Wolfgang in for declaring his desire to defect. However, even as the two titans bellowed at each other, a recording device concealed in the apartment at Stahlheimer Strasse 4 might well have been taking in every word. Ernst Schmidt became convinced as events later unfolded that the Stasi had bugged their apartment—just as they had bugged the suburban house where Wolfgang and his parents lived later. It was never proven for certain, but the likelihood existed that the Stasi listened in on all of Wolfgang's diatribes about escape.

On the other hand, it didn't really matter if the apartment was bugged or not, for the one great and terrible truth about life in a police state is that no evidence, no witness, no *reason,* is ever required to arrest a man.

The authorities could do anything they wanted to Wolfgang Schmidt. As a hero of the state, he was possessed by them far more than he possessed himself. For years, they had let him live in an athlete's utopia. Now they were taking it away and replacing it with prison.

They were also murdering him as an athlete. Under the best of conditions, the life expectancy of a great athlete is brief. It ordinarily spans little more than a brilliant decade or so between a man's late teens and his early thirties. Then it is over, snuffed out by the natural deterioration of reflexes and strength. All great athletes die twice—once as an athlete and once as a man. By locking Schmidt away from his sport in his prime, they had sentenced him to his first death at a tragically early age.

A LITTLE AFTER FIVE P.M., HE HEARD THE SOUND of keys turning in the locks. He stood transfixed as the doors were opened. Two new actors entered the day's drama. They looked more interesting than any he had encountered so far.

These two were definitely not of the *Null Acht Fünfzehn* type. They were men with distinct differences between them, and I didn't like either one. The taller one, the leader, was over six feet tall, with slick black hair. He was well dressed, very conservative, like a wealthy businessman in a dark suit and a tightly knotted tie. He was about fifty. His name, I learned later, was Wiedemann, and he was an *Oberstleutnant* [lieutenant colonel] in the Stasi. He was vain, stiff, and arrogant in his posture. I realized that he was a stuck-up twit who considered himself superior to everyone he ever met. But then I noticed that his fingernails were bitten down to the quick. So, I thought, the big boy is nervous. He bites his nails. The big boy has the manner of a field marshal, but inside he must be as jittery as a schoolgirl by the look of those fingernails.

The other Stasi was short and fat, with red hair and lots of freckles on his moon face. He was an *Oberleutnant* [a first lieutenant], about thirty-five years old, and I never did learn his name. He was a repulsive type and I came to think of him as Repulsive Red. When he smoked, he inhaled through his teeth with a hissing sound, and he blew out his smoke in fast puffs—*poh, poh, poh.*"

Neither of the newcomers introduced himself to Schmidt, so he asked them impatiently, "Who are you?"

Wiedemann said curtly, "We are from the investigation department of the Ministry for State Security." The redhead remained silent. The senior officer did all the talking. Not once that day did he address Schmidt by name.

Wiedemann went on very sharply: "What the hell is the matter with you?"

Schmidt was alarmed. "Nothing is the matter. Why have I been followed? Why have I been brought here?"

"We want to know what is the matter with you," said Wiedemann. "You cannot leave until you tell us what is the matter with you."

Schmidt again asked why he had been arrested, but Wiedemann pressed harder: "What the hell is the matter with you?"

Schmidt said in resignation, "Goddammit, I want out of this country. I want to throw the discus. If I can't do it here, then somewhere else. I am an athlete. I want to compete. Let me leave."

The Stasis were suddenly very still, letting his words hang in the air so there could be no mistaking precisely what he had said. Schmidt himself was momentarily stunned, too, for he knew he had put himself in great jeopardy. There was no taking it back.

Hearing myself say it scared the hell out of me. But at that moment, I didn't care, honestly. I just thought, Oh, go on, tell them and let's see what they'll do. Let's see what happens next.

Wiedemann grew calm and very authoritative. There was nothing of the nail-biter about him now. "Quietly now," he said to Schmidt. "Please tell us all about it, but quietly, very quietly."

Schmidt said, "No, I want to phone my parents first."

"Later."

"I want to phone a lawyer."

"It's not possible."

"Why have you been following me?"

"Traffic hooliganism. You were speeding, driving one hundred and twenty where only fifty is allowed."

"You are keeping me locked up here for that?"

"Not exactly," said Wiedemann. "We have some questions to ask about your future. You say that you are not happy in the GDR?"

Schmidt realized he could not retreat even if he wanted to. "Yes, I want to leave this country. I want out unless I can compete."

"It has gotten that far already? Talk to us about it. Tell us why this has happened."

"I can't pursue my sport anymore. I must go."

"How?" asked Wiedemann. "How exactly are you going to go?"

"I don't know," said Schmidt. "Apply for an exit visa. Leave by helicopter. Just split."

Wiedemann paused, then said, "Split? You mean defect?"

Though the interrogator spoke quietly, the sound of the word cracked in the room like a rifle shot. In the brief silence that followed, Schmidt became intensely aware of the fat Stasi, sitting on the bed, sucking in his cigarette smoke with a nervous hiss and exhaling with staccato puffs—*poh, poh, poh.*

Schmidt paused, then gazed directly at Wiedemann and said, "Yes."

Wiedemann's aristocratic face betrayed no surprise, but Schmidt did notice that the lieutenant colonel brought his left hand to his mouth and gnawed, ever so briefly, on the nail of his middle finger. It was only a matter of a second or two before the interrogator realized he was doing this and quickly put his hand in his coat pocket.

Then he leaned back in his chair and began to ask Schmidt many questions.

It went on for a couple of hours. I was very tired and my mind seemed mired down. I could hear shouts of swimmers in the lake, and I could see the blue sky through the window bars. Wiedemann was stiff, formal, but very calm. He was not threatening. He was quite civil. I was open with him. I didn't think I had anything to fear anymore. I didn't have any secrets that I knew of anyway. If they knew about my desire to get the hell out of the GDR, what more could I tell the pigs?

Wiedemann seemed most interested in learning which people in nonsocialist countries I kept contact with. Wiedemann came around to this more than once. I replied that my friends in the West were Mac Wilkins and John Powell from the USA, and Ricky Bruch from Sweden and Alwin Wagner from West Germany, who were discus throwers, too. Wiedemann seemed to think I should name more people. I mentioned a friend in West Berlin, not a discus thrower but a businessman I knew. Wiedemann pressed for more, but I really didn't have more to tell him.

It had got to be well into the evening, seven-thirty P.M. I suppose. It was still quite light outside, a long summer's day coming to an end. I could hear swimmers still splashing in the water and children playing on the shore. Wiedemann suddenly rose from his seat as if he had heard a signal. The redhead got up, too, fat and clumsy. He went to the door, knocked lightly, and the keys immediately turned in the locks.

Wiedemann said to me quite formally, "You will hear from us." Both left the room. The keys turned twice again in the locks.

Schmidt lay awake for a long time that night. He was disoriented and depressed and wondered if he had made a fatal mistake when he had confessed that he wished to leave.

Did he really want that? After all, he had been enjoying this athlete's paradise for all these years. He had had the best coaches, the best food, the latest drugs, the best sports doctors, dedicated trainers, revolutionary training techniques, superb facilities, as well as limitless time to do nothing but train. If he went West without the resources of the East German machine, he might be just another mediocrity.

Yet Schmidt knew that he really had no choice. He could not stay. The East Germans would never let him compete again at a world-class level. They would never trust him to leave the country again. He had sealed his own fate: Now he had to go West or give up all hope of competing again in his sport.

It was a daunting prospect. He knew well what had happened to Joachim Krug, a brilliant young discus thrower and shot-putter who had been Schmidt's rival in their teens. Krug had defected to West Germany when he was twenty, and he had never competed at world-class level. This was a tale Schmidt had never dwelled on before, but now he realized that the fate of Joachim Krug could well become his own.

They had first met in 1969, when both were fifteen. They had come from widely distant backgrounds. Schmidt's father had been the national throwing coach at the time, and he had seen to it that Wolfgang had access to the fine facilities of SC Dynamo Berlin when he was thirteen. Krug's father was a worker in a salt-processing factory at Bad Salzungen in Thuringia, and Joachim had been plucked from crowds of kids in district competitions by talent scouts from the DTSB. He was brought to Berlin and enrolled in a *Kinder- und Jugendsportschule,* one of the GDR's special boarding schools operated for budding young athletes. Krug did not possess the magnificent physical proportions that Schmidt had. He was a bit shorter and a lot more muscular. When he competed, he stood 6'4" tall and weighed more than 260 pounds.

These two budding child-athletes were so talented that, at fifteen, they trained with the best throwing athletes in the GDR, including Detlef Thorith, the European discus champion of 1966.

Schmidt always remembered those early years as a time of inspiration.

We motivated each other, the stars like Thorith and the tyros like Krug and myself. For us, it was like being on a par with our gods. Krug and I had our first successful competitions then. We traded them back and forth. In 1969, I became the champion discus thrower in the GDR in our age group and runner-up in the shot put. Krug was champion in the shot and second to me in the discus.

Krug was so talented then, more talented even than Udo Beyer [the GDR's Olympic shot-put champion in 1976]. Joachim was intelligent enough, but Udo Beyer became better than Krug because he was more intelligent and had more willpower. There was something missing in Krug's head. Still, he could have been one of the GDR's great heroes if he had remained in the system.

In 1971, a great prize was dangled before the teenagers of the GDR's sports program. The Friendship Games for Juniors were to be held in Havana, Cuba, an event open to competitors from socialist countries up to the age of eighteen. In the qualifying trials for the meet, Schmidt had defeated Krug in both the discus and the shot put, but both were picked to go to Cuba.

There were only fifteen of us nominated. Then two days before we were to depart, the functionaries announced that, due to financial problems, they could only send ten. Among the five they ordered to stay home was Joachim Krug. It was a terrible scene. One girl was crying. Krug slammed a wall with his fist. They had all trained so hard and now, nothing.

For Joachim Krug it was the turning point of his life.

The blacksmith's son was shattered. Until then he had been a model athlete. Afterward, he became an undisciplined troublemaker. The big-city temptations of Berlin suddenly became impossible for him to resist. He began climbing out a window of the boarding-school dormitory, spending the nights dancing and swilling beer. He said later, "I never got hold of myself again. The air had gone out of me. Looking back, I think it was wrong to let myself go as I did, but under the circumstances I just didn't want to go on." He continued to train at SC Dynamo Berlin for another year, but he was a changed young man.

He still had more talent in the shot put than anyone our age. But after the Cuba decision, he drank and smoked a lot. He was going downhill in every way. Once he was arrested for being drunk when he tried to pass a police car on his bicycle. Then he disappeared for a full week—didn't attend training sessions or school classes either. Coaches and the police hunted for him for three days. Finally he returned. It turned out he had been shacked up with a nurse the whole week he was gone. At that point SC Dynamo had had enough. Krug had to go.

The young man was ordered to go to work in the potassium salt mines of Kalibergwerk at Merkers. "They said they were giving me one last chance," Krug recalled. "If I proved myself in the mines, they might allow me to come back into sports. I thought that seemed ridiculous even then."

He worked underground with the crew that serviced the ventilation system in the mines. He recalled, "It was quite a good job, relatively speaking. We had a fairly good air supply. There were other jobs where people stood breathing in salt dust for eight hours a day." He began work in the mine tunnels in December 1972. In a few months, he judged his situation to be utterly without hope.

On a moonless night in September 1973, he set out to escape to the West. "My grandfather lived on a small farm less than five kilometers from the border at Empfertshausen," he recalled. "I had been visiting there since I was a child and I knew the area well. The night I planned to escape, I slept in my grandfather's home. I didn't tell anyone of my plan, not my grandfather either. I left at about eleven-thirty P.M. and walked through the woods toward the border. I knew there were supposed to be three or four fences, all about eight feet high with about one kilometer between each one. I climbed the first fence. It was not electrified, but there were five rows of barbed wire on top. Because I was an athlete, I had no trouble getting over the fence, but I tore my hands badly on the barbed wire. Between the first and second fence, I touched a trip wire that I hadn't seen and a flare went up, lighting the area ahead. I guess most people would have run back. But my reaction was to keep walking toward the border. I reasoned that when a flare goes up, the guards would assume that an escapee's first thought would be to go back on the assumption there would be border guards waiting ahead. But, I reasoned further, that is precisely what the authorities will think the escapee is thinking. I decided that if I turned back, they would be waiting for me. So I walked on, climbed the next fence and kept going toward the third fence. No one met me."

As he got closer to the border, Krug could see watchtowers with rotating searchlights posted every five hundred meters along the boundary. The lights kept sweeping over the ground he was crossing, and as he drew nearer, he had to seek cover whenever a light passed over him. Amazingly enough, in that black waste-land, he discovered there were cows. "I managed to reach the third fence by moving from cow to cow between two watchtow-ers, always making sure that I was in the shadow of a cow when a searchlight approached. When I got to the third fence, there was a sign mounted on it that read, '*Achtung! Minenfeld! Le-bensgefahr!*' [Attention! Minefield! Risk to your life!] I climbed over and I lay down on the edge of the minefield to think about my problems for a moment." After pondering the problem of the minefield Krug came up with a solution. "I grabbed some stones and threw them, one at a time, onto the minefield before me, figuring they would set off any mines they hit. They apparently hit nothing because nothing blew up. So I filled my pockets with rocks and proceeded ahead, throwing one at a time in front of me, then stepping from rock to rock until I crossed the minefield safely. I climbed the last fence, cutting my hands again on the barbed wire, and I was in the West. It was about three-thirty or four A.M. I walked into Hof, the first village. Dogs were barking, but no one was up. I rang a doorbell, but nobody came, so I walked down the street. Suddenly a police car drove up. They picked me up, drove me to a hotel in Tann, and told me to make sure I locked the door to my room. They said that it had happened in the past that refugees had been kidnapped and taken back to the GDR from that hotel. In the morning, I was taken to a hospital where my hands were cleaned and bandaged and I was given a tetanus shot."

Krug settled in Cologne, enrolled in a physical education course at the Sports College, and began to train again. He actually improved on his performances in the GDR in both the shot put and the discus for a while. Then he found that he could not support himself and still train as intensely as a world-class athlete had to. "I got the highest grant possible for my studies, six hundred marks [$240 at the time] a month, but I had to pay rent and buy food and clothes and it wasn't enough. I worked at every kind of job to survive. I delivered flowers, I loaded meat in a slaughterhouse, I was a bouncer at a theater and several discos."

Without the lavish support system of the GDR to give him endless free time as well as free coaching and free facilities, Krug simply had no hope of ever being a serious competitor again.

Schmidt had visited Krug once in Cologne during an international meet in 1977. He had long wondered what had happened to all that talent Joachim had shown as a teenager. Now he saw his old rival living in humble student digs, battling to earn enough to eat and stay clothed. Schmidt told Krug, "If they gave me a million marks, I would not stay here."

A year later, Krug, too, despaired of life in the West and wrote a letter to the East German mission in Bonn offering to return on the conditions that he not be punished and that he be allowed to try to return to world-class level in the sports program. The letter went unanswered. Eventually, things improved. Krug got married and took a job as a throwing coach in Qatar, Saudi

Arabia. Schmidt had heard that Krug was quite well off financially and that he was the father of four children.

That was certainly not Wolfgang Schmidt's idea of what he wanted life to be like if he went West. Yet, as he looked through bars at the clear night sky above Motzener See, he understood entirely too clearly the chilling similarities between his present plight and that of Joachim Krug ten years before.

I had always thought it was just Krug's fate, his bad luck, his bad temper, and I never considered it a lesson. Now I began to understand that I was experiencing the same things he had, only at a later age and after a great deal of success. He had been an outcast back then, but I was an outcast now. And I understood that I had no choice just as Krug had no choice: My life as an athlete was finished if I stayed in the GDR. If I stayed, I could end up the equivalent of digging in a salt mine, too. So I had to go West like Krug if I was ever to be a champion again. But I wondered if I, too, would have to live in a wretched room and become a bouncer at a disco in order to survive. I wondered if maybe being an outcast athlete in the East was a better fate than living like that in the West. And then I tried to stop wondering about these things since it was all driving me crazy.

He fell asleep as the sky was showing a pearly light. A short time later, he was awakened by one of the *Null Acht Fünfzehns* who knocked on his door and brought him breakfast. It was about eight A.M. by his watch and he had no idea where he was at first. Then he knew and a great lump of melancholy rose in his throat.

"Please, I must phone my parents," he said to the guard.

The man muttered, "No phone." Then he quickly scuttled out of the room, hurriedly slamming both doors behind him as if Schmidt were chasing him. Schmidt had no energy for such antics.

Later that morning the fat Stasi, Repulsive Red, reappeared in the room. He brought a sheet of paper with questions neatly typed on it, and he read them aloud to Schmidt.

"To which persons in nonsocialist countries do you maintain contact?"

Schmidt again ran down the list: Mac Wilkins, Ricky Bruch, Alwin Wagner, John Powell, and Ludwig Schura, the man in West Berlin.

"Do you exchange letters?"

Schmidt replied, "Only Christmas cards. Nothing else."

The man hissed in his cigarette smoke, puffed it out—*poh, poh, poh*—and eventually left.

The first full day in custody passed slowly. Schmidt kept demanding a chance to telephone his parents, but the guards refused, always replying flatly, "There is no phone here." He began to do calisthenics to keep himself from going completely crazy. Mostly, he did push-ups—dozens of them, hundreds of them. Despite the confinement of the room, he felt better, even felt as if he had somehow gained some control over his situation. This, of course, wasn't true.

After the first day, Repulsive Red came back regularly each morning, always with more cigarettes to smoke and always with more sheets of paper filled with questions:

What do athletes of the GDR think when they take part in competitions in capitalist countries? What do they think of the shopping there? What do they think about consumption in Western countries? What do they think of the clothes, the shoes, the food, the wine, the automobiles, the discotheques?

Schmidt began to answer, but Repulsive Red interrupted and told him he was now required to reply in writing. So he wrote with a pencil on sheets of foolscap: "When we athletes travel to competitions in nonsocialist countries, we are indeed a little impressed by what the shops have to offer, the volume of what is offered, and we like to shop there because we can buy things that are not available at home."

Schmidt went on to cover two pages with his slow, careful handwriting and gave them to the red-haired Stasi. The man read it all, squinting through cigarette smoke. Then he grimaced and shook his head. "Not enough. It doesn't suffice. Write it again."

That pig. I hated him so. Each day he kept producing pieces of paper with questions. Often they were the same questions repeated about what athletes thought of consumption in Western countries. And more stupid questions like, "Do athletes like to travel to Western countries?" They were typical GDR bigwig questions, unworldly questions. I simply didn't know what to write, but I wanted to be free of trouble so I scrawled answers on and on. They seemed to want papers filled with writing no matter what it said.

One day I was told to list all of my trips West in my entire life— every year, what months, what cities, what countries. It took a while, but I listed them all. From 1973 through 1981, to Canada, Mexico, France, Switzerland, Sweden, Norway, Finland, West Germany, Italy, Algeria, on and on. Then he said he also wanted a list of all my trips to socialist countries—all trips, whether private or sports-connected. I covered several pages, but when I gave them to him, he said, "That's not enough."

I said, "There are no more. This is all the trips abroad I ever took."

They had let him keep his wristwatch so he always knew what time and what day it was. On the fourth day of his imprisonment, July 5, the Stasi brought him a package from his home: a razor, toothbrush, underwear, pajamas. They did not tell Schmidt what they had told his parents—or even *if* they had told them anything.

The days passed, always with Repulsive Red appearing in the morning with more questions, demanding more lists. However, except for his nagging interrogator and his anxiety over what might happen next, Schmidt did not suffer. The two Stasi guards with the *Null Acht Fünfzehn* personalities were quite literally his servants, as it turned out. They apparently lived at the villa, and each day they brought him meals—breakfast, lunch, dinner, plus an afternoon snack of coffee and cake.

On the tenth day of his imprisonment, Sunday, July 11, he was allowed to watch television—the final World Cup soccer match between West Germany and Italy. The Italians won and

Schmidt was infuriated because downstairs he could hear the Stasis whooping it up as they watched the game.

The Italians scored a goal against West Germany, and downstairs, the Stasis were bawling like idiots, "Hurrah! Hurrah!" They were drumming the table with their fists, howling with happiness. The goddamn idiots! I, of course, was rooting for the Germans. Better, certainly, than being for the Italians. I really hated those Stasis that night for cheering against Germany.

They kept him locked in the villa room for eleven days. Through the bars, he could see the sun glistening on the lake, day after day after day. He continued his calisthenics with compulsive dedication, yet he was never really comfortable. Life had been reduced to the size of a shoebox and it was unbearable.

During the whole time, I constantly thought of breaking out, even though it was impossible. There were bars in front of the window, and it was a small window anyway. When I had to go to the toilet, I had to knock on the door. There was always someone outside. And always I would hear first one key turn, then the other. They never left me alone. They never left the doors unlocked. I was guarded day and night. Those pigs. And they didn't tell me why. The Stasi really were men without pity. People had told me this and now I understood for myself. I also understood that certainly there were other prisoners of the state—many others—who had it worse than I. Then on the eleventh day, at ten o'clock in the morning, things turned worse for me, too.

Three new and unknown men in civilian clothes walked through the doors of Schmidt's cell. Schmidt was struck by the fact that one of them, the obvious leader, very much resembled a toad. He was tall and thick, with broad shoulders, rather imposing except for his heavily lidded eyes, his wide, downturned mouth, the receding, chinless jaw. The other two were *Null Acht Fünfzehn*.

The toad opened the conversation. He spoke formally. "Are you Herr Schmidt?" he asked. His voice was deep.

I replied that I was.

Upon which he began to recite words in a singsong monotone as if he had memorized them: "On orders of the district attorney, a warrant for your arrest has been issued, and preliminary proceedings have been initiated against you on the grounds of the strong suspicion that you have made preparations for illegally crossing the border."

This surprised me. I had made no preparations. But then I thought, What should I expect? I had told the Stasi myself that I didn't want to stay in the GDR anymore. They had twisted it to make it sound worse than it was. I was angry, wrought up over it, but I didn't say a word in reply. What was the point?

One of the other men, not the toad, then produced an "eight"— a set of large cast-iron handcuffs. This was unexpected. I said nothing, though my heart pounded like a drum. The man held up the handcuffs in front of me and nodded at me. Like an automaton, I lifted my hands and held them out to him. He put the handcuffs around my wrists and snapped them shut. I was manacled as if I were a criminal. I felt helpless and humiliated.

They led me out of the room, downstairs to a car parked outside the villa. It was a Lada, an official Stasi car with no markings. They put me in the backseat, and then, to my even greater humiliation, they padlocked my handcuffs to a chain that was bolted to the seat between my legs. I was handcuffed to the car. I was suddenly very worried about what might happen next.

THE STASI CAR ROLLED AWAY FROM THE VILLA
and out the gravel driveway to the narrow highway that circled
the Motzener See. It was midmorning, and again, the weather
was superb. The car passed cyclists cruising along the road and
pedestrians dressed in their summer vacation clothing. The lake
shimmered through the trees.

Schmidt yanked furiously at his handcuffs in frustration. He
did it just once because it hurt. The Stasi next to him in the
backseat, a round-faced man, turned to stare with wide, startled
eyes. Schmidt glared back and the Stasi dropped his eyes immediately. He did not look like anyone's idea of a security policeman. He had corn-silk hair and apple cheeks and light blue
eyes. When he had turned to stare, Schmidt had been reminded
for a split second of the wide-eyed boys who used to come running
up to him when he left a stadium after competing. They would
be warbling with excitement at the sight of him, begging for his
autograph, elbowing each other to get closer, to touch him. When
his performance had been satisfactory, Schmidt was friendly and
humorous with the boys. Once in a while if his mood was dark,

he strode through them, muttering, "I have no time. I am in a hurry."

He wished he could hurry away from this boylike secret policeman and his grim partners. But he remained still and silent as the car sped down the country road away from Motzener See and turned onto the autobahn. The car hit a pothole on the freeway and lurched badly. One of the guards complained about the condition of the roads in the GDR. Schmidt almost blurted, "So now you understand why a man might want to leave." But he said nothing. One did not make wisecracks with the Stasi.

They entered the limits of East Berlin and went several miles into the city proper. At last they pulled up at a barrier across a narrow street. Beyond it lay several gray stone structures. Schmidt knew that he was at Grosse Leege-Strasse, at the corner of Gärtner Strasse, in the Hohenschönhausen section of Berlin, about three miles from his own neighborhood. This was a quiet part of the city with many gray apartment buildings. Schmidt did not recognize the drab, sprawling pile of a building where they stopped. It proved to be one of the special prisons run by the Ministry for State Security. It was known as an *Untersuchungshaftanstalt*— for short, a UHA. It was a holding prison where people waited before they were put on trial.

You don't see much from the outside, barred windows, blank walls. The barrier opened and we drove through. Ahead was a ten-foot fence with barbed wire on top. There were watchtowers to the right and left of it. Part of the fence slid open and we drove into the courtyard. We turned left and I saw an open gate, a gigantic steel gate, and we drove through that. The gate slid shut behind us. It ran quietly on tracks. It closed out the sun. We were parked in the dark in a big driveway and we got out of the car and walked up a staircase. Then through a door. Then through a steel fence that closed behind us. Then another door. Then we turned left and entered a small room. There were two warders there in blue uniforms. I had to give them my watch, my money, my belt, my gym bag. Everything I had with me I had to hand over.

They ordered me to take off my clothes, and they took them, too. Then they made me spread my legs, bend over forward, and they looked into my behind to make sure I hadn't hidden anything there.

They gave me a blue sweat suit, socks, underwear, felt slippers. I put these things on, then the Stasis—the damned toad and his stooges—who had brought me to the prison left. Two new guards in gray uniforms took me farther into the prison. First we went through a door with bars and it crashed shut behind us, making a great clashing sound that echoed down a long corridor. We continued down the corridor. The two of them stayed close to me, and that was the way it would always be—two guards with me, never one alone. Another barred door was at the end of the corridor. We passed through that. It, too, locked behind us. I think I passed through three such barred doors. All banged shut behind me. No more sunlight, I thought, no more freedom.

The Stasi were experts at making men vanish. As Schmidt moved ahead, he felt as if he were doing just that—disappearing from the face of the earth. The villa on the Motzener See had been unnerving, but the suburban furnishings, the lake outside, the sun, had at least made him feel he was connected with reality. Here he was moving deeper into a stony hell with gates closing and iron doors continually clashing shut behind him.

Schmidt didn't really believe the Stasi would let him die. But he knew that they could if they wished, and no one would know he was dead if they didn't want it known.

We walked up a staircase and I saw a longer corridor than any I had walked so far. Along the stone walls, both left and right, were cells like in a really proper jail, like the kind of jail you see on TV. With thick doors of wood and steel, an upper bolt and a lower bolt, a lock in the middle, a slit hatch at eye level that could be opened when someone wanted a spy hole to watch the prisoner inside. There was a hatch in the lower part of the door to pass food into the cell. The doors were gray, everything was gray. There were numbers on the doors.

And all along the corridor walls, up and down, were rip cords to sound an alarm. The cords were power cables with a low voltage in them, and they were there for the wardens in case of trouble. When the cables were pulled, an electrical circuit was interrupted, and the central office would know precisely where the trouble was.

They took me up yet another stairwell to the third floor. There was a green and a red light at the entrance to the corridor. When the green light was on, you were allowed to walk ahead into the corridor. But when the red light was on, you had to position yourself behind a white line, stand in a corner facing the wall, and wait like that until the green light came on again. This was to make sure no prisoners ever met on the corridors or staircases while in transit to and from their cells. I never saw another prisoner in the corridors there. I was always alone with whatever watchdogs were accompanying me.

They put me in a solitary cell. The number was 306 and it was small and narrow. Three or four steps long and one step wide. I felt suffocated when they closed that thick door on me. The cell felt no bigger than a grave.

There was no window, just a few glass blocks in the wall that let in a little light. The bed was made of planks with a dark gray blanket, a sheet, and no pillow. There was a toilet and washbasin. It was around noon, July 12, when they locked me in there. In a few minutes, someone gave me lunch through the hatch in the bottom of the door. It was slop in a plastic pot. Repulsive. Cheap sausage and white margarine. I tried to eat it, but I felt nauseous. I could barely look at it. I pushed it back out the hatch and someone out there took it away.

Nothing else happened that day. I slept as much as I could.

Schmidt was awakened in the morning by pounding on the door and shouts. "Wake up! Wake up!" For breakfast there was more margarine instead of butter, and Schmidt spread it on the bread and took a big bite. The margarine was rancid and he gagged. Then, an hour later, a guard shouted once more: "Get ready for recess! Get ready for recess!"

I was very pleased. I thought that now we were going to the courtyard of the prison—as I had seen on TV—and everyone would be walking in a big circle together, exercising, maybe talking. I put on the warm-up suit and a pair of sneakers they gave me and I waited. It took another eternity before the cell door was opened and I was led outside at last by two warders. The sneakers hurt immediately. They weren't too small, they were just manufactured in a way that made my feet hurt. I could hardly walk in them. But I went because I was anxious to breathe fresh air, and I was eager to see my fellow prisoners.

My two guards led me to the stairway I had come up the day before. Again we stopped for the red light. I waited, standing behind the white line with my face turned to the wall, for half a minute, maybe longer, until a warder said, "Go on." I had to wait my turn on my floor because another prisoner was moving through a corridor above or below me. They called it motion. You couldn't move when there was "motion" in another corridor.

The two guards took me down to the courtyard and turned me over to yet another guard. He was another redhead—not repulsive looking like my interrogator at the villa—and he was quite tall, about 6'3". The guards never said a word to me, they just did their job. They never spoke to each other and never to the prisoners. They just followed orders. *Null Acht Fünfzehn* all.

Schmidt found himself in an open courtyard about thirty-five meters long and ten meters wide. He was not allowed to see or to make any contact with other prisoners. Instead, he was ordered into an enclosed cubicle made of cement blocks. It was one in a row of eleven identical cubicles built along one side of the courtyard. Each of these outdoor cells was about ten feet wide by twenty-six feet long by fourteen feet high. They were open to

the sky, with a lacing of barbed wire overhead and a plank walkway running across the length of the cellblock. An armed sentry
strode back and forth across on this walkway, looking down
through the barbed wire at the prisoners as they worked out,
each isolated and alone in his own concrete box.

I had hoped to be able to see other human beings, perhaps someone
to talk to other than the sour Stasi or the mute UHA guards. But
here I was, alone in my open-air cell. There was someone in every
cell, but we couldn't see each other.

Of course, I could see the guard walking overhead. He stopped
to look down from time to time. When I was first there, the guards
watched me with great curiosity, as if I were some kind of rare
animal just brought into captivity. They never spoke. They just
stared.

When I was at recess in those cells, I exercised by running figure
eights from corner to corner, over and over, to get my circulation
going. Those were very small figure eights, and I felt like a mole
on a treadmill. I did discover early that cell number 8 of the eleven
in the courtyard was the most desirable because from it you could
see the top of a birch tree. That was the only sign of nature in the
UHA. I always tried to get into number 8.

As far as Schmidt could recall later, he was kept alone in cell 306
for three days and nights. He no longer had a watch, so
even that relatively short duration of time by himself became
confusing, and he lost track of hours and days. He was restless
and had uneasy dreams. He was worried about his physical condition and began to think he felt odd pressures in his chest from
a lack of exercise.

Time passed so slowly those first days. One hour seemed to last an
eternity. I didn't know what to do with myself, alone between four

walls. The world had broken into many pieces for me, and I wondered if it would ever be mended again.

I had a hard time sleeping through the night. It was so warm. It was so stuffy. I couldn't breathe. My body was screaming for work, for blood-circulation work. I needed to run, to exert myself in strenuous ways. I had no space, no freedom.

A high-performance athlete who suddenly cannot train his body anymore will suffer damage that might even threaten his life. The heart is too large. It is as if you had withdrawal symptoms because you can't give your body the activity it requires anymore.

He was allowed to write a letter to his parents and his sister on July 14, twelve days after his arrest. It sounded dark and self-accusing, couched in the submissive language of a man who seemed to have been brought near the breaking point by the incessant badgering of his interrogators. In fact, Schmidt had done this on purpose, knowing that the Stasi would read his mail. He thought that pretending remorse might make them go easier on him.

"Dear Mutti, dear Daddy, and dear Bettina:

"Today I have the possibility to write a few lines to you. At the time I am in *Untersuchungshaft* in Berlin. You must not reproach yourself, I alone am responsible for everything. I know now that I made many mistakes and I hope that I will be forgiven. It could be that I will ask you to get a lawyer for me. I still have to work on changing my attitude regarding many things. I want to prove what I can do in order to regain the confidence of the comrades whom I disappointed. This is my first goal that I have set for myself. I hope to see you soon again. Many dear regards. Your Wolfgang."

After the third day in the UHA, Schmidt was summoned from his cell after lunch. The door opened and the usual two guards stood there. One said in a monotone, "Come along for interrogation." They handcuffed Schmidt and led him down the corridor, past the green light and down two flights to the first floor of the prison. Here, in a warren of administrative offices, he was taken before a familiar person—Repulsive Red. The *poh-poh-poh* was still going on, and the man spoke in the same deadening voice.

He could hardly wait to tell me that he had just been informed that they had emptied my locker at the Sports Club Dynamo. They had taken my training clothes and my discuses away. I was no longer connected at all to any sports organization, he said.

Repulsive Red then ushered Schmidt into another office where he stood before a magistrate who was to sign the paper work that inducted him legally into the UHA. He was a pleasant man who gazed benignly over his glasses at Schmidt and said, "I was wondering why you didn't compete on the national team anymore."

Schmidt replied, "I was not welcome."

Later, the magistrate would cry out warm greetings to Schmidt whenever they met in the UHA, sounding much like a friendly maître d' at a good restaurant greeting a special customer. Now he simply laid the papers before Schmidt and watched while he signed them. The magistrate signed afterward, and Schmidt was now formally a prisoner held in detention by the state.

Schmidt rose to his feet and walked to the door without a word. Two warders accompanied him to his home away from home—solitary cell 306. It turned out to be his last night alone in the UHA. The following day he was taken by two more silent guards to cell 324, same floor, same corridor, just around the corner. It was a larger cell with three beds along with the requisite toilet and basin. He walked in, the guards slammed the door. Awaiting him was the first human being he had seen in the two weeks since his entry into the penal system who was probably neither a Stasi nor a prison employee. Schmidt thought "probably" because, like all prisoners, he never completely trusted anyone he met, knowing that many of the most popular and genial inmates turned out to be informers for the secret police.

Nevertheless, this particular inmate seemed an unlikely candidate for Stasi recruitment. He was a small, pallid young fellow. His eyes widened anxiously as Schmidt advanced toward him with his hand outstretched, and he took a step backward toward a corner of the room.

I realized that he was alarmed by the sight of me. I was very big and tanned and muscular, and he was so short and so pale and had already been in there for a long time. I was just too big for him to believe for a moment. But we introduced ourselves—his name was Bernd—and after a couple of minutes we were pretty friendly.

Bernd's crime was that he had stolen a car in Berlin and then had an accident in it. He panicked and left the scene of the accident, on foot, running. A cabdriver chased him on foot and grabbed hold of him for a moment. They wrestled, then Bernd tore himself loose and ran some more.

When he finally stopped and saw that no one was on his heels, he assumed that he had gotten away safely. Then he felt through his pockets and was shocked to find that he had lost his identification papers during the scuffle with the damned taxi driver. Now he really panicked because he realized that the police would immediately discover who he was and that they would arrest him the moment he went anywhere near his home again.

He was so scared by all this that he went berserk. This idiot ran all the way to The Wall and tried to escape although he had no ladder or anything. Of course, they caught him trying to get over a fence in front of The Wall and put him in the can.

By comparison, Schmidt's "crime" was lacking in drama. But both of them were charged with essentially the same thing: conspiring to leave the country without permission. Once this odd couple got used to each other, they got along very well.

Bernd was twenty-two, a mere boy in some ways, but very experienced in others. He explained to me exactly how to short-circuit the starter of a car and get it going without a key. I have never made use of this skill, but I remember that he taught me very well. We played chess together. We were quite evenly matched. I lost often and he lost often.

Bernd also spent a lot of his time memorizing a book by heart, some silly book, a utopian piece of work that I don't recall anymore. He would recite the sentences over and over, moving his lips and making no sound.

Whatever kind of a nut he was, being in the cell with Bernd was an improvement over counting the minutes alone in number 306. We were together for about six weeks, in all.

Privacy was unheard of. Not only were the two cellmates constantly in each other's company, they were also under twenty-four-hour surveillance while they were in the cell.

They spied on us all the time through a small watch hole in the door, even all night long. Every thirty minutes at night, the light in the cell would go on and someone would be looking through the spy hole. They claimed they were looking to be sure nobody was trying to commit suicide. It was enough to stretch your sanity to the limit, those lights coming on and those eyes in the peephole.

As always, Schmidt was anxious about his physical condition. He wrote a letter to the district attorney soon after his arrival at the UHA asking permission to do extra physical training while he was awaiting trial: "I am a high-performance athlete and I am at the height of my training. I am afraid my health will be damaged unless I am allowed to train consistently." He wrote out a thorough and specific training program for his prison existence that included the use of the prison courtyard for calisthenics and running, as well as working out with weights in his cell.

Requests for special treatment in prison usually ran to diets or medications for chronic illnesses, and they were handled quickly with an abrupt rubber stamp or the flick of a pen. Schmidt's request was apparently something that no one at the UHA had ever dealt with before.

The district attorney himself appeared during an interrogation to give his answer to Schmidt's request.

He was very unimpressive. He was short and thin, about 5'4" and 125 pounds. He seemed old and tired. Maybe he was sixty-five, maybe seventy. A real old doddering daddy. He had no teeth at all on one side of his mouth. He probably had some dentures, but he didn't wear them to the prison. When he spoke, he lisped and spit a little through his gums.

To look at him, he did not seem like a man accustomed to authority. But when he gave me my answer, I can tell you he was definitely an authoritarian. First, he had asked me about a few details in my training plan, then he said quite sharply that it was not possible to do my training the way I had imagined it. In fact, it was completely out of the question. He pointed out that I was in a prison and not a sanatorium. What training I could do, I would have to do in my cell, he said. That was the best he could do, he said, and then he turned and left the room, this little old man with missing teeth and such a bossy nature.

The next day I was given two dumbbells, each twenty-five kilograms [55 lbs.]. They were rolled through the door into the cell. "Here," said a warder, "train down all you want."

For the rest of his stay at the UHA—four months—Schmidt was allowed to train with weights for one hour a day. So as not to disturb his cellmate Bernd, he was allowed to use another empty cell.

I was still quite strong and had pretty good muscles. Once, when it was very warm and I wasn't wearing a shirt, I saw the spy hole open in the door and the two warders looked in. I heard one of them go "Aw! Aw! Aw!" as he watched me lift.

Despite the district attorney's refusal to allow extra training, Schmidt was occasionally allowed to run figure eights in the prison yard. In the yard, Schmidt sometimes mimed the movements of the discus thrower, starting with a motionless pose, then beginning his whirling rotation, accelerating until he flung an imaginary discus up and out and over the prison wall into the outside world.

He felt somewhat better after he began the daily exercises, but he was still weakened and occasionally nauseous. He was losing weight. He suspected at times that they were putting something in his food, perhaps a tranquilizer or a drug to keep him tamed. Once, early on, the warders sent him to a prison nurse to have a blood sample taken. The explanation for this was that they were routinely checking for anemia, but Schmidt suspected they were really keeping track of how some drug in his food was affecting him.

SCHMIDT HAD RECEIVED NO MESSAGES AT ALL from his parents. He had no idea whether his first letter had been delivered or what they knew about him. Actually, they had received his letter on July 23, but by that time, the Schmidts knew very well that he was in serious trouble.

The Stasi had visited the apartment three days after Schmidt's arrest and picked up the few personal items he was allowed. The policemen had curtly informed the family that Wolfgang was under arrest for "traffic hooliganism." On July 15, Ernst and his wife, Gretel, an energetic, intelligent woman who was every bit as strong-willed as her husband, had been summoned by an official at SC Dynamo and informed that Wolfgang was being held for "grievances against the state."

Then on July 20, the Stasi searched the apartment on Stahlheimer Strasse. Ernst Schmidt recalled, "They arrived with a search order. Three men. One photographed everything in the apartment, and two other snoopers, all in civilian clothes, searched Wolfgang's room. They looked for pictures, postcards, letters he might have received from the West, notes that might tell them whom he had contacted. They also searched his unfinished house in Hohen Neuendorf. There they found a flare pistol in the garden shack. This caused a lot of trouble later though the pistol was harmless and didn't work."

The day after the searches, a form letter arrived at their summer house, which was also in Hohen Neuendorf. Dated July 16, it was from the office of the attorney general of the GDR:

"Dear Herr Schmidt: Against your son, Wolfgang Schmidt, preliminary proceedings were initiated and a warrant for his arrest was issued since he is strongly suspected of having committed a punishable offense. Your son is being held at the Untersuchungs-haftanstalt Berlin. You have the possibility of writing four letters a month. Mention of the offense is not allowed in the letters. Packages cannot be accepted. Cash remittances up to fifty marks per month (though only through the postal service) are permitted. Underwear and clothing are only to be brought upon request. The following address should be used for letters and cash remittances.

"First Name and Last Name.

"1040 Berlin, Postal Box 84.

"Permission to speak will be granted as soon as the state of the investigations permits. After completion of the investigations you will be informed of the further course of the proceedings."

It was signed simply, "Haber, District Attorney."

On July 23, Schmidt's mother wrote him the first of many letters.

"My dear Wolfgang: On 7/21 the district attorney informed us that we may write to you. Today we also received your first letter, for which we thank you very much. We are well, our thoughts are always with you, and we'll also look after your property. On July 11 and 12, we harvested the sweet cherries, about 200 lbs. The garage is finished except for one wall in the back and it looks very good. Yesterday I mowed your lawn. We have wonderful summer weather right now, but everything is very dry. Father was in Kienbaum [a special training facility] for almost 2 weeks, but he came home a few times. On 7/17 we went swimming in Lindow Lake. It was a gray day but the water was wonderful, and that was great for the children. Annika [Schmidt's three-year-old niece] goes into the water all by herself, and one has to watch her closely. Now, my dear Wolfgang, I hope that we will see you soon again, and I send greetings from all of us. Your mother."

Before that letter was delivered to him, Schmidt had written yet another, again expressing abject contrition for his deeds: "I regret so much that I caused you so many worries and problems. That's what I get for fooling around and for my childish stupidity." He then said, "Surely it is now necessary for me to use a lawyer. That's why I would like to ask you to get one for me."

He sent a list of attorneys in East Berlin. Included was the famous Dr. Wolfgang Vogel, a mysteriously well-connected attorney of the GDR who had handled some of the Cold War's most dramatic and delicate East-West prisoner exchanges—including the sensitive transaction in 1962 in which US pilot Gary Powers, who had been shot down over Russia in his U2 spy plane, was allowed to return to the US in exchange for the Soviet spy Rudolf Abel, who had been captured by the FBI in New York. Over the years, Vogel had been instrumental in other major East-West exchanges including one in 1986 when the Soviet dissident Anatoli B. Shcharansky was allowed to go West in a complex deal involving eight other people. Vogel was a clever fellow who had often been involved in defending political prisoners of the GDR. At times, his techniques for springing them loose included raw barter with goods such as fertilizer, drugs, coffee, radios, and tropical fruit—and sometimes cold cash—given in exchange for a man's freedom.

How he got away with it, no one knew, but obviously he had good connections in both East and West. He was a confidant of Erich Honecker, yet he was also one of a handful of East Germans accredited to the West Berlin bar. His wife, a former West German swimmer, drove a gold-colored Mercedes and habitually shopped for her wardrobe in Vienna and Paris. Vogel liked to make his work sound like a divine calling, and he once said, "There is a kind of pastoral, priestly quality to the contact that a lawyer has with a prisoner and his family."

Gretel Schmidt went to Vogel's office and explained her son's situation to the great man himself. He turned her over to a partner named Dieter Starkulla. He was an unremarkable-looking man with a black beard, spectacles, and a low, soothing voice. He was pleasant, relaxed, and obviously intelligent. One of the first things Starkulla did was to try to arrange a meeting between Schmidt and his parents.

He did well. A letter dated August 2 arrived at the apartment on Stahlheimer Strasse, informing Ernst and Gretel: "You may visit your son on August 10, 1982, at 15:00 hours at the Untersuchungshaftanstalt Berlin-Lichtenberg, Alfredstr. 11."

This meeting was to be held at a different UHA from the one that Schmidt had now inhabited for a month. When he was taken from his cell and handcuffed, he had no idea where he was going. Someone told him he had some visitors. Two armed guards and a driver accompanied him in a "Minna" minibus through the streets of Berlin.

I was driven out of the dark UHA garage into the sunlight. We drove about fifteen minutes, and the destination turned out to be in a familiar neighborhood, at Magdalenen Strasse off Frankfurter Allee where my sister lived. We entered the UHA there, and my God, you can only imagine my joy when I was led into a room and there sat my mother and father.

We would have liked to weep and embrace, I suppose. But the Stasis remained with us at all times, so the meeting was not so emotional. My mother had tears in her eyes. But we couldn't even talk openly about how bleak our lives had gotten to be. The atmosphere was so damned oppressive. What a scene for black comedy. A son is in prison. I could not explain why. My parents couldn't explain why. They wanted to help me. How desperate, how hopeless, we all felt. Yet we couldn't talk about these painful things with those pigs listening, could we? So we made small talk, speaking of the lawn mowing at the summer home, the condition of the spark plugs on my father's car, the prune dumplings my mother had cooked for dinner.

I was so full of hatred for those dirty pigs who had made us into such a black joke.

Banal though the conversation had been, his mother was alarmed by his emotional condition. She wrote him the next day: "When we see each other next time, you will surely have calmed down. Read good books, take your mind off your problems, and especially don't reproach yourself about anything. Save your nerves because you have not done anything wrong. I can only repeat, remain courageous and strong even if it is difficult for you. Keep up some pride and don't crawl."

Ernst recalled, "My God, they had obviously been so inhuman to him. He had been taken out of a full training process where he was aiming for top-level performances and left with nothing— no training time, no medical advice, no medication. During that first visit, we thought he seemed to be psychologically broken. The impression we had was unbearable. How could the authorities be so irresponsible toward him? To take an athlete at the height of his preparations and slap him in a single cell without considering the consequences—the physical and the psychological damage. The state of his nerves seemed to be at the limit of insanity. He sat there pulling at his hair, scratching his head. We felt that psychologically he had already been badly affected, that he was perched right at the brink of despair."

Schmidt had been greatly moved by the visit. The next day, he wrote another letter that was heartbreaking. "Oh, I would like to return home so much. You, dear Mother, made me a bit stronger, but I am so helpless. I always think of you and often I have tears in my eyes. I am looking forward to your next visit. I am so sorry. Enjoy everything that is beautiful, everything that is nature; try not to be sad because then I'll feel better, too."

PRISON LIFE DRAGGED ON. THERE WERE HUN-
dreds of men and women in the UHA, but Schmidt rarely had
face-to-face contact with any but his cellmate. Occasionally, he
was touched by other prisoners in strange and impersonal ways.

There was one prisoner on our floor who must have had a wooden
leg. I never saw him. But whenever he was taken out of his cell for
interrogation, I could hear him limping down the long corridor.
Tak-tak, tak-tak, tak-tak. It was such a mournful noise, and I wondered what he looked like and how he had lost his leg.

One day I heard a prisoner being ushered into a cell next door.
The door crashed shut behind him. He wanted out but no one
came, so he began to weep. And it went on and on. I could hear
him weeping helplessly for hours. I never saw him either.

Throughout the first month of his stay at the UHA, to his
great discomfort, Schmidt had more contact with Repulsive Red

than anyone else. The interrogations went on, as endless as they were pointless, grinding over much of the same material they had discussed at the villa. Each morning Schmidt was taken to the Oberleutnant's office, a sterile cubbyhole furnished with a wardrobe, a desk and a couple of chairs, and a map of the GDR.

I sometimes stared at that map and I thought, Good God, is that the tiny territory where I am spending my life? Is it really that speck of fly shit on the planet where all this is happening to me?

The interrogation usually took place around nine or ten o'clock in the morning, and he always took his sweet time with it. Returning always, again and again, to the same questions. Why did I want to leave the GDR? Whom did I know in the West? He wanted to know everything—and more—about my relationship to Ludwig Schura, the West Berlin businessman. I told Red I had met him in East Berlin in 1980 through a girlfriend. Red accused me of planning to escape. He accused me of having asked Schura whether he could help me get out.

This happened to be true. I had talked to Schura about the possibility of escaping during the World Cup in Rome in the fall of 1981. He had been happy to help me, and he went to Rome for those competitions. Of course, I did not go because they had kept me off the team. I had kept contact with Schura into 1982, and the Stasi must have got wind of it. His wife was from the East and he often came to visit relatives. I was arrested in July, and one month later, while I was in the UHA, Schura was picked up when he crossed the border into East Berlin at Friedrichstrasse, and they questioned him for a full day.

He admitted that I had asked him to help me get out of the GDR. I admitted it, too.

But what was the point of all this? I had already told them I wanted to leave. I had already told them that it was only because I couldn't participate in sports in the GDR anymore. Again and again, I answered these same things. All of it was a waste of time. The only thing that mattered was that I wasn't allowed to pursue my sport anymore. I could not make it more clear to them. Yet they went on asking, asking, asking. And I went on answering, answering, answering.

After a couple of weeks, early in August, a new subject arose in Repulsive Red's questioning. The Stasi search of Schmidt's unfinished house had turned up the flare pistol. So what was an illegal firearm doing in Schmidt's possession? Was he planning to use it to escape? Repulsive Red grilled him for answers, but Schmidt could only laugh.

My God, what they had found was an old flare pistol from the Second World War—maybe it was forty years old. I had dug it up when I was a boy playing in the ruins of an old ammunition factory near my grandparents' farm in Klein-Schmölen. The pistol didn't work at all. It had been buried in dirt for years. I had come across it again recently in a drawer in my parents' apartment, and I took it with me to my house where I took it apart and oiled it. Then I forgot about it.

The redheaded idiot demanded to know where I had obtained such a vicious piece of hardware. I told him, of course, that I had found it as a boy, but naturally he refused to believe that. He went on probing, probing about that damned gun—a toy was really what it was. I laughed about it, but he really didn't believe my story.

By now, Schmidt had begun to wonder if he was going to spend eternity with Repulsive Red interrogating him. Then he got a reprieve.

I had been four weeks in the UHA, it was about the middle of August, when the fat redhead—that ugly Saxon—went on vacation. Of course, I instantly got a new interrogator, but anything was better than Red. The new one was an actor, a true thespian. Not a professional, of course, but he had all the habits of an actor. He was dark haired, small, and frail looking, in his midthirties. He would sit there behind his desk, asking questions quite calmly, and then suddenly he would start to twitch his facial muscles and his lips. As if he were having a fit of anger at me. As if he had suddenly gone crazy. He was trying to scare the piss out of me. It didn't work. Whenever he twitched, I began to twitch, too—exaggerating every move he made. This irritated him. Eventually, he stopped the twitching act and continued the interrogation exactly where Repulsive Red had left off. One was as bad as the other. Every day lasted a month.

Schmidt's old friend Wiedemann, the supercilious nail-biter, also surfaced again at the UHA.

As an Oberstleutnant, Wiedemann was the boss of several interrogators. He questioned me personally every three or four weeks. He would have me picked up in my cell and escorted to his office. He was as well dressed as ever with his hair slicked back, and his approach to life was as vain and superior as ever. His questions were more philosophical than the others had been. How did I want to go on with my life? What were my thoughts about life, about politics, about sport, about life after prison?

Whenever he questioned me, he had a meal brought for me from the prison kitchen. It was quite different food from anything we had in our cells. He would order me a nice steak with asparagus and potato croquettes or some such. And always he arranged for an enormous dish of ice cream.

I loved the food, but I knew, of course, that it was only part of the psychology Wiedemann was trying to use on me. He was trying to weaken my resolve and make me give in to him. It would have been a feather in his cap, I suppose, if he could tell his Stasi bosses that he had brought Wolfgang Schmidt to his knees.

Many times I would have liked to throw the whole meal in his fucking face and beat him up, too. But I didn't because I was interested in going through that whole period with as little trouble as possible. Besides, it would have been stupid to throw away such nice food.

He was pretending to be my patron. He tried to insinuate himself into my favor and he asked me private questions. How did I wish to pass my time in prison? What kind of work would I like to do? I told him, "Something with cars, I guess." I did not know, of course, that this would come back to haunt me a year and more later when I was forced to wash cars for hours every day.

In his letters to his parents, Schmidt did not mention Wiedemann and the torturous interrogations. He continued to write in a tone of abject resignation so the Stasi censors would think he was breaking down. On August 18 he wrote: "I miss you so much. Alone I am so helpless. I miss my daily training. I am losing more and more weight. I tell myself again and again, had I only listened to father from time to time, I could have spared us a lot of problems. Whenever this ends, I don't know, I only know that I need you very much and I ask you to help me." On August 31 he wrote: "I am terribly homesick and I worry very much. I wait, wait, wait, and am bored and nothing happens that would give me a goal again." On September 17 he wrote a birthday letter to his mother, and there was the sound of surrender in it: "I see everything in a different light now; I see the mistakes I made that I didn't see before, and I hope everything will be all right again. I hope the sports club will support me now. I know that my home is here [in the GDR] and that everything else that I desired was stupid. I would like to compete again. I must await a decision about that."

His mother warned him not to get his hopes up, that his career as an athlete for the GDR was indeed finished. She wrote him in late August: "During the GDR championships in Dresden, it was announced over the loudspeaker that the world-record holder Wolfgang Schmidt had retired from his sports career." And in late September, she said: "You write that you would like to compete again. I don't want to hurt you, but they won't permit this here anymore. Don't believe so easily and don't count on support from others."

At about this time, Schmidt and the young car thief Bernd were allowed to watch a telecast of the European Track and Field Championships from Athens, Greece. It was a strange experience.

It rained pretty hard during the discus competition, so I thought, Well, I am not missing that much, I guess. Imrich Bugar won. But as I watched, I thought of what Annette Tånander, a Swedish heptathlete, had asked me when I was competing in Stockholm in 1981. "Why don't you stay?" she said. I said no, but if I had any idea that Stockholm was going to be my last appearance in the West— my God, I'd have stayed immediately.

In fact, as I watched, I started to think of all the times I could have stayed in the West. Why didn't I stay in Düsseldorf way back in 1977 when I had just won the World Cup? The words of a song were running through my mind: *"Wärst du doch in Düsseldorf geblieben, kleiner Playboy."* [If you had only stayed in Düsseldorf, little playboy.]

As we watched the TV from Athens, I said to Bernd, "God, I should be there!" I wanted to add, "Because I'd never come back again." But I didn't know whether Bernd might be a Stasi stool pigeon, so I said nothing. All I could do was hope that I was missed by all my friends in Athens. All I could do was hope that athletes and journalists were asking everywhere what had become of me.

After six weeks residing with Bernd, Schmidt was moved to a new cell where he had a roommate of a vastly different type.

His name was—what?—Harmut? No, I can't be sure. But he had been a member of an army unit, an officer, and there had been a death of some kind, manslaughter through culpable negligence. He was guilty, all right, but he never told me the whole story. I imagine that he was probably in charge of training soldiers, and maybe when they were cleaning their weapons, someone fooled around and didn't know he still had a bullet in his gun and he shot one of his buddies through the head. The officer in charge had to take responsibility for that kind of accident.

This fellow had been pretty done in by it all. He was short and skinny and sallow and he had dark hair. He was from Dresden. He tried to change my outlook on socialism in the GDR, but he didn't have enough energy to launch any very good arguments. He ended up staying in the UHA even longer than I did, a lost soul with all of his years in the army wasted because of someone else's stupid mistake.

Schmidt's mother wrote the prescribed four times a month, and at times, her letters brought dark tidings from the outside world. She told him that her favorite uncle, Ernst Leist, an old man from West Berlin whom Wolfgang had adored, had visited them for a last good-bye and would soon die of cancer after a long and agonizing siege that left him weighing eighty-eight pounds. Also, she told him, his father was probably going to require surgery to correct a prostate condition, and worse, the wolves at the DTSB had begun to circle him.

In late August, Ernst had been summoned to the office of Manfred Ewald, the imperious little chief of East German sports. They had known each other as friends and colleagues for thirty years. But now Ewald began ranting about the visit the Schmidts had had from poor old Uncle Ernst Leist: "You in your position have no right to receive visitors from the West without reporting them. This old man was no exception. You broke the rules, Ernst!"

Ordinarily this sort of infraction would have been overlooked. Ernst reminded Ewald that the old uncle had been a benefactor for the DTSB long ago in its shabby beginnings because he had lent money for Ernst to buy a car that he used mainly in his work with the sports organization. "You know very well, Manfred," he said to the furious little man, "what Uncle Ernst did for us in the old days. You know the car he arranged built us up when we were still weak."

But Ewald was livid. "You should have shut the door in his face!" Ernst walked out of Ewald's office. This was the beginning of the end for him. During a track meet in Potsdam, word spread among officials of the DTSB that Ernst had suffered a nervous breakdown.

"It is the hammer for your father," Gretel wrote to Wolfgang. "Honesty has to be punished. The years of his work don't count, only this moment counts. His illness is only a welcome excuse. How would it sound if they had to say, 'You are finished because your son is in jail'?"

At last, late in September, word came from Schmidt's lawyer that the date for his trial had been set for October 12. His parents were told they would not be allowed to attend. Schmidt wrote them, "I am curious to see what the trial will produce, and I'll be happy when it is over."

He was very wrong about that.

Dieter Starkulla had had some sessions with Schmidt about strategy for the trial. Charges against Schmidt ultimately boiled down to two: plotting to leave the GDR and illegal possession of a firearm—the old flare pistol they had found in his unoccupied new house.

Starkulla warned Schmidt, "Paragraph two thirteen is the problem. The rest is not so serious." He referred to Paragraph 213 of the Penal Code, which dealt with the crime of attempting— or simply *planning*—to leave the country unlawfully. A sentence of "up to two years imprisonment" could be given to anyone who (1) "unlawfully crosses the state border" or (2) "unlawfully fails to return to the [GDR] or does not do so within the required time limit." A sentence of up to eight years could be given "in aggravated cases" that involved a weapon, a forged passport, or any action that "endangers the life or health" of others. Because Schmidt had confessed to the Stasi that he had discussed plans to leave the GDR, he was charged with "preparation to escape," a constitutional crime.

In the final analysis, having a lawyer was a joke. The law offices of Wolfgang Vogel had worked out so many big East-West deals that they certainly had to be collaborating closely with the Stasi. I knew this, but I figured that there might be a slim chance of obtaining freedom through this *Menschenhändler* [dealer in human lives].

But it was obvious that the state only lets you have a lawyer when they have their cat in the bag with no escaping. The case, the trial, all of it, was staged to suit the Stasi and the DTSB. Actually, it was the Stasi that insisted that I be forced out of sports and put on trial. They were afraid that if I left the GDR and then went on to have great success in the West and began living a life of wealth and enjoyment in the West, then other GDR athletes would wonder what the hell they were doing staying behind in their deprived little prison state. The Stasi had decided that I had to be jailed to keep that from happening. Starkulla could do nothing. Having a lawyer was nothing but a formality.

In those days, law in the GDR was an exercise in systematic hypocrisy and political manipulation. Amnesty International, the human rights organization headquartered in Switzerland, published an annual report on the East German legal system. In 1989, it summarized its findings with damning brevity: "Secrecy conceals the full truth about human rights violations in the GDR [because of] secret trials, secret directives to lawyers, laws forbidding sending information abroad. And the trials of prisoners of conscience are hardly ever reported in the press."

Prisoners of conscience were defined as people charged with crimes under "laws which curtail various freedoms" such as freedom of expression, freedom of assembly, freedom of association, and the freedom to leave one's country. All of these rights were guaranteed in the International Covenant on Civil and Political Rights, an agreement that the GDR ratified in 1974.

Erich Honecker had declared as recently as 1981 that "all citizens are equal before the law," but as Amnesty International pointed out, equality is meaningless when the law itself can be manipulated at will. Monika Maron, the East German author, wrote to the West German publication *Die Zeit,* "The law decides who is an offender, and if eating bread were to be legally banned in the GDR tomorrow, we would be an entire country full of criminals. I am a lawbreaker merely because I am writing you this letter."

Unlike criminal law in the West, which generally works to protect citizens against lawbreakers, criminal law in the GDR worked to protect the state and the party against threatening acts. An official textbook used in East German law schools described the nation's criminal laws as "a specific state-judicial instrument of the working class's political power" whose purpose "serves the realization of the historical mission of the working class." Thus, as Amnesty International succinctly declared, "criminal law [in the GDR] is officially intended to serve explicitly political ends."

Wolfgang Schmidt was jailed for expressing his desire to leave the country. As it happened, the particular "right" to leave one's country was one of the items included in the international covenant that East Germany ratified in '74. But that didn't matter.

The official rationalization of the East German state for making the desire to emigrate a criminal act was that it was really only for the citizenry's own good. A law school textbook, *State Law of the GDR,* published in 1977, explained this bit of propagandist hoodwinking in pure socialist boilerplate: "There is no social basis in the GDR for a basic right to emigrate. . . . The political and moral responsibility for every citizen requires the socialist state to consider also the class struggle between socialism and imperialism when deciding on applications to emigrate. It takes account of the fact that emigration to an imperial state means handing people over to a system that exploits them and compels them to serve an aggressive policy, that threatens their existence and is directed against socialism."

For what it was worth, Schmidt had not been singled out by the system for particularly harsh treatment. According to Amnesty International, most East German prisoners of conscience were dealt with in a manner pretty much identical to Schmidt's. Nearly all of them underwent immediate intensive interrogation in a detention center, and most made "incriminating statements during the investigatory proceedings" because most were "taken by surprise by their arrest, and during the first twenty-four hours, their shock and uncertainty why they are there often results in their making incriminating admissions." Also like Schmidt, political detainees were routinely kept in solitary confinement and "interrogated daily by state security police" who kept asking "exactly the same questions" day after day and week after week until, as one prisoner put it, "you felt that you were stagnating."

Amnesty International also described defense attorneys who rarely discussed a specific line of defense but rather advised their defendants on how to act in court. It spoke of vague charges that might or might not be delivered in writing to the defendant and his attorney, and it spoke of swift, secret trials "with few lasting more than one day" that inevitably led to a guilty verdict in a matter of hours.

All of this exactly matched Wolfgang Schmidt's experience with the judicial system of the GDR.

On October 12, 1982, after Schmidt had been in custody for 102 days, his trial was held in a small district court in Lichtenberg, a suburb of East Berlin. He had thought it might be something rather theatrical, a show trial perhaps in which the fallen champion was paraded about in eights and chains as an example of what happens to even the most famous and glamorous of East Germans when they break the laws of the state.

But there was nothing remotely sensational about his trial. The courtroom was small, a sleazy place where wife-beaters, swindlers, and real traffic hooligans appeared to receive their legal comeuppance. The major piece of decor was a large state emblem—hammer, circle, wreath—on the wall over the judge's bench. Instead of a rapt crowd of the curious and the worshipful—autograph hounds, sportswriters, sports fans—the spectators' gallery was empty. Not even his parents had been allowed to attend.

Starkulla explained it to him simply: "They are trying to keep it on a small scale or they would have brought it before a bigger court. They apparently don't want this known to the public. This is not something they want to shout from the housetops."

They took me to the door of the courtroom with handcuffs on, but then they took them off. The judge, three jurors, and a female prosecuting attorney all sat on a dais, and I sat below with Starkulla. Oberstleutnant Wiedemann entered, and to my surprise, so did a man I had seen around SC Dynamo, obviously a Stasi, I realized for the first time. They took places at the table for officials, listening as the prosecutor read the charges.

He accused me of having made preparations to escape from the republic and, of course, they had no trouble proving that. He said several times that I had spoken of wanting to leave by helicopter. *"Hubschrauber, mit einem Hubschrauber,"* he kept saying. He accused me of illegal possession of a weapon, too. It was a farce, nothing but a farce.

After they read the charges, they asked me to read my résumé. I told them of all the championships I had won, of the Order of Merit I had received from Honecker twice, of the silver medal I won in Montreal. And after that they summoned witnesses. And nothing that was said from then on made me sound like a champion of anything.

The most damaging of the witnesses entered the courtroom first, and Schmidt gasped in disbelief, for it was his ostensible friend and fan, Jochen Brüggmann. This fellow had for more than a year acted as if he were one of Schmidt's most adoring followers. He had displayed doglike affection, acted the sycophant and the gofer, put himself out constantly to serve Schmidt ever since he first appeared in April 1981 at a joint training camp in Cottbus with discus throwers from the Soviet Union. In those days, Schmidt was near the top of his form and was about to embark on some of the best competitions of his career. Brüggmann had approached him in a hotel restaurant and asked Schmidt to honor him with an autograph. Brüggmann had then begun a well-informed conversation about upcoming meets and about the comparative strengths of the East German and Russian teams. He made it clear that, to him, Wolfgang Schmidt was head and shoulders above the rest. Obviously well briefed about Schmidt's fascination with cars, Brüggmann insisted before they parted that Wolfgang borrow a Western magazine about automobiles.

I didn't want the magazine, but I think now that he wanted a reason to contact me again in Berlin. Anyway, I had thought he was a pretty interesting fellow. He said he was a collector and a dealer of antique porcelain. He said that he issued certifications for antique Meissen china, and he showed me some pictures of that china. He seemed quite well-off. Now that I know he was with the Stasi, I can see why. They often did deals in antiques smuggled West and sold for hard currency. Brüggmann had many connections, people in all different walks of life.

He asked me probing questions about lots of things, and he always seemed to listen to me closely, I now recall. He studied me. I was always talking about how I wanted to make my life better and that I was most limited by the fact that there was a border to the west and that I could not go beyond it.

He was very forthcoming to me. After Cottbus, we met next at a competition for throwers in Halle the following month, and he was pleasant, and soon after that he turned up again at a sports festival later in Cottbus. He seemed to be at my elbow always. I didn't mind. I was curious about him because he was out of the ordinary, a cut above the fans who followed us around. I was curious about him, very curious.

After the festival in Cottbus, Brüggmann had asked Schmidt, "What are you driving here?"

As Brüggmann well knew, Schmidt possessed one of the GDR's infamous air-polluting little Wartburgs. Brüggmann asked, "Ah, but do you really like it?"

Schmidt said, "Well, it's maintenance free."

"Ah, but you will like my Ford better. Get behind the wheel. See how this sweetheart takes off. Go ahead, drive it back to Berlin. I'll take yours."

Given his weakness for things American in general and cars in

particular, Schmidt was delighted to accept the offer. Brüggmann
followed to Berlin in the Wartburg, arrived at Stahlheimer Strasse
4 just in time for dinner, and stayed. From then on he insinuated
his way into Wolfgang's life and soon became a fixture.

He kept coming back, sometimes in the mornings when I was sleeping. My mother was very friendly to him and my father seemed to
like him, too. We would go out at night sometimes and he was at
dinner sometimes, always asking questions. He made me a little
uneasy, but I was still curious about him.

Though Schmidt had the impression that his father approved
of the unctuous porcelain dealer, Ernst had never been happy
about Brüggmann's presence: "Wolfgang seemed always to have
him in tow. I didn't like it at all because Brüggmann was about
fifty years old and he shouldn't be a buddy to a young man like
Wolfgang. I asked Wolfgang once, 'What's your relationship with
this man anyway? What does he want here?' Wolfgang replied,
'Oh, he just likes to make himself useful.' Well, now we know
how 'useful' his visits were. They allowed him to keep an eye on
our apartment and on our summer house and on Wolfgang's
house. We know how 'useful' it was for him to listen to Wolfgang's private musings and then report everything he heard to
the Stasi."

It was true. As Schmidt listened in disbelief to Brüggmann's
testimony at the trial, there could be no doubt. The man was a
professional Stasi informer.

Whenever we met, I am sure that he wrote down what happened
and turned it in to some central point where they would check his
information about me with some other Stasi sources who were
observing me. Maybe some team member or a coach or trainer
who kept an eye—and an ear—on me. Maybe some neighbor who
listened to everything. Then they would check each source against

the others to see who had what they wanted and whether the reports corroborated each other.

Brüggmann was the key. He told the Stasi after a couple of months, "Don't let him go West anymore. He is too easy to influence and he might break away at any moment." That's why I wasn't allowed to go West again after the track meet in Stockholm in July of '81 where I did exceptionally well—in fact, I won, although it was on a technicality. Nevertheless, it was my last international competition for the GDR. And it was all because Brüggmann had warned them to keep me in the country.

While I watched him testify, I couldn't believe this man was human. He looked like a younger brother of Honecker. He had wormed his way into my life. He was like a limpet, sucking my blood. I could not bring myself to look at him, this slug, this piece of filth.

What a witness he was, this goddamn porcelain smuggler, this eel. And I had never been smart enough to slam the door on him. Well, I learned a lot about life from that fellow. All the nonsense he spewed in court, I shut my ears to it.

Besides Brüggmann they also called my friend Ulf Leischner. He did not say anything derogatory about me. He had been ordered to appear. He had no choice but to come in and talk about me. They interrogated him about conversations we had had when we walked near The Wall together or when we rode to the top floors of the high rises there. He told them everything they wanted to know, even about our fantasies of flying to the West with a hang glider. Leischner was pale all during his testimony, a sickly white. He was on his feet to testify, and after a couple of questions, he weakly asked the judge if he could please sit down. I had to suppress a laugh, seeing Leischner, a man six feet seven inches tall, turn so weak and faint.

All the time I was thinking, How can you organize such shit as this and call it a trial? It was insane. The sum of it all was that I was a disreputable person on any number of counts and that I deserved nothing in life but a prison sentence. I would have laughed out loud if it hadn't been so depressing. There was absolutely no deviation from their plan from the moment the trial started.

I was, of course, in no position whatsoever to raise any points in my own defense. The verdict had been decided even before they chased me down and arrested me.

Starkulla put up a defense of sorts, but there was a rather tentative quality to his presentation. He did ask the judge and jury, "Can it really be possible that this young man can have turned into such a miserable human being after years of being a hero of the republic? Could we have all judged him so wrong that he could conceal such a dastardly character under the mask of the smiling hero?" This met with silence from the bench.

The lawyer tried to put a small dent in the testimony of Jochen Brüggmann by asking the Stasi, "If you thought Wolfgang Schmidt was such a bad person, a traitor to the state and a would-be defector, why did you visit him so often? What exactly did you want from him? And why didn't you prevent all this from happening?"

Brüggmann became uncomfortable in the face of such questions. But he was not required by the court to reply.

The trial took one day. It could have taken five minutes because it was all scripted ahead of time anyway. The verdict was announced the following day. Starkulla didn't even show up for it. He knew it would be a waste of his time.

The judge and jurors asked me questions, too. I guess my answers proved their case because when the judge announced the guilty verdict, he made it clear that I was a no-good with completely rotten character traits. The woman who was the prosecuting attorney demanded a sentence of fourteen months. When I heard this, I felt pretty good. I had thought I would get three or four years. If they deducted the time I had already spent at the villa and the UHA, my jail term would be less than eleven months. Then the damned judge sentenced me to eighteen months. This troubled me, but it didn't knock me really low. I thought, Well, I can sit that out on one buttock. When I get out in fifteen months or so, I'll still be able to throw again. I'll show them!

What Schmidt didn't know was that 15 months would be only the beginning of the time he had yet to serve in the killing limbo of Sportverbot.

PART 2

SCHMIDT'S SWIFT FALL FROM NATIONAL HERO TO enemy of the state would have taxed the sanity of any human being. But for him the shock was more traumatic because he had grown up in an uncommonly free and privileged style of life— free and privileged, that is, in the context of the oppressive conditions that prevailed under East European socialism.

Long before he was a champion, Schmidt was a prince of the upper middle class, socialist style.

This was due, of course, to his father. At the time of which we are writing, the average East German adult male was reduced pretty much to a lumpen clod trapped in whatever banal job the state had assigned him. By contrast, Ernst Schmidt's life radiated glamour and panache—especially in the eyes of a little boy.

From my earliest memory, he traveled abroad. No one else I knew had a father like that. Even more important was the fact that he came home carrying presents. When I was small, he always brought exotic clothes—Norwegian sweaters, Italian jackets, clothes few people in the GDR had ever seen, let alone owned.

He also brought home fascinating stories. Once he had been in Reykjavik with the decathlon team and he told us about the geysers, the hot water that came spurting out of the earth. We couldn't believe such things. He told it so it was like a fairy tale. He had also seen the eruption of the volcano Surtsey in Iceland when the team flew over it.

One of my main motivations as a child was to succeed at sports so I could travel and see the world as he had. Traveling to Reykjavik and beyond, that was my dream.

Ernst Schmidt functioned variously as mentor, tyrant, nemesis, and hero in the years the rambunctious boy was growing up. No one was as important to Wolfgang Schmidt as his father, and there is no way we can describe the life and times of the son without first describing the life and times of the father.

He was a man born to no silver spoons, socialist or otherwise. He arrived in the world on February 1, 1920, in a village called Semmelsberg, located about five kilometers from the manufacturing city of Meissen. His father, Max, worked as a boilerman at the jute spinning mill. His mother, Martha, worked in the shipping department of a factory that produced bricks and fired tiles. They were tough, brawny working-class people.

Ernst Schmidt was the youngest of four children. His brother died at the age of ten, and his two sisters both lived until 1980. Times were hard during his childhood, but there was usually enough to eat because his parents grew vegetables and potatoes on their small plot of land and raised pigs and goats as well. There was no extra money available, though. Ernst recalled that he wore wooden shoes on the farm so he would not wear out his single pair of good shoes. He had few toys. "I had a spinning top and some small animals made of plaster, but my best toy was our cat. I made a hoop from a willow rod and taught the cat to jump through it. My parents could not afford the nice toys some other children had," he said.

The 1920s were bleak years in Germany. The Great War had ended in November 1918. Germany had begun the conflict in the summer of 1914 by invading neutral Belgium, and the four years that followed had taken a terrible toll. More than 9 million were dead, along with 21 million wounded—Germans, British, French, Belgians, Italians, Americans. Nearly all of them were young men, the core of a generation. Because Germany was so clearly responsible for initiating this horror, a sense of national shame lay like a shroud over the country in the immediate postwar years. The smell of defeat was everywhere.

During the 1920s and early 1930s, the government of the Weimar Republic operated as a democracy, but the horrendous war debt plus inept economic policies trapped the country in mushrooming inflation and deep industrial stagnation. Germans soon became sick of being a nation of humiliated losers. Many turned to a new political party far out on the right wing of German politics—the National Socialist Party, nicknamed Nazis. The Nazis were led by Adolf Hitler, a decorated corporal in World War I who was a house painter before his fanatical politics galvanized Germany. He possessed a supernatural talent for public speaking, and he used it to deliver an enthralling message of German elitism and Aryan supremacy to his countrymen.

He was elected chancellor of Germany in 1933. Once in power, Hitler created a national network of militaristic organizations meant to appeal to all ages and all types of Germans. Perhaps the most effective of all was the Hitlerjugend—The Hitler Youth Movement—which introduced children and teenagers to the brown-shirted Nazi cult.

At fourteen, Ernst joined the Hitler Youth group in his hometown. It was what he called "a voluntary obligation" for students in his school. There were no goose-stepping parades, but the youth group did participate in quasi-military sports such as tracking "enemy" units in the woods and learning how to fly gliders. Ernst enjoyed these pursuits, but eventually found that they cut down too much on his growing commitment to track and field. He quit Hitler Youth after two years, explaining that he wished to concentrate on nonmilitary sports. The authorities did not object to his quitting: excelling at sport was considered a viable alternative.

"I had been smitten with sports as a child," Ernst recalled. "We had a *Turnverein* [gymnastics club] in my village. Our facilities were meager. We did our training in the ballroom of a restaurant in winter and on a lawn next to the restaurant in summer. I got absolutely no support from my father. I remember one Christmas, perhaps in 1936 or 1937, when I wanted a pair of spikes. I tried to explain to him how important shoes with spikes were to a track athlete. He couldn't even visualize what I was talking about, so we went to a store together. When I showed him shoes with spikes, he was completely shocked. He shouted, 'No way do we spend money on these things! You are getting a pair of proper sensible, strong shoes and not such nonsense!' Spiked shoes were like an idea from another planet and I gave up."

Spikes or no spikes, the young man pursued his passion for sport. He came under the wing of a club coach who seemed to have combined the qualities of a guru and a saint. "He expected us to enjoy training, not to dread it," Ernst recalled, "and he knew perfectly well how to keep us interested. Because I was a little bit talented, it didn't take long until I was the best youth in Meissen, then the best in the district of Dresden, and soon the best in all of Saxony. I was versatile. I especially excelled in a three-part event—100 meters, the long jump, and the shot put called the *Dreikampf*. I also competed in the decathlon."

The Olympic Games were held in Berlin in 1936, an unprecedented Nazi extravaganza that mixed sports, politics, and propaganda as no one had ever before. In the end, the grand irony of the Nazi Olympics was the fact that the individual hero was not an Aryan or a German: He was the magnificent American black, Jesse Owens, who won four gold medals.

At the time, Ernst Schmidt was only sixteen and not ready for Olympic competition. But he was an avid fan. He listened to the Olympics on the radio and gleaned the pages of a national sports newspaper for details on the competitions. He collected photographs of German Olympians that were included in boxes of a certain brand of cigars. He glued these pictures into a scrapbook.

He also clipped pictures of Jesse Owens from the newspapers and glued his likeness next to the German heroes. He recalled, "Jesse Owens was an idol for me."

In part because of the Olympics, Hitler had successfully maintained his charade of being a peace-loving leader throughout the late 1930s. On September 30, 1938, he signed the famous "appeasement pact" in Munich with the British prime minister Neville Chamberlain, which the Englishman trumpeted as the treaty that guaranteed "peace in our time." In August 1939, Hitler signed a nonaggression pact with Russia. On September 1, 1939, without formal declaration of war the Germans moved into Poland and World War II began.

Ernst was working as a journeyman lathe operator in Meissen. He was nineteen and was immediately drafted into the Wehrmacht. His first assignment was with a construction battalion working on a military airport in the town of Jülich, near Cologne. After a few weeks, he was transferred to an air-intelligence unit in Cologne where he helped install communications networks for antiaircraft stations. Typically, he participated in any and all sporting competitions involving his unit, and in no time, he attracted a crowd of high-ranking admirers. Sporting rivalries were spirited between units of the German army, and winning reflected well on commanding officers.

"Suddenly there were superior officers at Cologne calling me by my first name and treating me with great deference though I was only a communications technician," he recalled.

Soon, Ernst was relieved of his regular duties and allowed to train pretty much full-time. His immediate goal was the 1940 championships for the Central Rhine region. They were held in the Müngersdorfer Stadium in Cologne. Ernst won the decathlon. For the next year, his military duties became ever lighter, his training schedule heavier.

"In 1941, my friends and fans at the top arranged to post me to the Air Force Sports School in Berlin-Spandau, and there I was given a completely open schedule with responsibilities only to train and improve myself as much as I could. I remained there through 1942. Eventually, besides working on my own conditioning, I also taught classes for men who were in charge of physical training in their units of the Wehrmacht. My lectures and demonstrations dealt mainly with developing stamina, power, and speed. I was inventing my curriculum as I went along." As things turned out, his curriculum proved most effective. Soldiers in units trained by his students scored consistently better on standardized physical tests than the average German soldier.

Teaching didn't dull his athletic edge. In the summer of 1942, Ernst participated in the national championships for the first time. They were held in the Olympic Stadium in Berlin, and there was an aura of celebration. Ernst won the decathlon and scored the highest point total in the world that year. This made him certifiably the best all-around track-and-field athlete on earth as well as the toast of the Third Reich—a genuine superman in der Führer's super race. One would assume that such a champion would be protected and coddled like royalty. Quite the contrary. He was dispatched to the Russian front.

Ernst explained, "Sometime after my championship, Reichssportführer [minister of sports] Schamor von Osten issued a decree that all top athletes, record holders and champions, should be sent into battle in order to set a good example for the children and youth at home. A lot was written in the press—big headlines about how this and that great athlete was in combat, fighting for the people and the fatherland. The whole thing was considered a matter of public relations to raise the nation's morale."

For the record, the US used sports celebrities as wartime morale-raisers, too: Joe DiMaggio, the Yankee Clipper, joined the navy and gave hitting exhibitions for sailors; Private First Class Joe Louis, the heavyweight champion, staged prize-fight exhibitions at army bases. But the difference between the wartime use of US stars and German stars was literally a matter of life and death. America's celebrities rarely went near combat, while German champions were sent straight into the fires of battle.

In March 1943, Ernst joined a transportation unit in the Soviet Union near Nevel. He was assigned to drive an ammunition truck between supply dumps at the rear and gun emplacements at the front. Ernst recalled, "I was unenthusiastic about this assignment.

This was not only because I feared for my life—which, of course, I did, I am no fool. It was also because of an innermost conviction that I was committing an act of violence against the Russian people when they had never done anything to me. As I drove my truck to the front, I would think, This ammunition I am delivering is going to be used by our artillery to destroy people with whom I have no quarrel whatsoever. In a normal situation, people don't set out to destroy each other. Then why am I doing this to them? I knew, of course, that it was only because of Hitler and his territorial ambitions."

The ammunition caravans were favorite targets of Russian artillery, even though they often drove at night with their lights off. Ernst recalled, "One evening, we were in the small village that was our base. Our trucks were all loaded with shells and were parked in different spots around the town. A Soviet battery opened up on us and we all dove to the ground. One of the trucks was parked close to a crowd of us, and one of the drivers realized that if that truck was hit, it would annihilate us all. This brave fellow jumped into the truck, threw it into gear, and began to drive it away.

"I was lying in the path of the truck. He drove over both my legs because he couldn't see me in the dark. Both were mashed and the fibula was broken in one. They turned black and ballooned up immediately from internal hemorrhaging. I was driven from the village to a field hospital and a cast was put on the broken leg. Both legs were pretty bad. Within a week or so, I was sent back to Germany."

They put him in a hospital at Reichssportfeld in Berlin. But the Allies had begun heavy bombing of the city, and Ernst was transferred to a hospital in Brenslau. "There," he recalled, "my legs healed very nicely."

Nicely, indeed. Just four months after his legs had been crushed in Russia, he competed in the German track-and-field championships of 1943. He still had a bandage on one leg, and he was gaunt and weakened from his injuries. Yet he managed to finish second in the decathlon. That he did so well on virtually one leg was a tribute to his courage and his talent, but it also provided a terrible sign of how decimated German manhood was already in a war that still had almost two years to go.

Because of his wound, Ernst was not sent back to combat. He went to an air-intelligence unit in Döberitz near Berlin and returned to his prewar profession as a lathe operator making spare parts for air-reconnaissance devices. Everyone knew that the German cause was hopeless. As the Russians drove through Poland and Silesia and advanced on Berlin, Ernst's unit was transferred to the relative safety of Rudolstadt. It was common wisdom among German troops that it was safer to surrender to Americans than Russians because the Soviets were believed to be committing unspeakable atrocities as they charged through Germany.

This may have been true in general, but it certainly wasn't Ernst Schmidt's experience. He and several hundred colleagues surrendered to US troops in Rudolstadt in the cold days of early April 1945—and it was then that his worst wartime nightmare began: "The Americans transported us to Bad Kreuznach, a little spa resort that soon came to be known as one of the cruelest postwar prison camps. It was, in fact, a death camp. I starved there and I froze there. For a while, I subsisted on grass. Masses of us lived on an open field with no shelter over many acres. It was cold and it rained a lot. All I had to wear was my air force uniform, long pants, dress shoes, tie and jacket. We dug holes in the ground, forty, fifty centimeters deep, and we put cardboard in the holes and tried to sleep there, out of the icy wind and rain. Happiness was to possess a blanket. I still had my watch and I exchanged it for a blanket. Others traded watches or wedding rings to American guards for cigarettes instead of blankets. This was insane.

"We were exposed to terrible weather for two months. Sometimes we lay together in twos under a blanket so we could warm each other a little. During nights when it grew especially cold, the only way to keep from freezing was for all of us, the entire mass, to stand on the open field and huddle together, a vast dense clot of shivering men. Those in the front rank faced the wind, and they stayed there as long as they could, then they went to the back of the mass and sheltered themselves there while the next rank of men in front took the force of the wind. Those at the center of the mass were quite comfortable, although sometimes a man would fall asleep and slide to the ground, lying there while the rest of us trampled on him.

"After a couple of months, we were told we could apply for release. I put my name in immediately. Nothing happened. They started releasing men according to region. First the Rhinelanders went home, then men from Hesse-Nassau, then from other parts of western Germany, then Munich. I could not manage to obtain a release to Saxony. So I changed my application. Since I had been taken prisoner in Thuringia, I asked to be released to Thuringia. For some reason, this worked.

"The Americans assembled a group of POWs to travel to Erfurt in Thuringia. They loaded us into an open railroad freight car. Just before the train pulled out of Bad Kreuznach, they gave us canned food, peas and beans with meat. We had been starved, and now we tore open those cans and wolfed the food like animals. It tasted wonderful, but once it got to our stomachs, something horrible happened. We were not used to rich food. As the train rolled out of the station, many of us were stricken with diarrhea.

"There we were, at least sixty men, standing packed against each other in an open railroad car with at least half of us shitting helplessly in our pants. You can imagine the despair and the smell during the trip from Bad Kreuznach to Erfurt. I cannot even remember how long it took. All I know is that I was in bad shape from diarrhea and I did what I had to do. In Erfurt, I left the train, and as I passed through a walkway tunnel from the railroad station, a woman came toward me with a child, a little girl.

"She said, 'Where are you coming from?'

"I was walking very slowly because my trousers were full of shit. I told her, 'Bad Kreuznach.'

" 'Oh,' she said, 'we have heard about that camp. It must have been terrible there. Come with me. I will take you home.'

"I whispered to her, 'I cannot go fast.' I was embarrassed about my soiled condition, particularly in front of the child, who was about twelve.

"The woman said, 'That doesn't matter. We'll just go slowly.'

"We went to her home. She said, 'Now take off your clothes. I'll bury them in the garden.' She drew me a bath and brought me fresh underwear and clean clothes. Her husband had been killed in the war, and she still had some of his clothes. She gave them to me and I began to look like a human being again. She cooked me some semolina, a milk soup, and said, 'You won't get any meat from me. We have heard that some from Bad Kreuznach died because they ate meat after starving for so long. That will not happen to you, I promise.'

"After a few days of recuperation, I moved on to Bad Blankenburg near Rudolstadt. There another woman took me in. Her husband, too, had been killed in the war. She had plans for me right from the start. She was a little older than me and she had two children. She was sweet and accommodating in every way, and she gave me the right food for my condition. She wanted me to accompany her to Aachen, her hometown, but I told her that I wanted to go home to be with my parents. I had a girlfriend at home who expected a child and who later became my first wife. I was not going to get involved with anyone else for the moment. *Na, ja* [oh, well]. She didn't like the farewell at all when I got on a train headed toward Leipzig. She took it very hard."

It HAS BEEN SAID THAT THE IMMEDIATE POSTWAR period was a time of "national amnesia" in Germany as people tried to erase from their memory the atrocities they had committed—or allowed to be committed—under the Nazis. They fell deeper into shock as more was revealed of gas ovens, death camps, and the Final Solution. They could only wait for their conquerors to destroy them in retribution.

In fact, no such vengeance came to pass. The leaders of the Allied powers—Truman of the US, Stalin of the USSR, and both Churchill and Attlee, of Great Britain—made it clear at the Potsdam Conference in the summer of 1945 that Germany was not to be destroyed because of the Nazi crimes.

Instead, the country was to be disarmed and demilitarized. All Nazi institutions were to be eradicated, war criminals were to be put on trial, and huge reparations were to be paid to the victors. Besides that, the country was to be summarily divided into four parts with the US, the USSR, Britain, and France each controlling one section. Originally, all of the Allies—including Russia—fully intended that a divided Germany would last for only a short time.

All of them expected that the country would soon be reunited under a single neutral government. Even Stalin saw the Russian zone of Germany as a short-term buffer against the democracies of Western Europe. He saw a unified Germany as a continuing source of monetary reparation for the vast losses Russia had suffered.

The Allies had produced one of history's greatest war machines and had fought together well. But once they had defeated the Third Reich, the great alliance split between East and West. In 1947, the United States, Britain, and France merged their three German zones into a single political unit and tried to convince the Russians to put their zone in, too. But now Stalin became intractable, demanding outrageous reparation payments as well as impossible new borders between the eastern bloc of socialist nations and the West. Ultimately, the Western powers concluded there was no point in trying to placate the tyrannical Russian. In 1949, a divided Germany became a permanent political fact of life. On September 12, West Germany formally became the Federal Republic of Germany, and on October 11, East Germany formally became the German Democratic Republic.

There was nothing equal about the two. The GDR had 17 million people in a land mass the size of Indiana, while the FRG had 49 million in an area the size of New York, Connecticut, and Pennsylvania. West Germany soon came under the imperious but inspired leadership of Chancellor Konrad Adenauer and proceeded with great speed to rejoin the world of free and prosperous nations.

In contrast, the leaders of the GDR ruled in a brooding, defensive style that seemed to bind them inextricably to defeat. Theirs was a pariah land that many of its neighbors, including comrades in the Warsaw Pact, despised: The Czechs, the Poles, and, God knows, the Russians had been mercilessly pounded by Germans during the war. The Kremlin often seemed to regard the GDR with scorn. Stalin is supposed to have once said, "Communism fits Germany like a saddle fits a cow." And to the GDR's great humiliation the Soviet Union opened formal diplomatic relations with West Germany in 1955 without demanding quid pro quo recognition from the West for East Germany (the US didn't reciprocate until 1974).

Despite such insulting treatment, the leaders of the GDR insisted on kowtowing to the Kremlin. At one point not long after the war, the leadership ordered a particularly aggravating slogan to be plastered across the land: "To learn from the Soviet Union means learning to be victorious." This not only rubbed in the fact that Germany had lost the war, but it was also terribly offensive to Germans who had been raised from birth to believe that the Russians were a vulgar, inferior people. Moreover, it was common knowledge that Stalin himself was a blundering tyrant who had executed hundreds of German Communist exiles during his purges of the late 1930s and had cost his country millions of lives unnecessarily because of stupid wartime decisions. Nevertheless, East Germany soon emerged as Russia's most sycophantic satellite.

If relations with the Soviet Union undermined morale in East Germany, far worse was the constant knowledge that a stone's throw across the border their West German brothers—literally so, in many cases—were enjoying freedom and wealth while they were given nothing but lies and low wages. As David Childs wrote in 1984 in *The GDR: Moscow's German Ally:* "Many East Germans remain sullen, bitter, alienated, and angry. They do not necessarily identify with the Federal Republic as they do not identify with the GDR. They regard themselves as Germans and identify with Germany. They ask themselves therefore, why it is that other Germans, in Düsseldorf, Mannheim, or Munich, should earn more than they do? Why should they have better housing, social services, holidays, and pensions? They feel insulted that they have to pretend that they do not understand the mockery of elections without a choice. They feel sickened at the hypocrisy which surrounds everything to do with the Soviet Union, from its history and culture to its way of life, politics, and policies.

"Frustrated, they ask themselves why they should not be able to say, without looking over their shoulders, that they like the West Germans better than the Russians."

• • •

In early autumn of 1945, Ernst Schmidt wound up on the dark side of the Iron Curtain for the most natural and compelling of reasons: He was in trouble and so he went home. However, his political beliefs at the time were in complete agreement with the socialist regime. "I was twenty-five and I belonged to the group who later came to be called 'activists of the first hour,' meaning we were dedicated to the socialist movement from the start. It was pretty much a matter of course that if you were of my age at that time, you eagerly said, 'Yes! I want to be a part of it!' I believed deeply in 1945 that the time had come after that terrible war to build a society based on the theoretical ideals of Marxist-Leninist ideas. What came to be later is quite another matter."

He recalled his return home: "I arrived at my town and registered with the authorities. My parents were in good condition, considering everything. At one point, shortly before the end of the war, a shell had dropped through the roof of our house. Miraculously, it did not explode. My father simply put it in a sack and dropped it in the river—no damage done.

"Once I got home, sooner than I might have hoped, my body recovered from the starving in Bad Kreuznach and we discussed what work I should do. I was a good lathe operator, but at that time all the machines in the factories in my region were being dismantled by the Soviet occupation forces so they could be transported to the Soviet Union. I knew the Russians were unbelievably careless with these machines, shipping them so they arrived as often as not with parts broken or covered with rust. When I learned that my own lathe was supposed to go to Russia also, I was upset and I protested. But there were no exceptions.

"Somebody said to me, 'Why don't you work for the police force?' This was about the last thing that would have occurred to me, because I was no worshiper of the uniformed life. But I needed something and I said, 'Sure, good idea.' In the fall of 1945, I got a job on the police force in Meissen.

"I was mainly a traffic cop, but I was also supposed to be on the lookout for so-called criminals. Mostly these 'criminals' were cold, hungry people who stole from warehouses that stored food, and sometimes took handcarts into the woods and illegally cut down trees so they could bring a little heat into their homes. Everybody was scrounging in those days, for food, for wood, for coal. It was a cold winter. There was much suffering. Therefore, there was much 'crime' committed by pilferers who stole a few lumps of coal or a pocket full of rotten potatoes."

Much of his police work also dealt with traffic accidents, which were extremely common because most cars were ancient and had bad tires and poor brakes. Often these accidents were just nuisances, but not always. Ernst Schmidt's worst moment as a policeman occurred because of such a mishap in the spring of 1949.

"I arrived to investigate an accident in the foothills of the Erzgebirge [Ore Mountains] outside Meissen. It was not far from Semmelsberg, my village. I knew the location well. I had been told that a man had been hit by a car, that he had been carried into a nearby house, and that an ambulance had then taken him to the hospital. Only after I began questioning people at the scene did I learn that the injured man was my father. I was assured that he was all right and I went on with the investigation.

"It turned out that my father had been traveling along the road on foot, which was unusual. Ordinarily, he rode his bicycle to work in Meissen. Ordinarily, his schedule was such that he left for work at the jute spinning mill at one o'clock in the morning so he could start up the big boilers to get the mill warm by the time the main body of workers arrived. But everything was different on this day of the accident because it was my father's fortieth anniversary of working at the mill. He had the day off and his friends had organized a celebration. The day was beautiful, sunny, and brisk. He put on his good suit and took his walking stick and began to walk down the country road. He was walking on the right side and came to a slight bend in the road at a village called Buschbad. Two cars were coming toward him, one from behind and one from the front. They did not have enough room to pass each other. My father could not move farther to the right and the car from behind struck him in the back.

"When I got to the hospital after my investigation, I expected to perhaps ask him some questions. Instead, I found him dead on a stretcher. It was so tragic. He was a healthy man, sixty-five years old, on his fortieth anniversary of doing the same job, and he was dead. Nothing has hit me like that."

Ernst continued on the Meissen police force for a few more months, then was promoted to a police base in Grossenhain, where he served with an elite mobilized force that specialized in rescue operations and riot control. He was less enthused about the work than by the guarantee of a warm bed and good food— something one was never certain of in those hard days. He signed on for a three-year tour of duty.

He was still famous as an athlete, and when sports competitions began again as a kind of first rite of revival after the war, Ernst began training again. In August of 1949, he had his first opportunity to test himself against international competition. Sports authorities in Budapest invited athletes from the GDR, including Ernst, to compete in a Communist-sponsored World Youth Festival. Alas, when the team reached Budapest, they were told they couldn't compete after all. Because East Germany was still legally the Soviet Occupied Zone of Germany and had no formal standing as a nation, its athletes were not allowed to compete in an internationally sanctioned event.

Sympathetic Hungarian organizers tried to save the day for the outcasts by arranging a shadow competition between a Hungarian postal sports club and the GDR. It was disguised as a "training session" and took place in a locked stadium with only a handful of spectators present. Ernst Schmidt won the shot put, breaking the German national record in the process.

Back in the GDR, his police career was going exceptionally well. He was promoted to an elite police academy in Kochstetts that specialized in training future commandants of major police installations. This was a significant advancement, but Ernst hated the place. "Some of the instructors were veterans of the fascist Wehrmacht. They were very tough, very militaristic. They swore that they had always opposed everything Hitler stood for, but I wasn't sure I could believe them. Fortunately, I hadn't been at the academy long when I was approached by an acquaintance,

Rudi Rotkamp of the German Sports Committee, to join the committee in Berlin. My sports performances and the work I had done in army instruction during the war were the reasons they looked me up, I think. At the time, the GDR system for regional training centers—which eventually became the national network of sports clubs—was just beginning. I said yes without hesitation."

It was December 1949. Ernst's new job was with the Department for Youth and Physical Education. His overall boss was none other than Walter Ulbricht—then deputy prime minister, but soon to be first secretary, a position he would hold for more than twenty years. Ernst had little direct personal contact with Ulbricht then. Nevertheless, just being in the aura of this strange fellow offered him a rare glimpse of how the GDR was going to be in the coming decades.

For, as Ulbricht's personality went, so went East Germany. He was an austere, gnomish fellow almost entirely lacking in personal charisma and physical attractiveness. He was awkward on his feet, a monotonous speaker, a dull conversationalist. He was, however, a tireless worker and an eternal hard-line Communist. He had joined the German Social Democratic Party in 1912 as a youth of nineteen and had spent the war years in Moscow. When the war ended in 1945, he was fifty-one. Ulbricht's allegiance to the Kremlin was absolute to the point of being brainwashed. He had supported Stalin's nonaggression pact with Hitler in 1939 even though the Nazis were exterminating German Communists as fast as they could find them. After the war, Ulbricht went so far as to say that Germany's national guilt should be directed primarily toward the Soviet Union for its wartime suffering rather than toward the 6 million Jews exterminated by the Nazis.

In his ruling years as first secretary (1950–1971), Ulbricht produced his own East German economic miracle, pretty pitiful compared to the gold rush across the border, but not insignificant. Under him, the GDR had the highest standard of living in Eastern Europe and ranked eighth among industrial nations in terms of productivity per capita. By 1974 it had surpassed Great Britain in per capita income; the average in the GDR was $3,710 compared to Britain's $3,590.

Jonathan Steele wrote in 1977 in *Inside East Germany:* "The marriage of German traditions to the goal-directed philosophy of a Communist state has produced a particularly intense, disciplined, and orderly society. . . . [In the long run, Ulbricht] was arguably the most successful German statesman since Bismarck, although Bismarck's achievement was the unification of Germany and Ulbricht presided over its division."

The German Sports Committee under Ulbricht was a rigidly ideological operation, and it attracted future leaders of the GDR to its environs. One of these men was Erich Honecker. A Communist since 1926, Honecker had spent ten years in one of Hitler's concentration camps. He was freed in 1945 and the following year was appointed national director of Free German Youth (FDJ). The FDJ and the Association of Free German Trade Unions were the two major pillars on which the early sports organization was built. From there, of course, Honecker went on to far bigger things: In 1961 he became infamous as the man who supervised the building of the Berlin Wall, and in 1971 he replaced Ulbricht as first secretary—a position he still held when The Wall came down eighteen years later in November 1989.

Another future star whom Ernst Schmidt worked for—and ultimately befriended—at the Sports Committee was the tough, magnetic young Manfred Ewald. At the time, Ewald was a veritable child prodigy, only twenty-three. He had risen quickly because, as an ambitious FDJ leader in Mecklenburg, he had caught the attention of Honecker, who brought Ewald to Berlin as one of six vice-chairmen of the Sports Committee. From there, Ewald rose rapidly and was appointed chairman of the State Committee for Physical Culture and Sport in 1954 at the age of twenty-eight.

In 1977 a Canadian journalist named Doug Gilbert spent a lot of time in East Germany examining the sports system. Ultimately, he wrote a book, *The Miracle Machine,* which was published in 1979 and stood for years as the best study of the DTSB and its predecessors. In the course of his research, Gilbert interviewed Manfred Ewald at length.

Of the early days, Ewald told Gilbert: "There was more rubble in the German mind than on the German streets. For two generations we had been told we were supermen, the master race. For five years we were told we would have victory or we would have death, but no more German humiliation. Well, here we were in the spring of 1945. The war was over and those of us that were left were not dead. Reconstructing cities is one thing. How do you reconstruct minds? We didn't have anything. No stadiums, no universities, everything was destroyed and finished. We were a people completely down. But we had to get on with it [and] it was obvious sport was going to play a very strong role in the overall development of our national political reconstruction program. . . . The Soviet Union, of course, was the example for all of us. Most of our first leaders studied there. But although both we and they were faced with similar problems, each country had to develop its own possibilities. Thus, the USSR has built sports organizations on the foundation of large national trade unions. They have their state committee and their union clubs. We, on the other hand, have a municipally based system built around local enterprises and town and village committees. Theirs was the best for them, ours has proven best for us."

In April of 1957, Ewald got permission from Party authorities to reorganize the sports operation by forming a relatively independent fiefdom of his own—the DTSB. This was, in effect, an amalgamation of existing individual sports federations with its own budget and its own staff operating independent of the more politically controlled realm of the State Committee for Physical Culture and Sport. Ewald resigned his chairmanship of the Committee (which continued to operate as an administrative body inside the government bureaucracy) and took the position of president of the DTSB. It was a coup for Ewald because running the DTSB allowed him to concentrate more on the development of elite national athletes, which would ultimately be the key to the phenomenal success of the GDR's international teams in the years ahead.

Ernst Schmidt recalled, "The new structuring of the DTSB elevated our work to a higher level. Sports schools were established for potentially elite youngsters. We were able to conduct far more intense and more technical training camps. The performance level in the sports clubs around the country was elevated to higher planes. It was a central structuring that made all the difference in what was to come."

Ernst himself was not involved in the mechanics or the politics of Ewald's revolutionary restructuring, but he met often with him to discuss specific problems and developments involving athletes and coaches in the highest performance programs.

Ernst admired Ewald then for his pragmatic ability to cut through red tape and politics. "In those years, I can tell you, Manfred still had an open ear to hear how things worked out in actual practice. He did not depend on the theoretical mouthings of his office-bound underlings at that time. He listened to the word of men in the field and he acted on that word. Later, our relationship suffered when he abused his autocratic position and insisted on working hand in glove with State Security. He then made decisions I could not agree with. After that, our relationship worsened and we had hot arguments—not only in his office, but also in his home when he had us for social occasions."

Ernst recalled that he clashed with Ewald mainly over such things as the DTSB's reluctance to send competitors abroad and the official Stasi paranoia over who could and could not be trusted. "We received many, many invitations for our athletes from many countries. We coaches would have liked to send our athletes to all of these competitions where they would have been welcomed with open arms. He often said no. Ewald and I also clashed when he acted to drop athletes from a traveling squad because they had relatives in the West and had received gifts from those relatives.

Ernst Schmidt had never liked high-level bureaucratic manipulation such as Manfred Ewald specialized in. "I worked in Berlin for five months and I learned much—more than I wanted to know, I think—about the machinations of a monster bureaucracy," he recalled. "I was responsible for the organization of

Betriebssportgemeinschaften [the sports arm for industries and factories]. I cannot deny that I learned a lot in that time in Berlin. But I was at my desk too much and I was moving papers too much. I asked to be given a job in the field. I felt it was my fulfillment, my mission, to be a coach, responsible for the education and growth of the young."

He was assigned to the city of Greiz to supervise the renovation of a decrepit old school into a new sports educational facility. Ernst and a select faculty of coaches used the building to give centralized training sessions to elite athletes who showed unusual promise. "We invited only the very best, and we gave them two-week sessions of intense, expert training," he recalled. This school in Greiz with its full-time coaches and concentrated training was an important part of the genesis of the GDR's unique national sports-training programs that ultimately became the bedrock beneath the whole system. "These were the beginning years of the foundation," said Ernst. "Here we laid the basis for the elite sports clubs and for the use of professional experts specialized in specific events. We knew we needed more and more coaches in order to reach higher and higher levels."

Greiz proved providential for Ernst in more ways than one. A young woman bookkeeper had been assigned to the office there by the Sports Committee in Berlin. She came from the Schwerin district and her name was Gretel Leist. She was nineteen years old. What happened next, Ernst described succinctly: "We met there and became friends and later lovers, and we had two children."

The courtship almost didn't blossom beyond friendship. Ernst recalled: "She took me home to Dömitz to introduce me to her parents. She was from a small farm and there was not much there: two cows, a few pigs, chickens. A horse next door belonged to my wife's brother, and her father had one, too, and they swapped the horses back and forth when one or the other family needed to till the land. My wife's father had a small store in his house, a grocery. Later he gave up the store and began fishing. He spread nets in the spring in a flood area from the River Elbe where the fish came to spawn. He put out his nets and caught pike, carp, tench, also eel, and delivered them to the state store, which paid him for them. I often helped him. My wife also has two sisters, sweet, nice sisters. She comes from a good family.

"When I met her parents, they had just learned that I had already been married once, that I had a child, and was a divorced man. I had made no secret of this. My first wife had no interest in my interests. I had a motorcycle with a sidecar, and when I wanted to take her riding, she didn't want to go. When I wanted to teach her to swim, she didn't want to learn. When I asked her to go to a sports event, she was not interested. Besides that, she was telling the neighbors that she wasn't getting enough housekeeping money. This was not true since I was then, as I am now, a man who does not require much personally. I don't drink beer. I don't smoke. I am usually at home. I had a daughter with my first wife and she now lives in Neubrandenburg, and she just happens to be married to a coach at the sports club there, a coach who just happens to have trained many athletes quite successfully in the throwing events. In 1952 my first wife and I were divorced. *Na, ja.*

"When Gretel took me home, my marital past was greeted with icy stares. It took a while for her family to get used to it."

Ernst and Gretel were married in April 1953 and returned to Greiz briefly. "I had written many letters that were critical of the German Sports Committee in Berlin. Sometimes they were so critical that they weren't even answered. So they called me back to Berlin because they figured someone who is such a know-it-all should probably be stationed at the Committee itself to do things better if he could. I was assigned to *Sportschwerpunkt Einheit Nordost* [sports center unit for the northeast section]. I took part myself in some competitions in 1953, but these were my last. Mostly, I became a coach for young athletes, and then I was selected by the Committee leadership to be promoted."

That promotion put him at the top. From 1953 to 1962, Ernst Schmidt ruled as national coach of track and field for the GDR. He was a deft motivator, a good administrator, and a creative technical coach. He ran training camps, he coordinated a veritable army of coaching specialists in all track-and-field events, he acted as chairman of the Central Coaches' Council, which he founded in Greiz, and he selected the athletes who would take part in international competitions. He had been there at the birth of the most amazing sports organization in history, and he stayed for thirty years.

But if his timing was good as a coach, it could not have been worse as an athlete. In all his years of competition, he had never participated in a major world-class event—particularly the Olympics. The games of 1940 and 1944, when he was one of the best in the world in the decathlon, were canceled because of the war. The games of 1948 went on in London, and he might have done well in the decathlon or the shot put, but neither of the Germanys was allowed to enter a team. In 1952, Ernst was thirty-two and still young enough to compete, but the GDR did not send a team to Helsinki because it had not been sanctioned by the International Olympic Committee.

After that, Ernst was out of the running forever, a world-class athlete who would never compete against the world.

Then he was given something we might call a second chance once removed. On January 16, 1954, a son was born. Not long afterward, Ernst was pushing a pram containing the husky infant when he ran into an old friend, Klaus Huhn, a sportswriter for *Neues Deutschland*. Huhn dutifully admired the baby, then asked Ernst whether he thought this child would ever perform as an Olympian. Ernst replied without hesitation, "Beyond a shadow of a doubt, I believe that the passage of twenty years' time will solve the political problems in time for this little boy to grow up and compete for the GDR in the Olympics."

Wolfgang Schmidt's memories of boyhood were idyllic—recollections of jolly Christmases with roast geese, of summer trips into the country to visit an affectionate assortment of grandparents, uncles, aunts, and cousins, and of good cooking, fresh sheets, cozy furniture in the spacious prewar apartment in the Prenzlauer Berg section of old Berlin.

I liked this home. The apartment houses were clustered close together, and each had a courtyard in the back, and it was wonderful as a child to play there. We never had pets, but there was a small birdhouse outside one window, and we fed the birds there. A blackbird sometimes made its nest there, and I became fond of it and the baby birds it hatched.

My first memories go back to that apartment, when I was a tiny boy before my sister was born. On Saturday and Sunday mornings I ran into my parents' bedroom and we frolicked on their bed. They told stories and we laughed and played. It was during those times that my father taught me how to read the clock using the same rhyme his father had taught him: *"Viertel, halb, dreiviertel, um—oh, wie ist der Wolfgang dumm."* This rhymes in German, and in English it means, "Quarter, half, three-quarters, up—oh, Wolfgang is so dumb."

Even when I grew up and began winning competitions, I preferred going home to celebrate my victories. I always thought it was nicer to be with my family.

This certainly was not the life of glum deprivation that Westerners generally envisioned behind the Wall. To hear Schmidt talk, his childhood could have flowed from the pen of an East German Booth Tarkington. That he grew up inside a country that was effectively a penitentiary never prevented him from enjoying a continuous string of pleasant, prank-filled years. Of course, the Schmidt family was extraordinarily blessed.

All of them were uncommonly handsome and uncommonly smart. Gretel, fifty years old in 1982, was a graceful, humorous woman, fairly tall (5'8"), with a still-shapely physique and curly brown hair cut fashionably short. Unlike everyone else in her family, she had never seriously participated in sports—indeed, she boasted only a bit of leisurely rowing on the rivers of her girlhood. She was strong-minded, intelligent, and opinionated, yet capable of great gentleness and affection. She was a relaxed and sociable hostess, and later a consistent arbitrator between her autocratic husband and her hotheaded son. Wolfgang thought she was just about perfect:

She has always been a woman with both feet on the ground. When she was young, she was very pretty. She was generous and completely unselfish. She would only get into a bad mood when she burned a roast, and once when the Christmas goose didn't brown as it should have. This happened because our stove burned coal and cooking could be uncertain. I loved her Christmas goose. I also loved carp as she prepared it and prune dumplings, which were potato dumplings with a prune and a lump of sugar inside. These were eaten with brown butter and sugar with cinnamon mixed in it.

Schmidt's sister, Bettina, was twenty-five in the summer of 1982. She was a beautiful woman, almost six feet tall, with high cheekbones, blond hair, and the same radiant smile her brother possessed. She had once excelled in the javelin and the pentathlon. She might have had world-class potential, but she worked at an early age with a coach who forced her to train so rigorously that her throwing arm was constantly injured. Also, her parents did not want her to have to take steroids—a possibility if she competed at a world level. So Bettina had retired from serious competition, and in the summer of 1982, she was working as a secretary at SC Dynamo Berlin. She was married and living in an apartment with her daughter, Annika, and her husband, Wolfgang Knipp.

Schmidt ruefully recalled Bettina's arrival in his life when he was three.

It was a shock when she was born. I had been the baby sun god, all alone, and I had very much enjoyed it. Then, suddenly it seemed that nobody was paying attention to me anymore. Suddenly the earth began revolving around my mother and around the baby who would be coming home from the hospital. I was not allowed to go into the hospital. I had to wait alone outside. I was a little jealous. In fact, I was very jealous. It seemed to me that the sun was shining only on Bettina, and I was being ignored by all. Well, of course, as it turned out, I had nothing to worry about: Bettina and I were both spoiled very nicely by my mother.

His sister chuckled at Wolfgang's recollections and corrected him without rancor; "Perhaps we were spoiled equally by our mother, but he was spoiled by everyone else. From babyhood to manhood, someone was always doing things for him, admiring him, rewarding him because he could be so charming and so sweet. He also demanded it. He will get what he wants because he knows people adore him. That includes me, of course. We used to share a bedroom in the apartment. He was always writing in his training books at night, keeping the light on so I couldn't sleep. When I complained, my father let him write in the living room. Always Wolfgang, always his way."

Schmidt did not feel he was coddled. Quite the contrary.

I definitely got an authoritarian upbringing from my parents. Occasionally my father would slap me behind the ears, and I got quite a few beatings from my mother. Once or twice, she beat me with a wooden coat hanger for particularly bad acts on my part.

In Schmidt's memory, his parents' marriage was mainly sweetness and light.

My parents had a very open relationship with each other. Mother was on my side much of the time, and sometimes when my father wanted me to train, she would say, "Oh, why don't you just let him play today?" She never did any of this behind my father's back. If she disagreed with him, she said so.

One situation where there would almost always tend to be tensions occurred whenever we went on a trip in the car. The arrangement was that my mother did all the preparations for the entire family—including packing my father's bag—while my father took care of preparations only for the car. That meant he started the engine and drove it from the garage to the curb. She always took too long to my father's way of thinking. He would be angry and she would be red in the face, looking ready to weep, when she finally came to the car. They would fight under these circumstances, but other than that, almost never.

If the car trips caused a little trouble, they also gave the Schmidt family a lot of joy. In the 1950s and early 1960s, owning a family car in the GDR was about as rare as owning a family cyclotron. It was *the* symbol of influence in the GDR.

Father had a car for as long as I can remember. Some were better than others. The first one was a homemade job from a decrepit Opel, which he and my mother's uncle, a pipe fitter, welded together and painted gray. This homemade car had a few flaws, and sometimes, in the middle of a trip, it would stop dead.

Later, he was able to get a better car, a red-and-white Wartburg, through the help of the sports federation. He had to pay for it himself, though, and he had to borrow ten thousand marks [$2,500] from Uncle Ernst Leist, my mother's uncle. My father had a good salary, about a thousand marks [$250] a month, but he couldn't have bought it without the loan.

We kept this car for about four or five years, and his next car was a white Wartburg. He was always able to get a new car through the sports federation because he needed a car for his job in sports. Others waited ten or eleven years.

The cars also allowed the Schmidts to make regular vacation trips to his mothers' family in the country.

We often visited them in Klein-Schmölen, which was close to the border of the Federal Republic of Germany on the River Elbe. There were always newborn cousins around when I was a boy.

My grandfather was a wonderful man. When I was seven, he allowed me to ride the horse around a pasture. He took me fishing to the River Löcknitz, a tributary of the Elbe. Early on summer mornings, he would wake me to go with him to empty the nets. There was wet grass and mist along the river, and there would always be a catch of some kind in the nets. Pike, carp, eel. He would smoke the eels himself and sell them. It seemed he could do anything. He could make baskets. He did all the farming. He had been a fine hunter.

Wolfgang loved the country. His grandmother Dora Leist recalled, "Once as a boy he spent three months in Klein-Schmölen while his father was traveling, and when he returned to Berlin, he got sick. His parents took him to a doctor and the doctor said, 'He is not sick. It's his soul. He doesn't like to be locked up in an apartment. He loves to run free in the fields and sand hills of Klein-Schmölen.'"

Even in that idyllic rural world there was danger.

An old ammunition factory near the farm had been used during the Nazi regime. When the Russians marched in, they simply blew it up. But there were still a lot of ammunition and guns left behind. This was, of course, a favorite playground for us. We dug up old rusty guns and played cops and robbers on the haystacks nearby. We also found ammunition, which we broke open so we could ignite the black powder inside. The place was called The Factory. You could even find old rusty carbines and machine guns there. Three boys, not relatives of mine, were once digging with a shovel at The Factory and struck a buried grenade. It exploded. All three were badly hurt.

As a child, Schmidt was a relentless mischief-maker—not so different from the maverick who years later drove the martinets of the DTSB crazy. His father recalled, "He was involved in plenty of escapades. He got into fights with other boys. Like all children, he also stole things in department stores, little red Indians and little horses. Once we had to go to the police station because a theft had been reported. My wife always took it hard. 'Oh, God!' she'd say to him. 'How can you do this?' I'd say to her, 'We did the same when we were children.'"

Young Wolfgang seemed to bring an atmosphere of turmoil wherever he went—especially at school.

I was always fidgeting, always playing with something. I wasn't interested in school. I was always one of the tallest, so I stood out for punishment. There were others who fooled around, but I was always the one who got caught because I was so tall.

Schmidt saved every one of his report cards from school even though they were unrelievedly negative.

Here is 1960, the first grade. I entered school September third, 1960; the first report is dated February ninth, 1961. "Wolfgang is very bright and eager to learn, but he is easily distracted in class." The next report is June twenty-eighth, 1961. I am seven years old and my future in school has been perfectly predicted. "The execution of Wolfgang's homework is done in a very orderly fashion." That was when my mother was helping me. "But his involvement in classwork has become very erratic lately. Wolfgang has come to be very stubborn. He does not always succeed in fulfilling the demands of the teacher."

February 1963: "If he were more diligent, he could improve his performance in arithmetic. Wolfgang is very stubborn and defiant. He often has the last word when speaking to adults and is often admonished. Wolfgang has very bad manners. When in the company of girls, he often uses dirty words. He does not do his homework satisfactorily. . . . Wolfgang is often late."

July 1966: "Wolfgang received three reprimands for lack of discipline. He often showed an honest desire to change his impertinent behavior and to be more comradely with his comrades in class. Unfortunately, he always succeeded only for a short period."

July 1969: "Wolfgang was a lively student who spoke his mind openly and honestly. After initial difficulties, he was able to become more disciplined this year. Wolfgang must still learn to concentrate

more on the class action. This would lead to success in that regard
as well. It must be emphasized that he shows great diligence in
training in track and field."

That year, 1969, was his next to last in high school, and he seemed
finally to be on an upward academic trail. But not for long. His
final report was about as bad as ever, even though it was written
by a teacher who was a friend of his parents, and was bending
over backward to find something positive to say:

"July 1970: Wolfgang is a bright but still very unbalanced
student. His undisciplined behavior is reflected also in a certain
superficiality and thoughtlessness. He often had difficulties par-
ticipating in classwork in a disciplined and active fashion. If he
had shown more diligence in his homework and more interest in
class activities, Wolfgang could have performed better in several
subjects. However, his diligence in training in sports must be
emphasized. In 1969, Wolfgang became German youth champion
in the discus throw and finished second in the shot put."

If sports were Schmidt's favorite subject, his favorite teacher
was a tall, clever fellow named Joachim Hildenstein who taught
history and civics.

He was an expressive man who had the talent to tell a good story.
I liked the wars most. The Battle of Carthage, the Trojan Horse. He
told them like fairy tales. Joachim Hildenstein could make everything interesting, from ancient to modern history. He was the only
teacher I ever had who could get me excited about school.

This fellow had an original way with discipline, too. He once
caught Schmidt talking in class and instantly sentenced him to a
punishment as agonizing as fingernail-pulling:

Herr Hildenstein made me copy twenty pages from the Potsdam Treaty! I doubt that I've ever experienced a more effective punishment in my life.

Interestingly enough, unlike American high schools where a star athlete with a miserable academic record is often more admired than a student with straight A's, East German students put academic achievement first and sports second.

When I was honored after I had become German youth champion at the age of fifteen, I was embarrassed because I wasn't a good student in class and everyone knew that. Of course, it is true that nowhere else did you put the dot on the *i* quite as clearly as you did in sports. However, if you received honors at mathematics, it was more significant than a prize in sports. If I had been able to force myself to get better grades, I would have been more popular. But that wasn't my way.

THE CITY OF BERLIN PLAYED A MAJOR ROLE IN THE life and times of Wolfgang Schmidt. But of course, the Berlin he knew—oppressed, polluted, cut in two—was a dim image of the elegant metropolis it had once been.

Its origins went back to a twelfth-century commercial village on the banks of the River Spree that grew until it became the seat of government for the House of Hohenzollern, which ruled Prussia in the eighteenth century. Frederick the Great made it the capital of his empire and declared that all of its buildings were to be designed in the grand style that the French used in Paris.

By 1900, two million people lived in Berlin and the city had become one of the world's dominant banking and manufacturing centers. After the German defeat in World War I, the city wallowed in economic disaster like the rest of the country. Yet in the 1920s and 1930s, Berlin also became a wildly exciting center of madcap culture. Avant-garde movements such as absurdist Dada blossomed. Cabarets featured garish burlesque acts, brilliantly mixed with devastating political satire. Bertolt Brecht and Heinrich Mann produced vicious lampoons of the piggish bourgeoisie businessmen who ruled Berlin. The filmmaker Fritz Lang pushed cinema to new extremes. Walter Gropius founded the Bauhaus school of architecture and design. Arnold Schönberg performed the first concerts of his strange atonal music. It was a rare, mad time that came to an end in the ensuing Nazi years.

Hitler's major contribution to the city was to start the war that nearly destroyed it. The Communists who followed then made their devastating mark by cutting the city in two.

The building of the Berlin Wall began shortly after midnight on August 13, 1961. Until that date, the border between the East and West sections of the city had been essentially open, but now an army of men—soldiers, construction workers, civilian volunteers—waited quietly in the darkness. Batteries of flood-lights suddenly snapped on. Armed guards appeared everywhere. Tanks rolled up to block strategic points. And the grim construction battalions went to work.

They rolled in great coils of barbed wire. They unloaded cinder blocks, bags of cement, steel posts, and reinforcing rods from caravans of trucks. They built barricades of concrete blocks. They erected fences. They systematically shut down the streets, the alleys, the plazas. People on both sides of the boundary were at first confused, then shocked, then frightened.

By morning, everyone knew: They were sealing off the city with a wall! Passage to the West was choked off!

Panic spread through East Berlin. The rush to break out grew more frenzied by the minute. In some cases it was suicidal. People died trying to jump to freedom from buildings or railroad bridges. A few were shot as they tried to dash across the border. Some made it. Some jumped into rescue nets held by West Berlin fire-men or blankets held by friends. Some swam through sewers and canals. Some crawled through U-bahn subway tunnels.

Schmidt was a little boy of seven when this brutal melodrama unfolded. On the day it occurred, he and Bettina were vacationing in Klein-Schmölen with his grandparents. But Ernst and Gretel were in Berlin, and they became enmeshed in the event.

Like most men his age, Ernst belonged to the Kampfgruppe

der Arbeiterklasse (literally, Task Force of the Working Class). The group was organized for the express purpose of heading off potential uprisings among the citizens of the GDR. "As such," said Ernst sarcastically, "the Task Force of the Working Class was actually a force working against the working class. Nevertheless, it was the duty of good party members to belong to it."

On the day The Wall was begun—a Sunday—Gretel received a phone call before six A.M. from a travel agency she was then working for. "They told me to come to the office immediately. I hung up, half-asleep, and then I came fully awake and told Ernst, 'I better call back to make sure it's true they really want me in the office so early on a Sunday.'" She was told, yes, she had to come in. Ernst got up to drive her there, and they walked toward the garage where the car was kept. Gretel recalled, "The route was the same as walking to the subway, and people were coming toward us in large numbers. They said, 'If you plan to take the subway, you can't. Everything is closed. The borders are closed.' That was the first we knew of what was happening."

The streets were more crowded than usual, with trucks and cars and a large number of military vehicles. Gretel's office was on Unter den Linden, the main street in East Berlin, and not far from the Brandenburg Gate. Ernst decided that he had better go to his office at the DTSB to see what was going on. When Gretel got to her workplace, she was told quite abruptly that she was to draw up lists of all tourists who were abroad at the time and indicate when and where they were expected to return to East Germany. "No one told me why I was to do this," she recalled. "I finally finished in the afternoon and went home. Ernst was not there. He didn't come home the whole night. He didn't come home on Monday, nor on Tuesday, nor for the whole week."

At the DTSB, Ernst had been snared for duty. "The guys from the Kampfgruppe got me even before I could park my car," he recalled. "They told me to put on the Kampfgruppe uniform— dark gray with black boots—and I was given a carbine. Then we were dispatched to stand protection at factories, printing plants, the post office, and at the borders with West Berlin. At the border, our task was twofold: Nobody was allowed out, nobody was allowed in. We were bivouacked at a school where we slept each night for the full week."

He was not able to contact Gretel on Sunday, but she spotted him on Monday, August 14. "We all went into the street from the travel agency office to see what was developing. Unter den Linden was full of people, and a crowd was gathered at the Brandenburg Gate. At the Gate, there were lots of members of the Kampfgruppe pushing the crowd back. I saw Ernst among them—the first time I had seen him since Sunday morning. I was very disappointed to see him. He was pushing people back, too, like the rest of them. My own husband. He would have stopped me from advancing, too. There were lots of people who worked in West Berlin, and they were standing at the border, unable to go to work, wondering what to do."

Later, Ernst arrived at the travel agency and said to Gretel, "I was called to action and we all have to stay at a school. Will you come and visit me?"

Gretel replied sharply, "That is the last thing in the world I'd do."

Although the Schmidts were shocked by the sudden erection of The Wall, both realized that the government of the GDR was in a desperate situation. "I believe about fifty thousand East Germans worked in West Berlin, earning wages in deutsche marks, which they could exchange for east marks at a rate of one for five on the black market," said Ernst. "They were earning the salary of a state minister. It was an unbearable situation before The Wall went up. It was so unfair. West Berliners came to East Berlin and shopped with all those east marks they bought on the black market."

"They had to do *something,* they really did," said Gretel.

"Our state would have collapsed already back then without The Wall," said Ernst. "Because of the unequal economic development of the GDR compared to West Germany, many of our citizens could sympathize with the fact that The Wall had to be built. In addition to the economics, so many citizens were leaving the GDR for life in the West that it would have created a serious vacuum in available labor."

The Wall was a monument, quite literally, to the bankruptcy of the socialist regime. Over the years, as Ernst said, there had been a horrendous leakage to the West: Between 1949 and 1961, no fewer than 2.7 million East Germans left. The quantity of defectors was bad enough, but their quality made the situation worse. Many were society's stars—intellectuals, artists, doctors, scientists, teachers. Many were young. There was brief optimism in 1959 that the tide was ebbing when "only" 143,917 East Germans departed. This was the lowest number since 1950. But it was by no means a trend. In the first seven months of 1961, more than 155,000 East Germans had registered at reception centers in West Germany—the largest monthly average ever.

The attraction of freedom and prosperity so near was irresistible. Wolfgang himself had visited West Berlin a couple of times with his mother. It had looked like the Sugar Plum Kingdom.

I was always so excited, so thrilled. We would stroll by the shop windows and I would always beg her to slow her walking, to stop and wait in front of those wonderful windows. Then I would stand there and tell her, almost with my mouth watering, "I would like to have this and that and that and that . . ."

But The Wall was in place and it continued to expand. Hourly, daily, weekly, and for years it was lengthened, strengthened, thickened, until it encircled all of West Berlin. The first section put up in August of 1961 was 29 miles long. In its final form, The Wall covered a circumference of 104 miles, closing off 2.2 million West Berliners into an area 185 miles square. Sixty-nine miles of The Wall consisted of a penitentiary rampart from ten to eighteen feet in height. It was made of cinder blocks, cement, and steel, a mass that could be moved only by tanks or bulldozers. The top was festooned with coils of barbed wire and shards of glass. The other thirty-five-mile section was slightly less daunting, consisting of multiple parallel fences of steel mesh, barbed wire, and steel posts set in concrete foundations.

An open strip of no-man's-land from ten to fifty yards wide lay along the East German side of every section of The Wall. Attack dogs and armed sentries patrolled twenty-four hours a day. The open zone was floodlighted at night and filled with tank traps, car trenches, beds of spikes, electric fences, hidden trip alarms, self-triggering firearms, and sophisticated listening devices tuned to catch the sound of men digging tunnels.

The Wall did stem the flow of deserters: 30,415 had gone in July, and in August, 47,433 had fled the GDR. By December 1961 the monthly number had fallen to 2,420, and after that, attempts to escape became increasingly desperate. One involved a homemade submarine, another a homemade hot-air balloon. Others tried light aircraft, tunnels, and disguising themselves in homemade officer's uniforms. One young man scrambled over on a builder's ladder. Between 1962 and 1976, it was estimated that roughly 1,500 people were caught attempting to escape. The lucky ones went to prison for up to eight years. Others died in the act of fleeing. In all, eighty deaths were officially noted between 1961 and 1989 by the West Berlin police.

Yet none of this desperation and tragedy seemed to touch the boyhood of Wolfgang Schmidt. With or without The Wall, he used East Berlin as if it were a benign backyard, romping through the subways, hooking rides on trolleys, generally raising all forms of childhood hell.

My best friend as a child was Peter Spielmann, and he and I particularly loved New Year's Day in Berlin. We would get up early and go out in the streets looking for firecrackers that hadn't ignited during the night's celebrations. My parents had warned me to stay away from these dangerous things that could blow a finger off. But on New Year's Day the streets were full of them and we blew them up all over the neighborhood. The worst thing that could happen on New Year's was that it would rain during the night and the firecrackers would be too damp to explode.

Even the grim ruins from World War II bombings became just another exciting adjunct to young Schmidt's city playground.

Not far from our apartment was a great hill, a park really, that was made of rubble hauled there from destroyed houses all over the city. We used to climb it. It was called Mont Klamotte, which means Mount Rubbish.

There was also a church not far from my home with a huge cross on one wall. Under the cross was a big hole, made by a grenade probably. You could see how it had hit and exploded in all directions, fragments scattered across the wall. We would sit and study that church, discussing what had probably happened when the shell hit it.

Oddly enough, despite all the regime's fear and hatred of the West, leaders of the GDR never jammed radio and TV transmissions from Western Europe. Though it was officially frowned upon, East German citizens—children and adults—could tune into most anything they wished.

It was fashionable for kids to carry portable radios around the streets. I listened to West radio a lot, including a London station. Mostly it was beat music, the pop songs of the week. The kids in my school were sharply divided between those who liked the Beatles and those who liked the Rolling Stones. I was a Stones man.

Not only rock music wafted in over The Wall, but the news, too, as well as sporting events. This made for some unlikely idols in a society where hero worship was supposed to be limited to the likes of Marx and Lenin.

My earliest sports hero was Cassius Clay. All of his fights were on TV from the West. After Cassius Clay, my number two idol was Al Oerter [the American discus thrower who won four gold medals in four separate Olympics from 1956 through 1968]. My father brought home film of Al Oerter and of the entire discus competition at the Olympics in Mexico City. I was enthralled. It was like watching a film of gods. But what I wanted most of all was to be a boxer like Cassius Clay.

His parents said no boxing. And Schmidt had no choice but to follow in the footsteps of his runner-up role model, the discus thrower.

The metamorphosis of Wolfgang Schmidt from a rambunctious, headstrong child to a rambunctious, headstrong champion came about because of two irresistible forces. The first was his father, the second the mighty East German sports machine.

Ernst Schmidt had been quite serious when he declared that the baby in the pram could be an Olympian in twenty years, and there is no question that he set out to make him exactly that. But why? What were his motives? Was he a stereotype of the over-the-hill athlete driving his offspring to succeed where he hadn't? Or was he an enlightened mentor interested only in helping his son reach his maximum potential?

And what drove the son? Hatred of the old man? Love? Envy? Fear?

During one of her German-language interviews with Schmidt, which make up the heart of this book, Anita Verschoth questioned him closely about the relationship:

V: Did your father's past successes as an athlete motivate you to be like him?
S: My father's trophies had always been on display in our

home, but they didn't exactly kindle my desire to be a sports champion. As a small boy I had thought they were pretty, and I often said I'd like to have some of my own someday. But I saw them more as baubles, nice to admire. My father had also kept a scrapbook and I read his clippings.

V: So you worked hard to be like him—a great athlete?

S: No. I never thought about wanting to be like my father. My father was very authoritarian. When he began to coach me, he had to force me to participate. It was not pleasant. Believe me, in the early days, I was never inspired by the dream of becoming like my father. If I had had this inspiration, I would probably have enjoyed my early training at least a little bit.

V: He was tough on you?

S: He would bark, "Come! Let's train!" I was a normal little boy and I would rather have watched TV or run around with my friends in Humann Square. But my father made me do weight training in the hallway of our apartment. I was about eleven or twelve. Father had real dumbbells and a stool for bench presses. We trained for half an hour or an hour at a time. If he was free weekends, we went to the Friedrich-Ludwig-Jahn stadium. He took along two discuses and a shot, and we practiced and practiced. He taught me very well the rudiments of technique, but it was not fun in the early going, believe me.

V: Was he ever affectionate?

S: My father was a hard man. He'd say, "Get going or we are wasting our time!" It was more a teacher-student relationship. He was my father, but more my teacher, my authority. My mother was my mother, but there was a certain distance between my father and me. He was a strong man. His appearance alone was intimidating, tall, strong, powerful. But he gave me momentum. He'd shout, *"Los, ran!"* [Get going!] He never said you *must* become the best, but he never let me stop working either.

V: You have never thought of him as one of those aggressive fathers who try to pressure their children into accomplishing feats they could never do themselves?

S: Certainly not. I know there are plenty of crazy fathers like that. I saw them myself when I coached kids at Dynamo. Some of those idiots I would have liked to punch because of the way they bullied their children. One day we had a cross-country run. There was a little boy running in fifth, sixth, seventh place, and suddenly, with two hundred meters to go, his father appeared and began running next to the little boy, screaming like a lunatic. "Run now! Come on, run! Faster! Fight!" My father was never like that. He was a teacher no matter how harsh he seemed, and what he did was all meant to teach me. It was not neurotic. He knew precisely what he was doing. All the hard work and the pressure was done for me, not for him. Eventually, gradually, very gradually over the years when the learning process with him was more or less complete, I came to understand the great truth in his favorite saying: *"Ohne Fleiss kein Preis"*—no success without hard work.

V: How did he prepare you for a competition?

S: He would tell me how to warm up, what to look for in my opponents, how to adjust to the surroundings, to the weather. He saw to it I always took an umbrella along so if it rained, I didn't get wet and chilled so I might be injured. He'd tell me whether I had to warm up a bit more or not. He'd tell me to pay attention to the speed and direction of the wind. He'd tell me to study the officials for any personal quirks or odd habits. He'd tell me that I had to get a bit pushy with them sometimes so I could get in an extra warm-up throw. He'd tell me that I had to be as sharp in the mind as I was in the body.

V: Did he ever attempt to psych you up, to get you emotionally wired for a competition?

S: No. He would only say quietly, "Try hard. Give it your best." Of course, there were other times when I didn't seem quite sharp enough to him, and then he would raise his voice and become much more forceful. He'd shout, *"Faulpelz! Faulpelz!"* That means lazy bum.

V: Your father predicted while pushing you in the pram that you would become an Olympian. Did this serve as a goad to make you perform better?

S: Certainly not, although it was his sincere wish. After all, his life's work was in sports, and it was natural for him to say something like this about a son—like a shop owner saying that someday his son will take over the business, right? Fathers want their children to know what they know, to be what they've been. That's nature's way. His goal and maybe his fondest dream was that I should simply perform in the Olympic Games one day. He believed that would be truly beautiful in itself. He did not feel there would be a failure on my part—or his—if I finished out of the medals.

V: All in all, you feel what your father did for you was completely positive?

S: Yes. My father gave me a wonderful purpose in life. How many people are given such a gift? Most people work the same hours at the same job Monday through Friday, and they have no other purpose but to follow that narrow path. Some people don't work at all and become bums sleeping under a bridge. Thanks to my father, I have a purpose in life.

V: And he would not have been disappointed if you had never gone to the Olympics?

S: Come on now, I cannot answer that, that's speculation. You'll have to ask him. Maybe it is true that he would have been disappointed if I had never gone to the Olympics. In Moscow when I placed fourth, he was surely disappointed. But he didn't say anything critical to me. Just, "Better luck next time." And when I won my silver medal in Montreal in 1976, I was damned lucky and he was damned happy.

Ernst Schmidt felt he, too, was lucky with the son he had been given: "Of course, children develop. You don't get them presented to you all finished. But Wolfgang always preferred to go to training instead of working on mathematics or chemistry because he enjoyed it more. By comparison, training was for him fun. Of course, sometimes in order to get his willpower going, I'd give him a slap on the fanny. By the size of his feet and the way he was growing, I told myself that he would likely be an athlete who could accomplish great things in the throwing events.

Of course, he might also have become a good multiple-events man or a jumper or even a swimmer, the way his body build was."

Ernst Schmidt was neither so egotistical nor so domineering that he thought he could turn his son into a champion entirely on his own. Once Wolfgang had begun to show signs of special talent, Ernst arranged for special treatment.

When I was only thirteen, my father saw to it that I became a member of the SC Dynamo. I was just a tot, a pup. The throwing coach at Dynamo was Joachim Spenke, and at that time he also coached the throwers on the national team. They were strong, talented athletes, all older than I.

At first I was thrilled to be included in such company, but soon I came to dislike training with Spenke because he mostly looked after the older athletes. He had created a special training schedule for me, and it wasn't a bad schedule, but he expected me to carry it out entirely on my own. "Go do that," he would say, and then he'd disappear. I trained alone for a few months, then I stopped doing it. My father watched this and didn't like it. He spoke to Spenke, and soon, I got word that if I returned, things would be different.

In the summer of 1968 I made my first trip to a formal competition. It was in Schwerin. I was quite successful, maybe I even won although I don't recall. Later in '68, I competed in Weimar in the championship meet for SC Dynamo. Only the best members were invited and I was overjoyed. I don't remember how I did in the competition. I was in the top three, I know that.

Even better, Weimar was where I met Willi Kühl. He came with his group of throwers and discovered me when he saw me compete. A few months later, my life changed when he switched from Dynamo Luckenwalde to Dynamo Berlin. I very much doubt that I would have become the champion I did without Willi Kühl.

He was a small man, only 1.70 meters (5'7") tall, about forty-two years old when we met. When he saw me perform, he said he would like to coach me. Spenke agreed. Within one year under

Willi, there was an unbelievable improvement in my performances, an explosion.

He made my training more systematic than before, and he looked after me all the time. Willi had been a weight lifter and was especially good at weight training. He was also excellent at teaching technique. Under Spenke, I used to skip this or that exercise, and I used up lots of time just playing around. I couldn't do that with Willi Kühl watching me every minute, and my improvement was miraculous.

In 1969 I first tasted the real blood of victory. The competition for the youth national championships was held in Jena. Besides me, Willi Kühl was coaching a very good young man in my age group named Siegbert Hein, who threw the discus, the javelin, and put the shot. Just before the championships, he decided to drop the discus and concentrate on the shot and the javelin. He had a better technique than I, and he was also a bit more developed physically. I wanted badly to beat Hein at the shot, but he edged me out— barely, and only on his last put, 17.20 meters to 16.81. In the discus, the competition wasn't so tough without Hein, and I threw well under my personal best. Still, it was enough to win, and I was crazy with joy.

That night, I got drunk for the first time in my life. I had never even tasted liquor before. I guzzled beer, champagne, and vodka. I was staggering around, howling with laughter. Other athletes were plastered, too, a big fun-loving crowd of drunken, cocky kids. I drank to my victory and to my new friends and possibly to the glory of the German Democratic Republic and to Al Oerter and Bismarck and Beethoven and Berlin and the Beatles and the Rolling Stones. Then I got sick for three days.

I began throwing up right away and again the next day on the bus home. Soon, I was emptied completely, but I went on throwing up bile. At one point, I drank half a liter of nice cold milk. It tasted like ambrosia. A quarter of an hour later, the ambrosia came rushing up. After the bus ride to Berlin, I had to take a train for another three-quarters of an hour to my parents' summer home, and once I had to lean out of the train to throw up. At home, my mother and father said nothing. I looked like a ghost and smelled of liquor and puke. I could barely speak, but I managed to gasp, "I'll never drink again."

After that victory in Jena I was always the favorite in my age group. I always won the discus, and starting in 1970 I won the shot put as well. I won championships for youth Class B, then Class A (aged 17), then juniors (aged 18 and 19), and finally seniors (over 19). My rivals were Siegbert Hein and Joachim Krug. And I had to work hard, because they were very talented. If I look back now, I can be proud of what I achieved, but then I was never satisfied. I always wanted more.

THOUGH HIS FORTUNES CHANGED TRAUMATI-
cally in the summer of 1982, Schmidt had been a lucky man for
many years. Whatever powers in the universe dictate the fates of
mere mortals, they had seen to it that this man—born to be a
sporting superstar if anyone ever was—had spent his first twenty-
eight years in the embrace of a society that was obsessed with
the care and feeding of sporting superstars.

No system in history had ever been so efficient at turning out
world-class athletes. That such a dreary little country should be
capable of this was, of course, absurd—as if Albania suddenly
began producing crowds of great pianists. Now that The Wall
has fallen and glasnost has melted the ice of the Cold War, it is
safe to say that nothing like it will ever be seen again.

Measured against political logic, sensible economics, or even
simple arithmetic, it made no sense for a poor country to make
a huge investment—1.1 billion marks ($700,000,000) a year—
to produce a crop of world-class athletes. World politics had
always dealt in armies and navies, treaties and trade, guns and
butter. Imagine Napoleon including the results of footraces in

his strategy to conquer Europe. Imagine Alexander the Great calling on high jumpers to help him change the face of the world. Imagine Bismarck, Lenin, Metternich, using pole vaulters, shot-putters, swimmers, soccer players, to make a political point.

For such classic statesmen and strategists, it made no sense.

But in East Germany for forty years, it made great sense. Ernst Schmidt had no doubt about the political value of the GDR's athlete factory: "Our approach to sport was unique in the world. It was expensive, particularly in the beginning for a country whose economy was not cooking well. But our leadership decided that it was well worth the expense because producing a large crop of sports champions was a sure way to achieve worldwide recognition for the GDR. We selected sports as the vehicle because our best possibilities for public impact lay there. Our industrial production then was not so compelling that it would have caused the world to notice the East German presence. But sports? We specialized in it and we succeeded in it and we achieved worldwide notice because of it. People outside the GDR were amazed. 'What is going on in this small country?' they asked. Believe me, for the attention we got, the cost of the sports program was worth it."

Wolfgang Schmidt was well aware that, as an East German sportsman, he was in reality a warrior in a battle of ideologies.

The success of the sports program was intended to prove the usual point—that socialism was the best system. This was why the Russians were doing it, too, of course. But the Soviet Union did not have the problem of simply being recognized as we did in the GDR. Russia already was the big bear in the world. The GDR was a minor player, seen from the outside as a Soviet puppet, so the most important point for my country was to attract simple recognition from the world. The leadership chose sports as the branch of life that reached the global public most easily.

Ironically, the one event in all sport that made it possible to turn East German and Russian athletes into political currency was the one that had insisted longest and loudest that it was above politics: the modern Olympic Games.

They had first been held in 1896, and for the first fifty-plus years (through 1948 to be exact) Americans had won many more medals than athletes from any other country. No US politician or patriot, however chauvinistic they might have been, had ever tried to make the case that results from the Olympic Games proved democracy and capitalism better than other systems.

Hitler dabbled in the idea of using athletes for political propaganda during the 1936 Olympics. He had intended that a large harvest of Olympic victories would offer proof that the Nazis had really sprung from a super race. The Germans won 101 medals, while the US got only 57. But the harvest of four golds by Jesse Owens, and other medals by other American blacks, undermined der Führer's claims for Aryan superiority.

Ironically, members of the German Communist Party, Hitler's archenemies, had planned to use the Berlin Olympics to make a political statement. The central figure was to be Werner Seelenbinder, a loyal Communist and fierce anti-Nazi who also happened to be the world's best Greco-Roman-style wrestler in the 192-pound class. The Communists' original plan called for Seelenbinder to protest Nazi policies by not competing in the Olympics at all. But party members soon realized that just not showing up was not particularly dramatic so they changed signals. The new plan called for Seelenbinder to compete, win a medal as expected, and then when the moment arrived for him to snap the prescribed "Heil, Hitler" salute from the victory dais, he would instead turn toward der Führer and raise the middle finger of his right hand.

Unfortunately, Seelenbinder never got the chance. He lost the first match he wrestled and wound up fourth, out of the medals. When his party colleagues asked how he could have failed them so, Seelenbinder replied calmly, "Perhaps because what you were asking of me was no small thing. I could probably have expected to live about one day after the close of the games had I done what we planned." Seelenbinder became a legend and a martyr anyway because the Nazis executed him in 1944 for sheltering

Communist and Jewish fugitives. The largest indoor arena in East Berlin bears Seelenbinder's name.

The Cold War for athletes began in 1952 at Helsinki when the Russians sent a national team to the Olympics for the first time since 1912. The result of that first Olympic skirmish was essentially a standoff—76 medals for the US, 71 for the USSR.

The reason the Olympics became a major ideological battleground of the Cold War was that there were no other major international sports events in which the performances of different countries with different political systems could be compared directly. The soccer World Cup competition might have sufficed if the cast of Cold War opponents had been different. But none of the major protagonists—East Germany, Russia *or* the US—had been much good at soccer. American spectator sports such as football and baseball were unknown elsewhere in the world. Only the Olympic Games put everyone on ostensibly equal footing.

In fact, it wasn't equal at all. Olympic results were always skewed because of a couple of the IOC's crackbrained rules. Everyone who competed then was required to take an Olympic oath swearing he was an "amateur." This was absurd. Communist governments routinely paid elite athletes to train full-time. Although during the fifties and sixties some very good Western athletes were indeed amateur, most received stipends in the form of college scholarships and "travel expenses" from equipment companies and event sponsors.

It was not until the early 1980s that the IOC got smart. It effectively rescinded its bylaws on amateurism and let each of the various sports federations decide individually whether professionals could compete in their sanctioned events, including the Olympics. As of 1992, professional athletes were to be allowed to compete in nearly all Olympic events with the exception of boxers, cyclists, wrestlers, and soccer players over twenty-three years of age

Another Olympic mess in the early years of the Cold War was caused by the IOC's insistence that no country could compete unless it possessed a fully franchised national Olympic committee. This was all right except that the IOC insisted there could only be one such committee per sovereign country. Unfortunately, after World War II three formerly sovereign countries had been split in two—China and Taiwan, North and South Korea, and of course, East and West Germany. At first, the IOC tried to force these dual hostile governments to field a single Olympic team. The Chinese and the North Koreans refused even to consider competing until after the IOC agreed in 1968 to change its rules and accept both parts of divided countries as equals.

The East Germans, however, were so anxious to get their athletes onto the stage that from 1956 until 1968, Olympic competitors from the GDR were forced to stand in cold, angry ranks with the West German team because the only legitimate German Olympic committee came from the West. Ernst Schmidt recalled, "The Olympics in the fifties and sixties were very uncomfortable affairs. I had dozens of friends in the West with whom I had competed in the old days. Obviously, I felt a normal human affection toward them. But when we stood next to each other during the opening ceremonies, I didn't dare even exchange words of greeting with an old friend because there were always Stasi watchdogs spying to see which of us knew anybody in the West. I had to pretend my friends were enemies, even though we were officially standing together as teammates representing Germany."

The first time East and West Germany competed as a combined team was in 1956 at the Winter Olympics in Cortina, followed by the Summer Olympics in Melbourne. The two Germanys marched under a neutral flag with the five Olympic rings on it and shared a suitably neutral anthem—Beethoven's "Ode to Joy." East Germany gained its first gold medal ever in Melbourne when Wolfgang Behrendt won the bantamweight 119-pound boxing championship. For decades he was celebrated as a hero, signing autographs in the street and addressing banquets. In later years, he became a photographer.

Warped though the Olympic playing fields were for East Germans, they immediately made the games their pet hunting ground. Their production rate of medals was incredible. From the 1956 Summer Olympics in Melbourne through the 1988

Summer Olympics in Seoul, the GDR with its puny population of 16.7 million won 160 gold, 153 silver, and 141 bronze medals—454 in all. The USSR with a population of 250 million over that same period won 373 gold, 289 silver, and 277 bronze medals—939 in all. The US with its population of 200 million won 333 gold, 258 silver, and 207 bronze over that period—a total of 798.

That was the Summer Olympics only. In the smaller, more specialized Winter Games, the GDR was even more dominating. From the GDR's first competition in '56 to '88, it won 43 gold, 39 silver, 36 bronzes—118 in all. The Russians won 78 gold, 57 silver, and 59 bronze—194 in all. The US won a paltry total of 25 gold, 28 silver, 21 bronze—74 in all. Adding up all Olympic medals in winter and summer games won between 1956 and 1988, the GDR had 572, the USSR 1,133, and the US 872. The per capita ratios were stunning: A child born in the GDR had roughly an eight times better chance to win an Olympic medal than one born in the US or the USSR, and six times better than one born just across The Wall. It was a great record, and perhaps the most gratifying statistic of all was that the shabby, smaller GDR had beat its rich, booming brother country to the west by 572 medals to 335.

The secret of all this success puzzled people in the West. Some were suspicious that there was something quite sinister behind it all. But Doug Gilbert wrote in *The Miracle Machine:* "The answer, sad to say for those who would like to see a devious Communist plot behind every gold medal, and a series of Frankensteinian experiments and secret drugs behind every world record, is neither sensational nor miraculous. It is simply the result of some very thorough planning by a government that (1) gives sport a higher priority than it is given anywhere else in the world: (2) seriously promotes the unified development of both mass sport for the total population and elite sport for the international-level performer; (3) has processed more than 8,000 professional coaches through the Leipzig Institute since its creation in 1951 and, beyond that, has found them jobs within the system to maximize use of their talents; (4) has certified more than 200,000 volunteer coaches at the Little League and mass sport levels; and (5) has placed the country's medical research system at the disposal of sport."

The East Germans also employed a simple but efficient strategy to guarantee a maximum return of medals for the number of athletes in their program: They routinely emphasized individual events over team events for the reason that single athletes were cheaper to train and develop than teams were, and even though a couple of dozen medals might be awarded to members of a victorious team, the victory only counted as one medal in the national totals. Individuals also often produced more than one medal—sometimes many more, such as the swimmer Kristin Otto, who won six golds in Seoul; the swimmer Kornelia Ender, who won four golds and a silver in 1976; the sprinter Renate Stecher, who won two golds and a silver in 1972; and the swimmer Roland Matthes, who won two golds, a silver, and a bronze in 1972.

But these explanations for the GDR's success mainly addressed the cold mechanics of the miracle.

In fact, two quite different moral factors were the real key to it all: (1) the relentless recruitment and exploitation of children, and (2) a nakedly hypocritical willingness to create an elite class of people within the classless society that is the supposed bedrock of communism.

About the exploitation of children, Schmidt said:

I myself was not recruited by the system as a child because my father had already recruited me from the day I was born. But other champions were usually picked out as children through a very efficient network. In every municipal district there were full-time coaches, paid by the state, plus voluntary exercise leaders who went into the schools at certain times of the year to inspect the children and to pick out the prize specimens. They inspected children aged nine to twelve—except for those in the sports of swimming, gymnastics, and figure skating. Here they looked at younger ones. About six or seven.

At one point I was a coach working at the training center for SC Dynamo in Hohen-Schönhausen, and I went along with the local coaches in making inspections of children there. The Dynamo center at Hohen-Schönhausen, small as it was, also had its own sports medicine department and the two full-time doctors who always accompanied us during these school inspections. We gave the children physical tests and found out who could run the fastest, who were the best jumpers, the best throwers.

We always looked for tall children and children with big feet. The doctors would measure the children—the width of their hips, their height when sitting and standing, their arm span, the width of their shoulders, their fatty tissue. From all these results they could make a prognosis about how tall a child would grow—plus or minus three centimeters. There were no psychological tests, only physical exams.

After the tests, we'd select the best physical specimens and ask them to come for special work at the training center. This was an honor for them, of course. The children were not forced to participate in a sport if they didn't wish to. If a child was already a speedskater and liked speedskating, the child stayed there instead of becoming a track-and-field athlete.

The most promising children were enrolled in East Germany's unique KJS schools—*Kinder- und Jugendsportschulen*. These were institutions operated only for elite young athletes. They worked closely with the big sports clubs around the country and combined first-class sports training with a first-class education. The KJS had been established in the very early fifties. Ernst Schmidt had been involved then and he recalled, "We had to negotiate an agreement with the national education agency in order to organize the *Kinder- und Jugendsportschulen*. Eventually there were nineteen such schools, I think, with almost four thousand students. I believe that it was this marriage between education and sports development that was the significant key to the successful sports system in East Germany. It gave them the best of both worlds—a chance for sports stardom without sacrificing the excellent schooling that could give them useful, profitable lives outside sports."

Ironically enough, Ernst Schmidt's son never enjoyed this enlightened system.

I had such poor grades in school that I was never selected. In fact, that put me at quite a disadvantage because I had a much tougher schedule than people who went to the KJS school. Joachim Krug, for instance, could train twice a day while I had to go to school all morning and didn't even arrive for training until two or three P.M. I had to do in one session what Krug did in two.

Sometimes they found that a child in a KJS didn't develop as they had hoped; that child was promptly returned to his old school. There was no stigma in this. Everyone knew that it was supposed to be a very special institution where only the most talented were to be developed, and if an athlete didn't produce, then he certainly shouldn't be there.

You couldn't always predict what would happen. An athlete may have developed an injury or an illness. Sometimes a talented child may have been unwilling to train hard every day. KJS schools were expensive. They had to make them as productive as possible.

About the sport system's creation of an elite class in an ostensibly classless society Schmidt was quite blunt:

There is no other way of putting it: Good athletes in the GDR enjoyed great advantages over the rest of society. The powers made certain that this upper class not only excelled in sports, but that it also had an excellent general education. Athletes in the GDR also automatically became members of a politically elite society. They also became a part of an economic elite because they didn't have to deal with any of the hard realities of life—such as having a job or paying the rent.

I never had to find a real job because I was a *Leistungssportler*—

a performance athlete. I did train at one point, when I was in my middle teens, for a career as an apprentice electronics specialist. My father and I had agreed that electronics would be good because I would be sitting a lot, and that would not interfere with my back and leg muscles and make me tired when I went to train. I went to school four days a week, and one day I worked from seven A.M. until four P.M. in an electronics factory. For once, I had found a school I liked. But I would not have been there if I hadn't gotten special treatment as a *Leistungssportler*. My grades in normal school had been so bad that I was not eligible for the vocational school. My acceptance was taken care of by the Sports Club Dynamo Berlin.

In vocational school I got only one D and I finished my apprenticeship in February 1972. I never went to work in electronics. Instead, I was immediately employed by SC Dynamo Berlin at a monthly salary of six hundred thirty marks. My job definition was "sports instructor," but I never did that job either. I spent all my time training.

In 1973 I was admitted to the VP—Volkspolizei—and was paid a higher salary even though I never worked a day as a policeman either. This, too, was arranged because of SC Dynamo Berlin. The club also arranged for me to take evening classes to get a proper degree from high school so I could qualify to study at the DHFK, the German College for Physical Culture in Leipzig, if I later wished to be a coach or a physical education teacher.

SC Dynamo Berlin caused all these things to happen for me. I am eternally grateful to this club.

The SC Dynamo Berlin was the largest single sporting facility on earth, covering more than fifty acres in the center of the city. It dwarfed the Central Army Sports Club in Moscow, which was the largest sports facility in the Soviet Union.

On the Berlin grounds were the Sporthotel, a soccer stadium, a track-and-field stadium, an indoor competitive swimming pool with diving towers, an outdoor 50-meter pool with a diving tower, several large training buildings with individual halls for boxing, wrestling, judo, fencing, gymnastics, weight lifting, an indoor skating rink for figure skating, another for ice hockey, another indoor rink with a 500-meter speed-skating oval, and one of the largest indoor track-and-field training halls in the world. The KJS school and dormitories lay in a corner of the grounds beyond the track hall, and a separate sports-medicine clinic—complete with research facilities as well as treatment and therapy—was across the street from the main swimming hall.

The architecture was a classic socialist mix of tacky, blocky structures, big and small, and the premises had a pervasive run-down appearance. Nevertheless, this was the most celebrated sporting facility in East Germany, something like the Vatican in Rome—a vast separate, almost sacred community existing unto itself.

Now that I know the West, I can tell you there is no such thing available there. We had two full-time doctors only for track-and-field athletes at Dynamo. Every sport had its own doctors. They watched us like American government doctors watched astronauts.

Club Dynamo had us working with videos to spot flaws in technique years before they knew about such things in the West. The club had a big photo and video library for this purpose. Technicians would come to tape an athlete's workout whenever they were asked.

The club had a couple of nutritionists to check our diets. They made up menus in the dining room for each type of sport separately and issued different meal coupons for each category. Endurance-event competitors got more carbohydrates for example. I, being in a speed-and-power event, got a high-protein diet.

During my last few years at Club Dynamo, we also had a psychologist. Personally, I didn't feel any need for him. I was winning most of the competitions I entered, and I have never had trouble convincing myself that my psyche was quite healthy enough.

The same kind of sophisticated care was available on a smaller scale at each of the GDR's twenty-three other elite sports clubs.

The money for this club system came primarily from the budgets of the state and sponsoring agencies (State Security for Dynamo, the army for Vorwärts). Sports clubs were proclaimed by the regime as serving both elite athletes and the masses, but programs for the public were ill-equipped and underfinanced.

About 3 million citizens—not quite 20 percent of the population—belonged to sports clubs. Individual monthly dues ranged from 1.30 marks (78 cents) for a worker down to twenty pfennigs (12 cents) for children. For the masses, everything was free once an individual paid those minuscule dues.

For the elite, the costs were much higher. In return for their round-the-clock care and state-of-the-art training and equipment, they were expected to make an utterly sacrificial commitment to top-level performances. Among other things, they were required to sign a *Leistungsauftrag,* a contract promising to perform at a specific—and very high—level in their events. Ernst Schmidt explained it this way: "This was a matter of goal-setting for the athlete, and it was done in agreement with the national coach, the club coach, and the athlete himself. It meant determining what results the athlete would attain in the coming year, and then drawing up the contract, which committed him to reaching that level. If the athlete did not reach his goal due to injury or other unforeseen obstacles, we did not chop his head off. Considering the very large number of top-drawer performances we achieved through the *Leistungsauftrag,* it was of little importance if a few athletes missed their goals. Of course, if they didn't win the medals they were supposed to win, they got no premiums and their salaries were reduced also. Eventually, if they failed constantly to meet standards, they were no longer allowed to perform at all."

The *Leistungsauftrag* was only the most obvious commitment demanded by the state. Elite athletes were also expected to perform in public—particularly in the West—as if they were in total thrall over socialism. They were expected to play the role of perfect socialist puppets, no deviations in behavior allowed.

For years, Ernst Schmidt had watched preparations of groups

of athletes before they ventured out of the GDR. "It was normal to tell athletes about the places they would visit—about the politics, the economics, the customs they would encounter. This was a good thing, part of good intellectual development for young people, and we had knowledgeable experts talking to them. On the other hand, there was too much pressure, in my opinion, for our athletes to disassociate themselves from athletes in Western countries. At all times, we were told to view these athletes as enemies. Not opponents, *enemies*. Our only friends, we were told, were athletes from socialist countries. Those from capitalist societies were not to be spoken to, not even looked at. Everyone was afraid not to obey."

This included young Schmidt for several years.

I willingly lent myself to all of this when I was competing in my earlier years. I was giving one hundred percent to win for the GDR. I was the perfect parrot repeating what I had been taught to say. We were always given extremely strict guidelines before we left the GDR about how we should behave in a capitalist country. The result was that we were nervous, frightened that we might do or say something wrong in public. That was the main reason why GDR athletes have gotten the reputation for being such a dreary bunch of earthworms with rarely anything interesting to say. It happened many times that people in the West would observe a GDR athlete staring glassy eyed at a press conference, and they'd say, "Well, there is another typical boring GDR robot who never opens his mouth."

We were elite, all right, but we were elite without true self-esteem. If someone asked us a political opinion, we were allowed to repeat only the rote drivel that the system approved. If we got it wrong or varied from the rote, we were in instant trouble. In the end, my motivation was no longer to win for the GDR. I was giving one hundred percent to win so that someday I could open my mouth and say what I believed myself.

Schmidt's open mouth, of course, cost him some of the ripest years of his career—a lesson that certainly did not go unnoticed by other members of the GDR sporting elite. Most of them were loyal party-liners, and the idea of prison never entered their minds.

What they feared most was losing their special privileges. The opportunity to travel, to own a car, to have an apartment or a house, to eat the best food, to be paid well for simply training—all these were such rare treasures that they had to be protected at all costs. In Schmidt's view, this was the drive that gave East German athletes their winning edge.

The outside pressure from coaches and the authorities was hard, of course. But the inside pressure you felt from yourself was even harder. Certainly there was pride and joy in being the best in your events, but uppermost was the fact that if you failed, you would then lose the beautiful life.

That was the supreme motivation in the GDR—and in all other socialist countries—the fear of losing what little freedom and favor we were given. This made internal competition among socialist athletes much nastier than it was in capitalist countries. We had so much more to lose if we were dropped from the team. We had so much farther to fall that the relationships among members of socialist teams were already extremely tense, even bitter. There were not many friendships made, I can tell you—certainly not among athletes competing in the same events.

No athlete could be absolutely positive that he would make the team. He trained for months, learned his political propaganda perfectly, and in the end there would be a test event against his mates, and if he failed badly enough—bang!—back to the lowly life of an average citizen of the GDR. It was always a matter of absolute performance. A dictatorship is a dictatorship. You only made the Olympic team if your performances indicated you could place among the top six in the world. Anyone who couldn't rank in the top six stayed home. It was ruthless, but it was efficient—like a factory testing its products to see there are no flaws before it sends them to market.

In 1973, Schmidt was chosen to be a member of the superelite
group that was preparing for the 1976 Olympics.

We lived in a tiny world not unlike prison life. Everything happened
for us in quadrennial cycles. But I was nineteen and still had respect
for my superiors, and I believed in the socialist system because I
believed it was giving me the opportunity to become the best I could
be.

Much of Schmidt's time was now spent at the DTSB's secret
sports facility in Kienbaum, a village about thirty-five miles east
of Berlin. It was a futuristic training center where athletes went
for a final tune-up before they went to major competitions in the
outside world.

Kienbaum simply provided the best conditions enjoyed by any athletes on earth. It was equipped to handle two hundred athletes at
a time, and it spread over many acres. There were two track-and-
field stadiums as well as a big indoor running track for use in the
winter. A lake on the grounds was used for rowing, canoeing, and
recreational sailing. There were two weight-lifting gyms, a twenty-
five-meter pool, and a special indoor throwing area devised by my
father, which allowed us to practice in any weather.
    One facility was so secret it was camouflaged. It was built inside
a partially underground bunker that had no windows and from the
outside looked like two hills with grass growing over it. It was
pressurized inside so the air pressure could be adjusted for training
endurance athletes—cyclists, distance runners, walkers. The pressure could be changed so that athletes felt as if they were training
at an altitude of, say, three thousand meters [9,000 feet]. This allowed them to have the same high-altitude training conditions that
gave the great Ethiopian and Kenyan runners and Mexican walkers
such endurance. They rode or ran on a moving belt adjusted to

speed. They stayed in there for hours every day; walkers sometimes stayed in there for as much as three weeks.

Athletes in other sports were never allowed in there.

The day-to-day routine at Kienbaum was strict and militaristic.

Breakfast was at seven-thirty A.M. sharp, but before we ate we had to line up for *Morgenappell*—morning roll call. Our leaders shouted commands—*"Still gestanden!"* [Halt!], *"Richt Euch!"* [Right dress]. Sometimes the national flag was hoisted as we stood at attention. The day's agenda would be announced. Then breakfast, then the various training groups broke up for separate discussions. From time to time, this involved a political briefing. A Party secretary or some other politician would give us a speech on current political issues. To me, all of this was of the utmost seriousness, and I swallowed it all as if it were my morning vitamins.

Training didn't begin until nine-thirty or ten A.M. There were always several groups, and we went our separate ways. After morning training, we showered, lunched, then took a rest or some therapy, maybe looked at videos from the morning workout for technical analysis, then went back to training for the afternoon. Dinner was at six-thirty P.M., and sometimes we would have yet a third training session that lasted until nine P.M. We had to be in bed by ten-thirty P.M.

We slept two or three to a room, beautifully appointed rooms with a shower. The food could not have been better. The personnel who staffed Kienbaum were the best available in the GDR—from the overall manager to the chambermaids, the custodial staff, the caretakers of the facilities, the kitchen staff, even the gardener. All of these people lived in the village of Kienbaum not far from Kienbaum Lake, which had a floodgate and a lovely little stream, an idyllic spot.

Before every important international competiton, we were given a dose of time—a couple of weeks—at Kienbaum. It helped bind us together emotionally as a national team and got us into peak physical shape. You could put it this way: In Kienbaum, our athletes were bred—pardon the ugly expression, but it is true—*bred* to go forth and be gladiators for the GDR.

Schmidt recalled the way it was when the national team sallied forth to do battle in Helsinki in 1973 when he was a mere child of nineteen.

As always, there was a heavy final briefing at Kienbaum, someone barking: "Breakfast at seven! Bus leaves for the airport at seven-thirty sharp! In Helsinki you stay at the hotel and do not leave it alone! Do not forget that you are there as a national team! You are loyal representatives of the socialist state of the GDR! There will be no unpleasant incidents! When you leave your hotel, inform your coach! Never go out without another team member! . . ." On and on.

But even under such strict rules, I found it beautiful to be in Finland, to belong to such a big team, and to actually be a member of my nation's team. It was all so new and I was still only a boy. To me, Finland was the Land of a Thousand Lakes. We were staying in a hotel and I had rarely done that before. We had been given a little money—one hundred or two hundred Finnmarks [about $25]—and the shops were full of things we didn't have at home. I bought fishing gear and I wanted jeans, but I couldn't find any my size.

We moved together in a group—training, meals, shopping, sight-seeing. To me the togetherness seemed a wonderful form of friend-ship, but in reality we were being very restricted, very controlled. There were about six officials with us, including the coaches. Al-ways, at least one of them was a member of the Stasi. They appeared for trips abroad and then were not seen again until the next trip. In the early years, I never gave it a thought that they were Stasis. I had no contact with any Finns at all. I was so warmly wrapped up in being with my team that I didn't care. I didn't want any other contact.

The older guys on the team would make jokes about the watchdogs. They didn't like being watched so closely. But I was still a young boy then, so I didn't mind being treated like a young boy. That came later.

THOUGH HE EVENTUALLY REBELLED AGAINST ITS
oppressive ways, Schmidt never stopped being an admirer of the
scientific and medical functions of the East German machine.

In the West, everybody has to find his own doctor. If he is lucky,
he might be as well taken care of as we were, but it is definitely a
gamble for athletes in the West.

Our doctors were always there for us—and only us. They worked
out an individual program for every one of us individually, including
massage, physiotherapy, sauna, mud packs, muscular stimulation
by electricity. Each athlete got specifically prescribed vitamins, elec-
trolytes, and minerals. Our doctors performed a full blood analysis
two or three times a year on each athlete.

The practice of East German sports medicine was always an object
of envy and curiosity in the West, as well as a subject of bizarre
conjecture and sensational rumor. One report had it that the

authorities arranged for female athletes to be impregnated by male athletes as part of a sports breeding production line set up to turn out continuing crops of flawless world-class baby athletes. Wolfgang Schmidt scoffed at this.

A relationship with a partner who is an athlete was considered to be good for you and officials encouraged it. This was not because of the offspring it might produce, it was because an athlete understands the needs and problems of another athlete and this makes things easier. Sometimes I was so tired at night from my training that I could hardly eat supper. Other times I was so hyper I couldn't sleep all night. These things caused certain frictions with women I was with. If I had been dating another athlete, she would have understood and no explanations or apologies would have been necessary.

Ernst Schmidt, the dedicated socialist "activist of the first hour," was deeply offended by the suggestion that the GDR organized the mating of athletes: "To try to breed superior athletes would be returning to the evil ways of Hitler when all dark-haired, dark-skinned people, Jews particularly, were persecuted, and all blue-eyed, Nordic blonds were put on pedestals. His official state policy called for SS men and properly qualified German women to couple in attempts to breed a blue-eyed race. They would meet at 'breeding institutes,' so-called, have sex, and hope for pregnancies. That was Hitler's unspeakable idea, and I shudder at the thought that anyone would ever accuse the GDR of wishing to repeat anything like it."

Interestingly enough, Hitler had attempted to breed master-race babies as a sort of sideshow experiment to the 1936 Olympics in Berlin. Adjacent to the Olympic Village he created a sylvan retreat called the Love Garden. What we know of this breeding nest came from an interview in 1971 by a *Sports Illustrated* correspondent with a Swiss osteopathic surgeon named Paul Martin. Bizarre though his report was, Dr. Martin was no quack or crackpot. He was a reputable citizen of the Zurich medical community as well as a world-renowned Olympic competitor. Dr. Martin had raced for Switzerland as a middle-distance runner in five consecutive games from 1920 to 1936—the only track athlete in history to compete so many times. Dr. Martin's only medal was a silver in the 800-meter run in 1924, but at the 1936 games in Berlin, this distinguished fellow was awarded a Diplôme de Mérite from the IOC. Thirty-five years later, he had this to say about Hitler's Love Garden: "The Olympic athlete in Berlin was elevated to a godlike creature. We were gods of the stadium. The Germans had even reserved a sort of heavenly forest near the Olympic Village for us gods. And there the prettiest handpicked maidens would offer themselves to the athletes—especially the good Aryan types. Olympic babies born out of such encounters were cared for by the state. There was every indication that this Woods of Love was a matter of state policy by the Nazis. The maidens were usually sports teachers or members of Hitler's Bund Deutscher Mädchen [German Girls' League], and they had special passes to enter the Village woods and mingle with the athletes. It was a lovely beech forest which had a pretty little lake, and the place was tightly ringed by *Schupos* so no one would disturb the sportive couples. It was interesting that before submitting to the Olympic god of her choice, the girl would request her partner's Olympic badge. In case of pregnancy, the girl would give this information to state or Red Cross maternities to prove the Olympic origin of her baby. Then the state would pay for the whole works." Dr. Martin said that it was obvious the willing maidens had been ordered to maintain racial purity because they avoided blacks and sought out Americans, Scandinavians, Dutchmen, and Finns as well as Germans.

Production-line breeding aside, the East German sports-medicine machine was the key to a great deal of the success its athletes enjoyed. Verschoth questioned Schmidt about his own experiences with it.

V: Did your doctors as a rule rely heavily on injections of drugs?

S: Not particularly so. Surely, some athletes in the GDR got lots of shots. Some that were injured may have gotten a hundred shots over their careers, too. I've heard of cases where someone got one hundred injections in the knee because of damage to the cartilage. Whenever I was supposed to get a shot, even a tetanus shot, I personally was scared! But if, for instance, I was hurt two weeks before the Olympics and my doctor told me, "We can get rid of it in a week with a lot of shots," then I'd certainly put up with shots. Sometimes it took shots, sometimes surgery, sometimes a little vitamin pack.

V: You refused to have shots?

S: If I could. However, in 1975, I had a serious back injury suffered in weight training. I couldn't throw at all. I went to the SC Dynamo hospital, and a doctor diagnosed my problem as a blocked vertebra in the lumbar section of the spinal column. The European Cup competition was almost at hand. With time so short, I let the doctor convince me to have shots—procaine, I think—to eliminate the pain. It didn't work at all.

V: But you won the European Cup in 1975. What happened?

S: That is when I came upon the golden hands of Arno Staudinger, a blind chiropractor and acupuncturist. He lived in Bernsbach in the south of the GDR. He worked often at the Army Sports Club Potsdam, but he helped all national-team athletes when necessary. He did manual therapy with those magic hands. He had a theory that a diseased tension is created in the muscles by work and strain, and that this tension causes more injury and more pain as it increases. He had a great feel for the muscles. Like no human who ever touched me. He was more like a friendly alien from outer space.

Arno Staudinger would merely touch me, and instantly he would realize what the problem was. Then he went to work with his fingers and his acupuncture needles—

V: Acupuncture needles? They didn't frighten you?

S: They didn't hurt, they soothed. With his needles, Arno dissolved the blockage in the spinal column. It took only a few hours and the pain was gone. One or two days later, the inflammation had subsided, too. I was free of pain and I won at the

European Cup. Arno Staudinger suited me best because I could be sure that he would not pump my body full of chemicals. I stayed with him from that time on. I had other back injuries, and I always went to his place in Potsdam or drove all the way to his home. He always made me healthy.

V: His techniques were copied by many other doctors in the GDR, right?

S: Wrong. Arno Staudinger was a man of great controversy. Most of our other doctors called him a quack. He had never studied medicine formally. He was not a licensed medical doctor. The other doctors saw that the athletes turned to him for help and they were jealous.

V: Did the blind chiropractor ask for extra fees because he was so popular?

S: He did not expect to be paid at all. I gave him money sometimes, not enough to be worth mentioning. He had a truly altruistic nature. When there were cases he couldn't cure, he would tell us to go to a regular doctor and get a shot. It happened to me once. The inflammation in my back had returned. Arno's fingers defined the tension in my muscles and he knew immediately that he couldn't help me. He sent me to a doctor to get a shot.

V: The man sounds like a saint.

S: He never got any recognition because he was too unorthodox for socialist thinking. But I had him to thank for many of my medals—and so did the GDR.

The East German sports-medicine complex routinely offered a menu of anabolic steroids and other performance-enhancing drugs. In its simplest application, the stuff is used to bulk up muscles and increase strength. Originally, it was used by athletes who specialized in strength events—weight lifting, bodybuilding, and throwing. In recent years, it has proved useful—perhaps essential—to athletes who need bursts of explosive power such as sprinters, cyclists, and swimmers. Multiple-event athletes such as decathletes, pentathletes, and heptathletes have found it helpful, too, and even athletes in endurance events such as long-distance running have used it. Steroids also tend to speed up the healing of muscle injuries for all kinds of athletes.

The use of such substances has been outlawed in most major international competitions since the early 1970s. In recent years, urine tests have been required after major events in an attempt to catch violators. There have been a few—but very few—disqualifications based on these test results.

The most notorious occurred at the 1988 Summer Olympics in Seoul when a urine test indicated that the great Canadian sprinter Ben Johnson had used steroids before he won the 100-meter race over the American Carl Lewis. The IOC instantly stripped Johnson of his gold medal, as well as the new world record he had set of 9.79 seconds. The medal went to Lewis. Johnson was banned from further competitions sanctioned by the IAAF. At first, the sprinter denied using illegal substances. Then, in hearings held in Toronto in the spring of 1989, he confessed that he had indeed been ingesting great quantities of the forbidden drug. The IAAF then voted to expunge Johnson's earlier 100-meter record of 9.83 seconds, which he had set in Rome in 1987 at the world championships where he did *not* test positive for drugs.

Ben Johnson's suspension was soon followed by a worldwide campaign—joined by both East and West—to force major athletes to take year-round random drug tests. If they tested positive once, they faced a two-year suspension. Twice, they could be expelled from international competition for life.

Some people, such as Mac Wilkins, felt the punishment was way out of proportion to the seriousness of the "crime." He said: "I don't think steroids are a good thing. I think we should be able to compete without them. But I think if you measure steroids versus marijuana or alcohol or crack or cocaine or heroin, the amount of social damage caused is inversely proportional to the punishment. There are guys on the street pushing heroin and crack, destroying lives, costing the economy billions in lost lives, lost resources. Those guys just cycle through the judicial system and end up right back on the streets, ruining lives and costing billions.

"With steroids, the public damage is almost nil. By and large, the only negative effect is to your own body. Maybe a couple of people have died from it, but compared to other substances the punishment for using steroids is out of line. You won't go to prison for it, but you face international ostracism and the public perception that your moral character is lower than low."

Once the IAAF handed down its retroactive punishment to Ben Johnson, everyone clammed up about steroids because no one wanted to risk having his greatest athletic achievements—including world records—erased forever. That included Wolfgang Schmidt.

I am not saying that I took anabolic steroids. However, I must say one thing very forcefully: The success of the GDR was not based on steroids. It was the system, the coaches, the exercise leaders, the sports functionaries, the sports physicians, the sports scientists, the sports facilities. Who started with steroids? The US. Who started with the atom bomb? The US. Others had to follow suit to keep the balance.

Americans did indeed start the steroid epidemic forty years ago. The precise genesis is lost in the decades, but it is likely that the earliest application of the stuff for a sport occurred in the late 1940s in York, Pennsylvania, the mecca for weight lifters and bodybuilders. After that, American shot-putters and hammer and discus throwers followed, and soon, it was not a secret any longer.

Ernst Schmidt recalled: "American and Soviet weight lifters and throwers had suddenly begun to excel in a very surprising way around 1960. There was always such a great gap between their performances and ours that we came to the conclusion that the Americans could not possibly do what they were doing if they were using only the traditional training methods we were using. We evaluated scientifically what would be required in terms of training methods and training time to produce the results Americans were getting. Eventually, we realized that anabolic steroids were being used. I, as head coach of all track and field then, made the suggestion that we should explore this matter also.

"We started testing steroids in a methodical way in relation to training. Soon we learned that where the load bearing was the highest [meaning the training load an athlete had to carry in order to achieve a certain result], the dosage of steroids had to be accordingly adjusted because it translated directly into a higher performance ability for the athlete. We found that these higher load-bearing tolerances simply could not be managed without this medication. We began to experiment with steroids, always under strict medical control, fine-tuning the dosage in exact relation to the resulting improvement in performance. It was always done under the closest medical scrutiny."

"We had a motto: *'As little as possible; as much as necessary.'* We felt the great danger lay in the uncontrolled use of very high doses. For men who took high doses there could be a negative effect on potency. If they took drugs for many years in big doses, they might be hardly fertile in the end. A chemical castration, we called it. With women, there could be virilization—growth of beard, deep voice, other side effects. Usually this was temporary. When our women stopped competing, they had children and there were no problems."

There was nothing illegal or unethical about taking anabolic steroids for many years. They were not outlawed by the IOC until 1976. However, the proper medical use of anabolic steroids was to build up emaciated cancer patients, to cause stunted children to grow, to speed up rehabilitation after a serious illness or operation. In the West they were supposed to be available only with a prescription. Any American athlete who wished to use steroids had to find a sympathetic physician or pharmacist willing to deal without prescriptions. This was not so hard to do early on, although in recent years steroids have become harder to get over the counter and a thriving black market has grown up. In the early years, however, many athletes thought the more they took the better because they possessed little information about the effects of large doses of steroids on their hearts, livers, libido, and behavior.

Because of consistent supervision, the use of drugs behind the Iron Curtain was less threatening to athletes' health than in Western countries. Mac Wilkins said, "What we were looking at were two basically different approaches to sports medicine. The East European research people looked at the anabolic steroid as another tool to help the athlete advance his performance at the international level. The American sports officials looked on it as something akin to heroin."

In an interview with the West German magazine *Sports* in the winter of 1990, Dr. Hermann Buhl, deputy director of medical research at the formerly top-secret Research Institute for Physical Culture and Sports at Leipzig, admitted that anabolic steroids were "systematically" used by athletes of the East German republic. He declared, "The secret was always to find the exact moment in the training regime when it was the best time to give an athlete such drugs. But we were always guided by the precept that we should consider not only improved performances, but also the physical condition of the athlete whose body and organs were burdened by such a high volume of training. We didn't have a bad conscience over the use of drugs because we kept everything under strict medical supervision."

One of the most sensational reports on performance-enhancing drugs in the GDR appeared in June 1989 in the West German tabloid *Bild*. It came from a certifiably expert source, Dr. Hans-Georg Aschenbach, then thirty-eight, a gold medal Olympic ski jumper in 1976, a trained sports physician, and winter-sports team doctor for five years before he defected to West Germany in August of '88. Aschenbach was on both receiving and dispensing ends of the drug operation in the GDR. His story in *Bild* was told with plenty of lurid tabloid flourishes but it rang of truth:

"I took drugs over the entire period of my sports career. I swallowed and injected anabolic steroids for eight years. We had to take these substances. We were forced to do it. If you refused to take them, you were fired from the national team and the sports club, and you faced many problems in your private life as well.

"At the beginning, I didn't know what I was taking. The people who looked after us spoke of vitamin pills. Later the older athletes explained it to me. We were instructed not to talk to anybody about this. If you talked, you'd be fired.

"During our preparations for the Olympic Games in Innsbruck, I had refused to take the pills. I was terribly afraid I would be caught. I was told, 'Either you let us inject you or you don't go to the games.' I let them inject me."

At the time, Aschenbach was taking a daily dose of thirty to forty milligrams of Nandrolon, which is a composite of several male sex hormones. Nandrolon filled him with a powerful sense of aggression as well as a monumental sexual hunger. "Sometimes you could hardly stand it. These things increased your potency to the point where you suddenly started to masturbate—in the woods, shortly before training began behind the ski jump, in the men's room, anyplace at all. It was crazy, but you simply had to do it. Actually our cross-country ski racers had a good arrangement. There was always intense sexual intercourse between the men and women. Top female athletes were often satisfied by their coaches. Alas, there were no women ski jumpers."

In his work as a doctor, Aschenbach knew precisely how drugs were dispensed: "Doping treatment occurred two or three times a year during training buildup to competition and weight training. Each treatment lasted between three and six weeks. One hundred milligrams of Primobolan Deposit was injected into muscles each week. It builds power. Turinabol was administered in tablet form. It is a mixture of Nandrolon and the natural male sex-hormone testosterone. It was especially bad for women. Pubic hair grew up to the region of the navel, as you see it on men. The breasts got smaller, the clitoris became very large. A special problem was the change in voice. After the dosage was stopped, everything else went back to normal, but the deep voice remained for life." Aschenbach recalled that a GDR swimming coach was asked at the Montreal Olympics about the deep voices possessed by his female swimmers. He replied, "We are here to swim, not to sing."

A colleague of Aschenbach's, Dr. Hans-Jürgen Noczenski, former general secretary of the judo federation in the GDR, defected in February 1989. He explained in *Bild* why no East German athlete has tested positive in a competition since 1977: "Very simple, every athlete stops taking medicine before the competition. But before he or she is allowed to leave the country, so-called 'piss cars' drive around the country collecting urine samples from every competitor. These samples are then driven to the doping laboratory in Kreischa near Dresden. Those found clean can compete. Those who are not clean are forced to announce that they are injured."

Only a couple of East German athletes were ever caught outside the country. The last one was the shot-putter Ilona Slupianek at the European Cup in 1977 in Helsinki, and it happened only because she had been given an injection, which stays in the body longer than pills. She was suspended for eighteen months. Reinstated, she won the Olympic gold in Moscow. Now in her thirties and retired, she is married to Hartmut Briesenick, a former shot-putter. She is the mother of a child and her voice is that of a normal woman.

Aschenbach claimed that drugs were also part of the routine in the *Kinder- und Jugendsportschulen*. "Six A.M. is wake-up time, then into the woods for a run. Six-thirty A.M., a shower; seven A.M., breakfast; eight A.M., first training session until ten A.M; then school classes at ten-thirty A.M.; then lunch at two-thirty P.M. Next to the plate, a knife, a fork, a spoon, and for the best young athletes, three pills. Yellow, red, blue. 'Vitamins,' say the coaches. Yes, the yellow pill is vitamin C, the red a multivitamin composite. But the blue pill contains Nandrolon. The children are being doped without knowing it. Also, it is not widely known, but before these children are admitted to the sports schools, they must undergo special liver tests. If the result is not good, they are not admitted because it means they cannot then use drugs."

In the winter of 1990, another insider from the GDR spilled to the West German magazine *Der Spiegel* what he knew about blue pills. Michael Regner, thirty-seven, had been a swimming coach for teenagers in Potsdam until he defected to Hungary in August 1989. He said that the chief physician for swimmers in Potsdam had given him an envelope of a dozen blue pills of oral Turinabol one day in the summer of 1987 and told him to give one-half pill each day to two thirteen-year-old swimmers who were going to compete in the European championships in Rome. "The two were exceptional talents," recalled Regner. "I was told to say nothing to the girls, but to mix the pills into a vitamin drink." One of the girls—Grit Müller—won a gold and two bronzes at the championships. Regner was required to sign a document swearing that he would reveal nothing about the medications his charges were taking.

After the Ben Johnson scandal broke in Seoul, there was panic among leaders of the DTSB, according to Regner. In October of 1988, an order was issued nationwide to stop all doping of athletes. Then in January 1989, at a meeting of swimming coaches, trainers, and doctors, it was reported that East German athletes in other sports—such as canoeing—had been using drugs since Seoul and had not been caught. The head swimming coach announced to the assembly, "We have received an order from the sports Medical Committee in Berlin to continue as before."

Later that year, Regner was at an altitude training camp in Armenia, and each night he and Stefan Hetzer, the coach whose two best swimmers had produced eight gold medals in Seoul—six by Kristin Otto and two by Silke Hörner—sat together counting out pills for their charges. Regner decided to try the same dosage his athletes were taking just to see what might happen. The results? He gained six pounds of new muscle over a cycle and felt great new surges of energy. "It was only then I realized exactly how important doping was to the success of GDR sports," he said. "Now I know why there is a saying among all top athletes in the world: 'No dope, no hope.'"

Even as tests get better and authorities turn to all sorts of new tricks and techniques to catch the violators, athletes, sports physicians, and coaches will keep searching for—and finding—new ways to fool the experts.

This is not because athletes are cheaters at heart, but because they are, as a rule, quite pathologically competitive. They have been given magnificent physical gifts, but they have them for no more than a limited few years. Thus, they are driven to force absolutely maximum results from their bodies while they are at their peak of potential. Most of them will stop at nothing in the attempt.

Hal Connolly, the American hammer thrower who won a gold medal in the 1956 Olympics and competed in three more, put it well: "I knew any number of athletes on my Olympic teams who had so much scar tissue and so many puncture holes in their backsides that it was almost impossible to find a fresh spot to put in a new shot. I relate this information merely to emphasize my contention that the overwhelming majority of international track-and-field athletes I know would take anything and do anything short of killing themselves to improve their athletic performance and win."

Wolfgang Schmidt at one and a half years old, in the summer of 1955.

Wolfgang in kindergarten.

Ernst and Gretel Schmidt's
wedding at Klein-Schmölen in
1953.

Ernst Schmidt putting the
shot in 1953.

Christening of Bettina, born
August 5, 1957.

Wolfgang starting school,
with his sister Bettina.

Wolfgang and Ernst in 1969.

Wolfgang and Ernst in 1978.

Wolfgang in 1980. *(Credit: Peter Kroh)*

Wolfgang congratulating
Mac Wilkins at the 1976
Olympics in Montreal,
where Wilkins won the
gold medal and Wolfgang
won the silver.

Jochen Brüggmann, the spy, visiting the Schmidts on New Year's Eve, 1981.

Wolfgang in 1981.

Wolfgang in Budapest in 1986.

Passport photo of Wolfgang smuggled out of East Germany in 1986.

Jürgen Schult refusing Wolfgang's handshake in 1988. *(Credit: dpa)*

Ernst protesting the bug found in Wolfgang's house, in front of Stasi headquarters in Berlin, after the Wall came down. The sign reads, "On January 3 in 1989, removed from the living room— bug behind wood paneling."

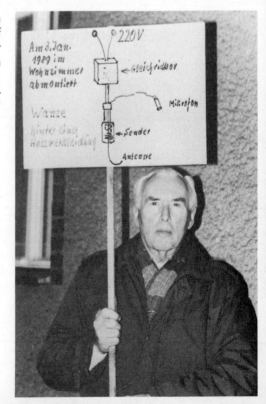

Wolfgang in California in 1990. *(Credit: Heinz Kluetmeier)*

7

SCHMIDT'S TRIUMPHS WERE MUCH ADMIRED BY men at the pinnacle of power in the GDR. When he won the Olympic silver medal in 1976, Erich Honecker himself sent a telegram saying, "Dear Wolfgang, Congratulations! I wish you many more beautiful athletic results. Good luck. Good health." Both times he was given the Fatherland's Order of Merit, the nation's highest honor, the First Secretary chimed like a bell, saying, *"Mach weiter so!"* [Go on doing it!] Four times Schmidt was honored as a Master of Outstanding Merit. Erich Mielke, minister of State Security and chief Stasi, once gave him fatherly advice at a banquet: "If a man has dedicated himself to a goal, he should do it with his whole life."

For years Schmidt was treated with deference and respect by just about everyone in the GDR from party chairmen to charwomen—by everyone, that is, except for the peculiar breed of martinet who seemed attracted to the coaching ranks of the track-and-field federation.

A surprising number of them treated me as if I were a puppy who had just peed on the carpet.

This was what stuck in my throat. I considered myself a mature champion. They saw me as a little boy in short pants. They would sit in the hotel lobby at night to find out which athletes were observing curfew. They would give you the cold eye when you came in, even if you were on time. If you arrived late, you were in a lot of trouble. I remember two well-known decathletes, Hans-Dieter Michalak and Herbert Wessel. During the European championships in Helsinki in 1971, they accompanied a Finnish female official to a bus parked near our hotel after a banquet. They didn't stay long, but both were kicked off the team when they got home because they had had contact with a foreigner.

There were other bizarre examples of East German sportsmen banished for ludicrously minor violations of the rules. Two shotputters—Gerald Bergmann and Roland Höhne—were competing at the 1979 University Games in Sofia. A group of athletes from West Germany invited them to a hotel room for some champagne. The Stasi watchdog barked, and both were dropped forever from high-performance sport. Carola Zirzow was a gold medalist in the women's single kayak event at the 1976 games in Montreal. That night she dated an Italian athlete in the Olympic Village. A smiling Manfred Ewald accompanied her to a TV interview the next day, but no sooner had they returned to the GDR than he told Zirzow she was out of performance sport. It was not only athletes who were hit with capricious punishment. A sports-science researcher at the Research Institute for Physical Culture and Sports in Leipzig, one Dr. Erdmann, once wore a Marlboro T-shirt during a competition in Dresden. He was fired on the spot.

Thanks in large part to his father's protective presence in the DTSB, Schmidt survived for years despite his maverick ways. However, a constant thorn in his side was Joachim Spenke, who became his coach again after Willi Kühl had been reassigned. In the winter of 1980, the team was on a two-week altitude-training stint at the Bulgarian ski resort of Aleko in the Vitosha Mountains.

It was January sixteenth, my twenty-sixth birthday, and we were staying in a nice hotel. I was sitting with the team masseur having a birthday beer in the bar. We were talking pleasantly enough when, about eleven-thirty P.M., Spenke suddenly appeared and said, "You there, Wolfgang! Eleven-thirty! Bedtime!"

I did not like the sound of his voice and I thought, Wait a minute. I must be crazy. My twenty-sixth birthday and this asshole tells me to go to bed as if I were a child being punished? I stayed in my chair and said, "Yes, yes, we'll leave soon."

He left, then he came back a second time and he was upset. He said, "Bedtime you hear?" I said, "Yes, yes, I hear!" Spenke was furious, but he couldn't get me into bed by brute force. Of course, the fun was gone and the masseur was a little worried—and soon we went to bed.

This was the way it was with the GDR—even if you held the world record. It was not often possible to have a party. The only thing you had was training, eating, bedtime. Always training, eating, bedtime. And Marxist-Leninist lectures. They were always so afraid that something would happen out of their control if we stayed up at night. Something with women or someone from the West. They were always terrified about our contacting Westerners who came to Bulgaria and stayed at the same hotel.

I am absolutely in favor of a regimented lifestyle in sports. It is necessary. But when you have delivered, when the good performance or the good day of training is over, you need to relax a little, too. They didn't allow that.

Team and sports-club administrators felt they had the right to meddle in every aspect of their athletes' lives—especially their sex lives. Schmidt had had his experience in 1977 because of his married lover. Others were treated just as crudely.

Once, in 1980, Axel Weber, a pole-vaulter who was married, and Ellen Streidt, a 400-meter runner who was not, got into bed together during a training session at Kienbaum. Edwin Tepper, the coach, probably wanted to score points with the higher-ups. He went after them, watched through the keyhole, and then flung open the door to find them in bed together. It was a sneaky, cowardly act, but the authorities backed Tepper and sent both of them home immediately. Their careers were in great jeopardy.

In the *Bild* exposé, Hans-Jürgen Noczenski, the former judo expert and official, recalled: "My girlfriend was asked if I was a good lover, how often we did it, and which positions I preferred. Always, they were looking for weaknesses to enter in your file so they could put you under pressure."

Obsessed as the authorities were with sex lives and curfews, they feared most that their athletes would be negatively affected by what they saw, heard, felt, tasted, or bought while they were in the West. This xenophobia pervaded every trip abroad that Schmidt ever took—starting with his first journey in 1973, when he went to the European junior championships in the bustling West German City of Duisburg. He was only nineteen.

We had prepared well at Kienbaum. They had sent us off to confront our enemies in the imperialist Federal Republic. We crossed at Friedrichstrasse into West Berlin, then took a train to Duisburg where we were driven by bus to a sports boarding school. It was a world none of us had ever dreamed of. Cars everywhere. Everything so clean. The people so friendly and so content. They frightened us by being so friendly because we weren't supposed to have contact with anyone.

I did allow myself to talk to the West German who looked after us at school. He drove a splendid BMW. We went places as a team, wonderful places. We went to Bonn by bus and visited the East German mission. We took a boat trip on the Rhine and went shopping at the big Rhine-Ruhr shopping center. This was the biggest adventure I had ever had. And our team won twenty-one gold medals, by far the most successful country there.

We had all been looking forward to shopping in the West. On this one morning, I had nothing to do, so I left the boarding school by myself to do some shopping. I had won the discus event the day before, and I was going to compete in the shot put that afternoon. I ran into some coaches right away, including the head coach, Werner Trelenberg. He looked at me queerly and said, "Well, Wolfgang, I think you had better go back to the school. It would be better for you to rest for the competition." They were going shopping and could as well have invited me along, but I had to go back and I sat around alone and got more and more mentally tired out of boredom. I finished second.

The following year, 1974, Schmidt made the trip to Italy for competitions in Siena and Turin—no longer a junior but a bona fide member of the national team. Four GDR athletes and one watchdog made that trip, and Schmidt managed his first man-to-man contact with the forbidden Americans.

Here were John Powell, Al Feuerbach, and George Woods, another world-class shotputter. They were very interested in us because East Germans were such good throwers. I was very curious about them, too. Powell won both competitions and I was third in both. He treated me like a little boy, but he was okay. We exchanged T-shirts. He gave me one that said "Pacific Coast Club Long Beach"; I gave him one with the hammer, circle, wreath symbol of the GDR. He wore it everywhere, but I didn't dare wear his anywhere. We talked about training and test performances in weight training. I asked Al what kind of car he had, and he said in an embarrassed way, "I own two cars, big American cars."

This trip to Italy made a big impact on me. I saw immediately what a beautiful life it was to travel from meet to meet, and I realized what a rare reward it was for an East German to be allowed to do that.

The following year, in Helsinki again, he competed against Mac Wilkins for the first time. John Powell was there, too, as holder of the world record. Besides them and Schmidt, two great Finns were there, Pentti Kahma, the European champion, and Marku Tuokko.

When we arrived at the Helsinki airport, we were picked up by car and a newspaper was lying on the seat with a big article about the great discus duel coming up between Powell, Wilkins, Kahma, and Tuokko. My name was not mentioned. This didn't surprise me, but it made me all the more determined to beat them all. And I did on my last throw. It went 65.56 meters [215'1"] and won the meet— my first big international victory. I was given a Swiss watch, an Atlantik, which I still wear every day. Later in 1975, I also set a new East German record and I beat Kahma at the Europa Cup. I was then ranked number one by *Track and Field News* for the year.

As it turned out, the mid-1970s produced just about the greatest field of discus throwers in modern memory. As Wilkins recalled it, "there were maybe seven or eight guys in the world who were in a pretty elite group then. There was myself and Powell, the two guys from Finland, Ricky Bruch from Sweden, the Czech Ludvik Danek, and of course, Wolfgang. And since that time, there have only been a few other guys of as high quality as our group was then. Imrich Bugar of Czechoslovakia for a brief period; Ben Plucknett, who threw a couple of world records but performed really well during only maybe five competitions over three years; and Jürgen Schult, who came after Wolfgang in East Germany. But it was in '75 and '76 that we really broke some barriers."

During that period, Wilkins produced a veritable hailstorm of great throws, breaking the world record four times in one week. On April 24, 1976, in Walnut, California, he broke Powell's record with a throw of 226'11" and followed that with three other record-breakers, the best a 232'6" on May 1 in San Jose.

On May 21, Wilkins and Schmidt met again in Cologne for a meet.

The team from the GDR was staying at the Esso-Hotel near the stadium, a beautiful hotel on a pond. I ran into Mac in the lobby. He was already dressed for the competition and I was not. He simply invited himself to come with me to my room, and he stayed there while I put on my competition clothes. This made me uneasy. We were not allowed to go to the rooms of the Americans, and they were not allowed into our rooms. But here he was. Strange, because athletes generally like to be alone when they prepare before a competition. I guess he was just curious and I was curious. We took the bus to the stadium together.

Schmidt's uneasiness at the hotel did not affect him at the stadium. He loosed a throw of 68.60 meters, 225'1", a new European record. Wilkins was second with 67.44 meters, 221'3".

The night after the meet, Schmidt and Wilkins went partying.

A man from Cologne, a fan of ours, said we should all go to the discotheque Marco Polo. Mac and I got into one taxi and this guy followed in another. When he arrived at the disco, to my dismay, I saw that he had brought along our GDR team watchdog. The guy had invited himself. So he sat at our table where he could watch and hear everything. Finally, I got up and beckoned Mac and we asked two girls to dance. Then we held a conversation on the dance floor.

Even with disco music thundering and dancers bumping them, they managed a conversation. As Wilkins recalled: "We hadn't seen each other since Helsinki, but it seemed as if our relationship had grown. Probably that was because our achievements had increased and we had established ourselves as clearly the only two people who really had a chance to win a gold in Montreal. This gave us something in common we hadn't had before. We were talking both languages on the dance floor—he spoke ninety percent English, I did about sixty-five percent German. He asked me how I could stand to live in a country that was doing what we were doing in Vietnam. He said he had seen some atrocities on television. He also mentioned crime and poverty and asked me how I could stand to live in a place like the US. I didn't argue. I said that I agreed there were some bad things, but it was a huge country and no one person or one opinion represents the whole place. I told him that some things the US does are good, some are bad. I read somewhere that he told his father after he got home—probably during one of their arguments—that he had liked it that I hadn't come back with a lot of antisocialist statements to shoot down his anti-US ideas. That had surprised and impressed him as being a nice, civilized thing to do."

The girls we were dancing with asked for our autographs and I wrote "GDR" after my name and one exclaimed, "You're from the GDR? How did you ever get out?" We danced some more, then sat down with the watchdog and drank glasses of Cinzano until shortly after midnight. Then the watchdog began to bark and whine. "Back to the hotel, Wolfgang, let's get going. Okay?" He even followed me into the men's room, saying, "So, let's go! Now, Wolfgang, now."

So we went back, all together. The next day on the train back to the GDR, the watchdog spoke quietly to me. "Wolfgang, that wasn't quite correct what you did last night. Normally, I would include that in my competition report, but I will refrain from doing so. It remains between you and me. I will never talk of it again, it is forgotten." I was amazed. A decent man who was also a watchdog. I believe his name was Grundmann, a good fellow.

Even if Grundmann had turned him in, it is doubtful that Schmidt would have been severely disciplined. The most important event in sports, in the eyes of East Germans, was only a matter of eight weeks away.

THE GDR HAD HIGH HOPES FOR ITS TEAM AT THE
Montreal Olympics. Manfred Ewald himself saw them off in a
farewell ceremony in Berlin. He feverishly begged them to give
their best in Montreal and to come home with the maximum
medals possible. The team departed two weeks before the games
began in order to get used to the time change and the free-world
atmosphere. It took them twenty-four hours to get there, including an endless series of plane changes and bus rides from
Schönefeld Airport in East Berlin to Shannon, Ireland, to Montreal to Toronto, and finally, to Sudbury, Ontario, where they
had set up a training camp at Laurentian University. Sudbury
was a squalid nickel-mining city set in a bare, stony landscape
that had been stripped of vegetation years before by pollution
from smelting plants. The land was so barren that American astronauts trained there in the late 1960s to familiarize themselves
with the terrain they would encounter on the moon.

To the East Germans, Sudbury was paradise.

Everything was new to us. The GDR was training by itself in Sudbury, and we loved the place, so quiet, so open, so deluxe. Such a vast country, we thought.

It wasn't only open space and a pleasant campus that captivated Schmidt in Sudbury.

I met Louise there—Marie-Louise Kelday, a French Canadian and a physical education teacher at Laurentian University. The team ate in the university canteen and so did she. We met at a meal. It was not a real affair then, just *schmusi-bussi* [smoochy-kissy], but we met every day for meals and sometimes in the evening for an hour or so. She was pretty and pleasant. Brown eyes, dark hair, a real beauty, five feet seven inches tall, slender. We spoke English and I improved my English with her. At night, we stole away for a walk sometimes. We went to a golf course and sat on a bench and watched beautiful sunsets across the beautiful lawns. It was summer and we hated to say good-bye.

East German competitors stayed in Sudbury until only a short time before their individual events were scheduled, then flew to Montreal. This, of course, was to minimize contact with athletes from the West. Schmidt arrived two days before the qualifying competition for the discus.

He and Wilkins met again and the American recalled, "When our paths crossed in the Olympic Village, Wolfgang had now decided that the US maybe wasn't half so bad as he first thought. He asked me what it was like in San Jose where I was training, and I told him I thought he'd prefer it to a mining town like Sudbury. He then asked me if I thought he could train with us in California, and I said the invitation would be open anytime he could arrange it. That's the frame of mind we were in at the time of the competition. Two friends who happened to be struggling for the same gold medal."

The setting for the discus throw in Montreal was rich with suspense. Because of his binge of world records, Wilkins was the favorite. Powell and Schmidt were considered next best, with the Finn Pentti Kahma and two other East Germans, Norbert Thiede and Siegried Pachale, next. In the qualifying round the day before the final, Wilkins finished first with a strong throw of 68.28 meters, (224'). This was below his record, but considering that the Olympic Stadium was partially roofed and thus, offered none of the lifting breezes necessary to produce truly herculean throws, it was considered a remarkable effort. Schmidt threw 206'8¼". That was good enough for third in the qualifying round from which fifteen competitors would go to the final.

Nevertheless, Schmidt wasn't well.

Foolishly, in Sudbury I had ruined my stomach and intestines with drinks that were too cold. I always drank 7-Up and it was always too cold. It gave me stomach cramps, and I wasn't up to par on the day of the competition. I had been eating lots of oat soup, but my stomach kept cramping. I had to run to the bathroom all the time. The night before the final I was nervous. I woke up at eight A.M. Still, my stomach wasn't right.

One could not predict who would win the final. Mac and I talked a little before the competition, really very little. In the drawn order of competition, both Mac and John Powell threw before I did. This was not my preference. I like to go first. I feel that if someone who throws ahead of me lands a good one, he is in the superior position.

The weather was beautiful. The sun was shining through the open roof, but the ring was a bit slippery. I didn't like it much.

Mac was nervous, but on his second throw [each competitor had six], he was pretty strong—67.50 meters [221'5½"]. Because of the slippery ring, I had to start my turn more carefully than I liked. After my fifth throw, I was in third place. After their sixth throws, Mac remained in first place and Powell was in second with 65.70 meters [215'7"].

Then it was my sixth throw, too. I was really mad at myself because I had been starting my rotation so cautiously that I hadn't gotten off a real good throw. So this time, I let it all go with great force, and the discus flew 66.22 meters [217′3″]. I had stolen the silver medal from John Powell. I was elated. I lifted my arms to the crowd. And then, suddenly, I saw Mac running toward me.

To some people, the scene was touching, even inspiring. But to a number of American sportswriters covering the games it was disgusting. They saw it as a blatantly un-American act—a citizen of the US rejoicing over the success of a communist at the expense of a fellow American. The hostility of their questions at the press conference surprised Wilkins. He snapped, "Listen, as far as I'm concerned, I'd be just as happy if I got my gold medal and all the rest of the medals in Montreal were won by East Germans!" The right-wing element in the sports press—of whom there were a lot—left the press conference and wrote rabid denunciations of Wilkins.

"They painted me as a kind of black sheep, anti-US-establishment radical. I got a lot of hate mail," he recalled. "But I wasn't knocking the US, I was knocking the US Olympic Committee. I was tired of the mythology that things were still like they had been when Jesse Owens competed and you could train on weekends and for an hour after work and you'd win a gold medal. I knew what I had to do to prepare for an Olympics, and the US Olympic Committee had no idea what that meant. They ran their system so it was a benefit to the administrators, but that happened to be of practically no benefit at all to athletes. I said that I did not win an Olympic gold medal because of the sports system we have. I won my gold medal in *spite* of it."

As it turned out, Schmidt was in hot water, too, though not with the press. While they were still in Montreal, the leaders of the East German delegation kowtowed and congratulated him again and again for his silver medal. The moment the team got home they turned hostile.

This was typical. They always saved the reprimands for when we got back. They left you alone as long as you were in Western territory for fear you might tell them, "You have a screw loose, boys," and make a dash for freedom. But back in Berlin, they called me up in front of the head coach and the directors of SC Dynamo. They accused me of isolating myself from the team because I ate lunch with a Canadian woman. I told them Louise had merely asked me a lot of questions about the GDR and that I had answered them. My accusers strongly advised me to refrain from such behavior in the future.

One year later, Schmidt showed what he thought of their advice when he entertained Louise Kelday for a week in East Berlin.

One day in the summer of 1977 she called me from the Hotel Berolina and said she was waiting for me. I was amazed. I was also delighted. I had told her in Sudbury, "If you ever want to visit me and they ask you at the border where you are going, do *not* say you wish to visit me." They had questioned her at Checkpoint Charlie for half an hour, and she had not mentioned my name. They had found it strange that a Canadian woman, traveling alone, wanted to visit East Berlin. But she told them she was a tourist and they had to accept that. I visited her at the Hotel Berolina and I took her home with me. I took her to a discotheque. None of this was legal.

She said she would move to the GDR to be with me, but I discouraged that. I was still with Uschi.

His parents knew of his relationship with Kelday and of her visit to Berlin. Gretel recalled, "When she was in the city, we all felt uncomfortable." Ernst berated him constantly for all his contacts in the West, saying, "Now you are putting your foot in it again. You are getting nothing but black marks against your name." Typically, Schmidt ignored all of this, and his relationships with people in the West blossomed. Besides Powell, Feuerbach, and several other Americans, he had met discus throwers Alwin Wagner of West Germany in 1973 and Ricky Bruch of Sweden in 1976.

But his best friend and greatest competitor was Wilkins. They competed frequently through the seventies. In all, between 1975 and 1981, they competed eleven times, with Schmidt beating Wilkins nine times. Schmidt won the first World Cup competition in 1977 in Düsseldorf, with Wilkins second, and he won the second World Cup in 1979 in Montreal with the American second again.

When Schmidt broke the world record in East Berlin on August 9, 1978 with a throw of 71.16 meters [233'5½"], it was Wilkins's mark he surpassed. Friend or not, it didn't particularly please Wilkins when he heard about it. "I was about to walk onto a competition area in Reykjavik and some guy comes up and says, 'Hey, let me be the first to greet you at the competition today, Mr. Former World-Record Holder.' Somehow, he said it in a way that I didn't belt him. It sort of stuck in my mind during the meet though, and I got one throw of 236 feet or so that went out of the legal sector. I was sharply aware that if it had been legal, Wolfgang's new record would be kaput. I saw him a couple of weeks later in Warsaw. I congratulated him. I really didn't feel any sentiment one way or the other about his breaking my record, although I might have been disappointed if someone less talented had done it because of a lucky wind or something like that."

The record-breaking throw occurred under banal conditions without TV or press coverage, without even much of a crowd. It happened at a local evening meet at the SC Dynamo Berlin stadium. Even Schmidt had difficulty generating much excitement over his accomplishment.

It happened on my second throw. I had been training hard for the European Championships to be held at the beginning of September, and I had, during the days before this club meet, reached a new personal plateau in my throwing and also in my weight training. It was all part of a tough, goal-oriented plan that I had systematically begun the previous October.

When I released the discus, I knew it was going far. I wasn't surprised when I learned it was a world record. I felt very good about it, of course. Setting a world record had been a goal of mine for a long time. But I wasn't ecstatic or crazy or anything like that. I would have much preferred to do it at a bigger meet, throwing against Mac and John Powell and Ricky Bruch. It would have meant a lot if they had watched me do it.

The world record brought a reward that was rich indeed by East German standards, but Schmidt had been collecting good money all that year.

In 1978 alone, I received bonuses totaling seventeen thousand marks [$8,500] for the world record, the European championship, and performances in dual meets. It was my best year for financial profit. It broke down like this: world record, three thousand marks [$1500]; European championship, eight thousand marks [$4,000]; third place in shot put in European championships, three thousand marks [$1,500]; for throws over sixty-six meters in competition, two thousand marks [$1,000]; and for winning the discus in a dual meet between the GDR and the Soviet Union, one thousand marks [$500].

My biggest premium was ten thousand marks [$5,000] for the silver medal in Montreal. Only international competitions drew cash bonuses. We were paid nothing extra for winning the East German championship.

I always kept careful records of what they paid me in premiums. From 1973 through 1981, I received eighty thousand marks [$45,000] in bonuses beyond my performance pay.

Schmidt was performing at the top of his game in those years. Then came the great fiasco in Moscow.

None of Schmidt's Western friends were there because of the boycott, but Mac Wilkins wasn't surprised when he heard about the hooliganism at the games. "I had been to Moscow for competitions, and the spectators were always incredibly vicious—anti-everybody except Soviets. It would have been real tough for a non-Russian to win there. But then in Los Angeles during the 1984 games the American spectators' behavior wasn't that much different."

Did Wilkins think that Schmidt might have choked under the pressure in Moscow? "I have never seen him choke. The pressure was heavier than it had been in 1976 because he was the favorite. To win a gold medal, you have to be very good, but you also have to have things just right. There is a real thin crest you ride. Things were very negative in Moscow, very difficult. There was the blatant cheating, of course. The Soviets won all four throwing events in Moscow, and the only one they deserved was the hammer throw. Unless you were a Russian, to win a gold medal in Moscow you had to be far superior to your competition, and you also had to have all the luck in the world going for you."

Unlucky or not, Schmidt felt the noose begin to tighten after Moscow.

There were discussions about my finishing fourth, but nothing about my behavior. There was to be the meet in Malmö, Sweden, and I was very much looking forward to that because Malmö was the home of my friend Ricky Bruch. However, due to my performance in Moscow, they said that I was scratched from Malmö.

This was the first hint that I was in trouble. I went immediately to General Secretary Heinz Czerwinski and demanded to know what was going on. I argued with him that I was in great shape and that Malmö could be a great meet for me.

He shook his head and said I had finished too poorly in Moscow to be allowed to go. He explained that because I had missed my formal performance goal in Moscow—which was to win a gold medal—I had failed to fulfill my contract with the DTSB. My behavior in Moscow was never mentioned.

Even his father, the consummate insider, had no inkling of how bad things were. Said Ernst: "Moscow triggered it, we now know that, because he had threatened our class brothers. But they said nothing to me about Wolfgang's actions either. There was never any word in our papers or on TV. The crowd's whistling and jeering were erased from the sound on TV. There were reports in the Western media, and they probably led authorities to decide that they had to throw him out of sport. That is what I suspect. But it was unfair and unjust. Wolfgang was badly served. It was not only Wolfgang who didn't win for our team. Ruth Fuchs was eighth in the javelin, Udo Beyer was third in the shot put, and Wolfgang Hanisch finished third in the javelin. I was sitting in the section of the stadium reserved for coaches, and I suffered as I watched how the Russian referees were cheating. The big disappointment was that these people were supposed to be our friends, our big brother. After the competition, I told Wolfgang, 'It was only bad luck. Our plan did not work out.' But I had no idea that he would be removed from competition for the things that happened in Moscow, since they were not his fault."

The Malmö meet was the last of the 1980 season, and Schmidt began preparing for the next year with renewed vigor because he wanted to avenge his defeat in Moscow. He was on very thin ice, but he did not know how thin.

AT ONE POINT THAT SPRING, HE HAD DEMANDED
a meeting with a DTSB vice president named Thomas Köhler
and had the cheek to lay down a list of personal complaints against
the system. He complained that he had not been given permission
to compete in California on the famous *Segelwiesen* with their
great winds for discus throwers. He complained that invitations
for athletes to compete abroad were too often lost in the bureaucracy of the DTSB and that athletes were seldom told of
invitations to compete in the West. And he complained that, even
though he had set the world record three years earlier, he had
never received his plaque from IAAF headquarters in London.
He pointed out that when other East Germans set world records,
the IAAF plaque was presented with great fanfare in front of the
entire team.

Then, in June—on *Olympischer Tag* (Olympic Day), to be
exact—Schmidt made some inflammatory remarks to an American journalist in Potsdam. Schmidt's world record had just been
broken on May 16 by the American Ben Plucknett in Modesto.
Irked, Schmidt told the journalist that he had tried to get per-

mission to compete in California, too, but that the DTSB refused to let him go. He complained openly to the journalist about the lack of freedom in the GDR.

Despite his obstreperous ways, Schmidt was performing with consistent success.

I competed in Lille, France, and I won. There was a dual meet against Great Britain in Dresden in June. I won and I threw a stadium record of 69.60 meters [228'4"]. I celebrated a little that night. The following morning, I overslept and didn't show for breakfast. I also didn't show for the roll call. They grated on my nerves, those morning roll calls: "Halt! Right dress! Eyes front!" All in dreadful military fashion.

Back in Berlin, I was ordered again to appear at Czerwinski's office at the DTSB. He said to me, "This can't go on, the way you conduct yourself. You are sitting here in my office for the second time, but let me tell you that nobody sits here a third time and stays on the team."

I couldn't stand Czerwinski. He was such an arrogant guy, small and good-looking with his gray hair combed without a hair misplaced. I could do without people like him, but they seemed to be all around me.

In July, Schmidt was still competing and was one of a select group of athletes sent to Stockholm for a meet. The date was July 7, 1981, not quite a year to the day that he would be picked off Indira-Gandhi-Strasse by the Stasi. A strong field had been assembled for the discus, including Mac Wilkins, John Powell, Knut Hjeltnes of Norway, and Ben Plucknett.

Schmidt was feeling extremely well and produced a series of fine throws, the best being 226'7". As it turned out, only Plucknett beat him, and he blasted off a stunning throw of 237'4", almost *four full feet* beyond his world mark. Like everyone else, Schmidt was dazzled by the throw and rushed to shake Plucknett's hand.

That night, Schmidt celebrated at a Nike shoe party. Wilkins was there, as well as Plucknett. Wilkins recalled, "We got pretty involved in the party scene. Wolfgang was talking to Ben and he was having a hard time of it. Plucknett was a real defensive kind of guy, a pretty closed person, and Wolfgang couldn't figure out what was wrong. He kept asking Plucknett real direct questions, but he got all kinds of hemming and hawing and finally he gave up. I went up to bed fairly early, but I think Wolfgang went on."

Indeed, he did.

I went to town in a taxi. I had hard currency and I went dancing with Swedish women. I returned to the hotel two hours before our departure at six-thirty A.M. and I slept one and a half hours. I didn't know whether anybody noticed and I didn't care. I had done extremely well. Five of my throws that day were good enough to beat everyone in the meet except for Plucknett.

As it turned out, Plucknett's monumental throw was soon wiped out. Drug tests taken after an earlier meet in New Zealand indicated Plucknett had been using steroids. Both of his world records were ruled illegal. Schmidt's 1978 world record went back on the books, and he was declared the official winner of the Stockholm event.

His spirits soared. He was on top of his game, and he had just begun a complex new training program calculated to bring him to his peak just in time for two major international events—the Europa Cup in Zagreb in late August and the World Cup in Rome in September. Before those meets, he did have to defend his national championship in Jena on August 8, 1981. Schmidt had won the title for six straight years beginning in 1975, and he had little doubt that he would win again.

Two days before the competition, he had gotten special permission to take a train from Berlin to Jena instead of going there on a bus with the rest of the SC Dynamo team. He had a legitimate reason:

I had to take my political examination at the sports club. This was routine. We had political classes at the club and were required to take tests to prove that all the propaganda had sunk in. I wanted to get this behind me before the Jena competition, so I stayed in Berlin, took the test, then took the train a day later than the team. My coach Spenke was supposed to pick me up at the station, but my train was two hours late. I arrived with my gym bag and my competition discus and he was not there. I didn't know where the team was staying, so I took a taxi to the Interhotel in Jena.

Two women clerks greeted him at the reception desk, and he asked if they could accommodate him for the night. It was past ten P.M., ordinarily too late to register, but they agreed. He took his suitcase to his room, then returned to a bar off the lobby and ordered two glasses of Russian champagne for the women to show his gratitude. He was carrying the wine on a tray to the reception desk when he saw Thomas Köhler, the DTSB vice president he had complained to in the spring. Schmidt greeted him.

Köhler glared at the glasses of champagne. "What are you doing in the bar at this hour?"

Schmidt replied airily, "I just came to check up on our leadership to see that they weren't getting out of line."

Humor was never a strong point among officials in the GDR. The next morning word spread that Wolfgang Schmidt had been up after midnight drinking champagne.

This might instantly have been forgotten, except that, to his—and everyone's—immense surprise, Schmidt failed to win the national championship the next day. A perennially mediocre member of the team named Armin Lemme had come up with the best throw of his life—218'10". Schmidt had exceeded that distance many times, but on this day the best he could do was 217'5". It was shocking, but Schmidt knew very well why it had happened.

All my training had been aimed toward the big meets later in the summer. I had made no attempt to peak for the national competition. I had bad luck and Lemme had a hell of a day. I wasn't very concerned. There was no condition that I had to win the national championship in order to qualify for the Europa Cup or the World Cup. I had already been officially nominated.

But they were after me. The Jena meet ended on Sunday. On Monday I went on to Kienbaum with the team to prepare for the Europa Cup. When I arrived, there was a note for me at the gate that I should immediately report to Werner Kramer, the club director of SC Dynamo in Berlin. In Berlin, Kramer took me immediately to Heinz Czerwinski at the DTSB. As I entered the office, I was very aware that Czerwinski had told me last time: "I can tell you that you won't be sitting here a third time!" But here I was. So now Czerwinski began to lecture me. He raved about how I had stayed away from the team in the hotel in Jena, about how I had been late for the morning roll call in Dresden, how I was so often late for breakfast.

He brought up an idiotic little thing that had happened earlier that summer. A bunch of photographers at the Potsdam stadium had wanted to take my picture as I released my discus. There were six or eight of them, clustered together, so I flung it over their heads. Well, I do know how to throw a discus so it won't hit someone, but Czerwinski accused me of throwing the discus *at* the photographers.

Then he said that worst of all my sins was that I had finished second in the championship because I had been drinking champagne the night before. Then he said, "Your *Leistungsauftrag* is terminated! We don't need athletes like you. Enough is enough! You are finished, Schmidt!"

He asked me if I had anything to say. I glared at that vain little rat with the perfect gray hair. I said, "No, I don't have anything to say to the likes of you."

Ernst Schmidt was appalled by the decision. "Wolfgang's mediocre performance was simply connected to his methodical buildup to a peak for the Europa Cup. This was common among athletes. Other athletes who took second at Jena were allowed to go on to the Europa Cup competition. We had always seen to it that our best individuals competed."

The DTSB didn't back down. Armin Lemme replaced Schmidt in both Zagreb and Rome. Amazingly, Lemme won both competitions with relatively unimpressive throws—the Europa Cup with 210'2" and the World Cup with 217'9". The DTSB now officially declared that Schmidt had *Entbindung vom Leistungssport,* meaning literally "deliverance from performance sport." He could still train, but he was off the national team and exiled to a sporting purgatory where he could only wait and see whether the leadership would restore him to good standing.

Schmidt's father went through this with painfully divided loyalties: "I was powerless. It was a collective decision among Ewald, Köhler, and Czerwinski. It was a complete surprise to me when he was dropped from the team. Of course, in my position I had to insist that my own son adhere to the rules that were binding for all. He and I had always had serious differences concerning his behavior. I'd tell him, 'For God's sake, do it differently! You can speak with foreign athletes, but you don't have to go on doing it while others are watching.' He didn't ever listen.

"Wolfgang's biggest difficulty was what happened in Moscow, but he was never good at observing discipline of any kind. In training camps he was expected to make his bed like the other athletes. But no, he said that's what maids are for. Another matter was punctuality. I told him that he had no right to appear fifteen minutes later than he had agreed with his coach. He should have overcome this laziness about discipline. I told Wolfgang that there would be serious consequences. That he would not be able to continue in his sport if he so blatantly did things that were not allowed. Always he'd say, 'How so?' and I'd repeat, 'You are running into an open knife! Someday you'll see!' "

SUDDENLY IN SEPTEMBER, THE KNIFE WAS NO longer open. His fortunes reversed completely after a surprise meeting with Erich Mielke, number one Stasi, president of SC Dynamo and Mielke's deputy in charge of intelligence, Rudi Mittig. Mielke had always taken a shine to Schmidt, and on this day he was like a kindly Dutch uncle. He did all the talking.

"Well, my boy, where do we go from here?" Mielke asked.

Schmidt replied, "I would like to get back into the sports program."

The chunky little Stasi spread his short arms and crooned, "Of course, my boy, of course. And I tell you that is possible, Wolfgang, but you must be a good boy. If you promise to behave well, I will see to it that you can continue after all."

Schmidt rose to thank Mielke. But the minister waved him back to his chair. "Is there anything else I can do for you?" he asked.

"I would like to compete in California," said Schmidt.

"We'll talk about that later. Anything else?"

"Well, it would be nice if I got a new car."

"No problem."

Schmidt could not believe his ears. He decided to plunge ahead. "And I have had problems purchasing a house and I need some help with some permits and such, getting gas piped into the house, for example."

Mielke waved his chubby hand. "Everything will be arranged. I will have the house equipped and furnished for you."

Schmidt left wondering if he had just had a wonderful dream.

Two days later, it all began to come true. He received his white Lada 1600, a 25,000-mark ($12,500) vehicle ordinarily available only to top officials in the Stasi, the military, or the government.

As for Schmidt's house, a partially finished suburban cottage in Hohen Neuendorf not far from his parents' summer home, Mielke ordered the leadership at SC Dynamo to step in and solve Schmidt's problems. He had initiated the purchase of the house in 1979 by giving the owner a customary bribe of eight thousand marks ($4,000) to guarantee he would sell the house to him. Before the deal was completed, members of the district council of Hohen Neuendorf stepped in and blocked the transaction.

Under the law, as a single man, I only rated a one-room apartment where I would barely have room for my suitcases. However, Mielke and SC Dynamo believed that having a beautiful house might encourage me to get married, have children, and settle down a little more.

Acting on orders from the number one Stasi, SC Dynamo simply circumvented the district council by arranging for the official state housing agency, called Building Economy, to make a formal purchase of the cottage and then sell it back to Wolfgang. Dynamo had already arranged for a bank to give Schmidt a mortgage for thirty thousand marks ($15,000) to complete the deal.

The house had only partial plumbing and the roof on the garage was unfinished. Schmidt and his father worked feverishly on these things because winter was coming. SC Dynamo did its part by hiring Czechoslovakian workers to complete the job. The boiler had been equipped to heat the house with coke, but SC Dynamo got permission for Schmidt to install a gas heating system.

Schmidt had planned to enhance his house with expensive hard-to-get trappings such as first-class locks, top-quality doors, wood paneling, plaster walls instead of wallboard, a hobby room in the basement, a fully equipped workbench, and a garage. Even though he didn't ask for these things, everything was done.

What was going on here? Schmidt was never sure whether Mielke's generosity was genuine or a cruel psychological ploy to make his coming demise all the more painful.

I always thought that Mielke liked me and was being a good guy to me. But also, it could have been a tricky way of getting to me. They give you sugar, then they snap the snare. You catch mice with bacon, and maybe the car and the house were supposed to be my bacon. That's how the Stasi were.

The World Cup competition was underway in Rome at the time Mielke restored Schmidt to good standing. Ernst was officially informed of his renewed eligibility by a vice president of the DTSB, Hannes Resch. It seemed to be authentic and Ernst rejoiced. After he returned to Berlin, however, he found a critical flaw in the situation. "Though both Wolfgang and I had been told he was reinstated, no public notice ever appeared to that effect. I thought this was strange, but I didn't pursue it."

Nevertheless, Schmidt's reinstatement as a bona fide member of the national team did seem genuine through the winter of 1982. He was involved in a complete training cycle, working out daily as if there had never been any trouble at all. Unfortunately, he also continued to misbehave with reckless disregard for the fact he had been on very thin ice with the authorities.

There was the case of the illicit tires. Ludwig Schura, his old friend from West Berlin, had relatives in East Berlin who wanted to install a new kitchen but had no ready cash. Wolfgang and Schura made a deal: Schmidt wanted some top-quality West-made tires for his Lada to replace the cheap Russian tires, and also a stereo radio for the car. If Schura could get him these, Schmidt would pay for them by giving the relatives GDR currency. Schura produced the tires and the radio, plus some fancy doorknobs for Schmidt's house, and Schmidt paid five thousand marks ($2,500) to the family to buy their new kitchen.

Ernst was upset by this: "As innocent as all this may sound, these were all things that were against the rules of the DTSB. He did not specifically violate any currency laws, but this was not a wise thing to be doing when he was in such a sensitive state with the authorities."

Later, Schmidt got himself in quite a different kind of trouble. He was attending a winter training camp in the Bulgarian mountain resort of Boroveč when he was approached in a hotel corridor by a young woman. She asked with a flirtatious smile, "Could you please give me an autographed photo?"

Wolfgang flashed his Sunny Boy smile. "I have my photos in my room. Why don't you come to my room later?"

When she knocked that night, he invited her in and said, "Well, I didn't bring any photographs along. I must have left them in Berlin. Why don't we have a drink instead?"

Early the next morning, a young man knocked on Schmidt's door and asked whether he had slept with his wife. "Of course not," said Schmidt, closing the door.

The next morning, just before breakfast, the man came to Schmidt's room again. He accused Schmidt of having raped his wife and threatened to beat him up. He took a boxer's stance, but Schmidt simply said, "I think it would be best for you to leave." The man did.

I felt bad all morning. I hoped that team officials wouldn't hear about this thing. This was our day to depart, and just before we boarded a bus for the airport in Sofia, the husband came up to me one more time. "You pig," he said, "you'll never win a competition again."

He could well have been a Stasi. In any case, I assume he reported the incident to the authorities.

Ernst Schmidt later pointed out, "The husband and wife were both citizens of the GDR, and I would assume that they were following the instructions of the Stasi. Maybe they were paid for it, maybe as much as five thousand marks or so. That sort of thing was possible in our country."

So the case against Wolfgang Schmidt was building, and finally, the end arrived.

In March of 1982, I was summoned to meet with Mielke's deputy, Rudi Mittig. He told me there would be no more performance sports for me. He said the authorities had other prospects for my future. The reason for this, he said, was my long record of disciplinary violations.

It was all a pretext. They were afraid I would run for it if they ever let me compete outside the country again. They thought I was a dangerous character. They had already begun to warn my teammates to keep a distance from me.

Mittig did not speak of this. He only told me that my personality did not fit into the system. He said quite jovially, "So, Wolfgang, performance sports is out of the question for you from now on. However, we can offer you future work as a coach."

I was very direct. "I cannot accept that," I said. "I will have to look for other possibilities so I can continue to perform my sport. Coaching is no answer for me."

He became very cold. "Well, then, the day may come when preliminary proceedings will have to be introduced against you, Wolfgang Schmidt. I am quite serious."

That pig! That was a frightening thing to say. He knew very well that the Stasi only instigated preliminary proceedings against someone when they wanted to arrest him. At that point, I couldn't think of any reason they'd have to arrest me.

At this time, his father was in Damascus, Syria, managing a training camp for sprinters and throwers. He got the word there about Wolfgang. "I was told he had been assured support in his studies to be a coach, and that SC Dynamo had offered him an immediate position as an instructor in the training center and a future position as a coach. But he was finished as an athlete." Ernst was devastated, but he was not surprised by the verdict. Nor was he totally unsympathetic toward it: "After all, Wolfgang had been taking full advantage of what our state was dishing out to him. Everyone knows the old saying: *Wessen Brot ich esse, dessen Lied ich singe*—'You sing the song of the man who feeds you.'

"I won't say Wolfgang was ever an angel, but he was no more difficult or complicated than other great athletes such as Udo Beyer or Marita Koch or Marlies Göhr or Heike Drechsler. They all had their problems. I had a lot of experience dealing with such athletes. There were always violations of discipline that one could easily blow out of proportion. Personally, I always settled such matters in private talks with the athletes. I never sent reports about them to the Central Office where they would be pawed over by snitchers and snoopers who lay waiting to pounce on something they could use against somebody."

The snitchers and snoopers had already sealed Schmidt's fate. Rudi Ortmann, head of track and field at SC Dynamo, summoned him and advised him to take "a nice vacation" and begin to train down. No one used the word *Sportverbot* specifically at that time, but that is what had happened.

Ernst viewed his son's demise with a sinking heart and increasing alarm. "As more and more of these things happened, Wolfgang was beginning to sound a little crazy. 'If I can't pursue my sport here, I'll do it somewhere else! If I find a hole, I'm gone!' The Stasi surely heard about it from the rat Brüggmann. They heard about it on the bug in our apartment, I think. They were extremely well informed about his feelings. 'Preparations to escape,' they called it, a crime against the state, a crime worth eighteen months in prison. That is a lifetime in the world of a young athlete."

I did not share my father's views. I always had a yearning for freedom and I wanted to do as I liked. Not even my father could influence me in that regard. Sometimes I thought that I might have caused some of my own trouble, but on the other hand I knew that I could not act differently. I always thought that I wanted to do things my way. I was stubborn. I was not interested in the restrictions; I always tried to circumvent them.

PART 3

A WEEK AFTER THE VERDICT, ON OCTOBER 19, both Gretel and Ernst visited him at the UHA and were stunned to find him so distraught that, at one point, he said that he would rather shoot himself than spend so much time cooped up in a cell. His mother wrote him immediately after the visit: "Father and I had a long talk, and we both are very worried about your psychological condition. Your statement about putting a bullet through your head certainly does not present a solution to your plight. That would be a far bigger tragedy than going to prison, especially for us, but also for your sport and for the country. We feel deeply the pain you have gone through during the last several months. We assure you that you are no criminal in our eyes. Your violation of the laws and this resulting punishment is something that you unfortunately must accept now. We can only hope that you use your energy to find inner peace to carry you through and bring your personality back to normal."

Schmidt sounded less desperate a week later when he replied in a letter, "My dear mother, my dear father: Last week you visited me and it was so beautiful to see you. I was especially happy that father came all the way to see me because it is he whom I disappointed the most. Only during the time here [at the UHA] have I understood what a fine development I had experienced and what good, solid prospects I had. These times, hard as they are, will pass, and with your help I will be able to achieve something again. Alone I am helpless."

The awful enormity of what was about to happen to her son had dawned on Gretel Schmidt. Shocked and frightened, she wrote, "We have been told that life among prisoners can be problematic. We hope and pray that you will resist persuasions and temptations. Don't allow your body to be tattooed or sexually misused. Despite all the crucial tests of nerve you will face, remain steadfast in your normal, respectable way of life. In such difficult situations as may be forced on you in prison, it is especially important that you maintain a mighty will, the same mighty will you have displayed so many times in your competitions."

Schmidt spent twenty-four more days in the UHA after the trial, waiting for his transfer to the prison at Frankfurt on the Oder, a town of seventy thousand, about fifty miles east of East Berlin, not far from the Polish border.

The day before I was moved, the boss interrogator, Wiedemann, called me to his office once more. Always, like the Lord of Alexanderplatz, he said, "I have been looking around in Frankfurt on the Oder to find you something suitable, a place where you can do the kind of work you like to do. Where you can work on cars."

I was surprised that Wiedemann would have anything to do with my life in the new prison. What I didn't know then was that I was not going to lose Wiedemann by merely leaving the UHA. He had become my official Stasi educator, so to speak. Even when I was in Frankfurt on the Oder, he would travel over from Berlin and talk to me once a month for one or two hours.

Now, he asked me some pretty large questions: "What do you want to do with yourself when you get out of jail? Life will have to go on somehow for Wolfgang Schmidt. Would you perhaps like to open a café? Or would you like to own a car wash? Exactly what occupation are you thinking of in your future?"

I told Wiedemann I was thinking of only one occupation: "I'd like to get back into performance sports." And he replied in that arrogant way, "Oh, no, that's not possible anymore. Not anymore, not at all anymore. Oh, no, no more sports for someone who has violated the law as you have, no more sports for a man who wanted to betray the republic."

The day came for Schmidt to leave the UHA and move to his new home in Frankfurt on the Oder. It was November 6, 1982— 127 days since he had been picked up on Indira-Gandhi-Strasse. He was as pale as all the other prisoners now, and he had grown quite gaunt.

We left early in the morning. I was taken into the "lock," which was a huge garage below the UHA. There I got into a Barkas, which is a small bus made in the GDR. It looks like a Volkswagen bus. The bus had no windows in the back section, and it was dark in there. There were three guards, no less, to accompany me. I was in handcuffs. Still, the guards were nervous and one of them said to me, "We have to advise you that we will shoot if you try to escape. Any attempt at all and I promise that we will use our weapons." They all carried big automatic 9-mm Makarov pistols in their holsters.

They slammed the rear doors of the van, the garage gate slid open, and we drove out toward Frankfurt on the Oder.

He sat cramped and confused in total darkness, handcuffed to a bench. The roar of the motor and the howl of the tires filled his consciousness during the sixty-minute ride on the autobahn from Berlin. His thoughts disintegrated and he could not concentrate. He had no sense at all of the direction or the distance the van was traveling. He realized that he had no more control over his fate—his destination, his destiny, his life or his death for that matter—than if he were a head of livestock on the way to the stockyards.

In Frankfurt, the van finally came to a stop, the noise stopped, and I was let out of the back. I found that I had arrived in a "lock" like the one at the UHA—a gloomy sort of garage inside the prison walls with its doors closed so I had no sense of what kind of a building I was in. I was very confused, completely out of touch with where I was. It was as if someone had blindfolded me and turned me in circles ten times.

They first put me in a room that was one meter square, about the same size as a public-toilet booth. There was a stool on the floor and a light in the ceiling. I stood there for a while, still dazed. I turned around a couple of times, just to prove that I could move by myself.

I had to hold my pants up because my clothes didn't fit anymore. At the UHA, they had given me back the jeans, shirt, and Adidas shoes I had been wearing the day they arrested me. The jeans hung loose around my waist and hips, the shirt was baggy. I had lost about twenty pounds.

I sat down on the stool and waited beneath the light for a long time. Then I was taken out of the cell and told to take a shower. I handed my own clothes to a woman attendant. In return, I was given another blue warm-up suit, and then I was taken to the *Oberst-leutnant* who was in charge of the prison.

The warden was a hulking fellow, about 6′3″ tall, thick as a tree through the torso with a huge block of a head and the droopy, likable features of a basset hound. Schmidt was never told the man's name, so he called him Shultz because his face and plodding seriousness reminded him of the man who was then US secretary of state, George Shultz. The warden knew all about Schmidt, of course.

After a brief talk with the warden, Schmidt was taken to another cell, this one of normal size with a toilet, a glass brick window, and a bed with an iron frame and mattress that was covered with a quilt. The walls were clean and white instead of the grimy shroud-gray they had been at the UHA, and Schmidt was pleased to notice that everything was newer and in better repair. After four months in custody, he had settled into life as a prisoner so thoroughly that he was able to judge subtle differences in jails with the same casual expertise he had once used to compare accommodations in various stadiums around the world.

I was in the cell only a short time when the *Oberstleutnant* came and told me that I would be joining a work battalion, a *Strafkompanie*. He said that I would be working in the *Kraftfahrzeug-Dienst*, KFZ for short—the motor vehicle department. Shultz explained to me that the prison had a forge, a carpentry workshop, plus divisions of painters, gardeners, and car servicemen. Then I was taken to my new digs with my comrades in the *Strafkompanie*.

Schmidt's *Strafkompanie* numbered twenty prisoners in all. All twenty lived together in a four-room apartment with barred doors and a couple of windows made of glass-block brick that let in light, but were too opaque for inmates even to be certain whether the sun was shining or not. This would be home for Schmidt's unforeseeable future.

The first room you entered from the prison corridor was a long, narrow kitchen with a barred door at each end. Both led to the prison corridor. There was no stove in the kitchen—that was in the bathroom for some reason—but there was a refrigerator and a cupboard in which every inmate had his own small compartment to store his cups and plates. There was also a huge bread knife, sharp as a razor blade. I don't know why they allowed that to be there. I was always afraid that one of my more peculiar cellmates might go berserk some night and start carving us up in our sleep.

After the kitchen there were two living rooms, each about five meters by four meters. Both had television sets, and in one of them chairs were set in rows like a theater for watching the TV. The bedroom was off the first living room. It was really a dormitory, very large, about ten meters by five meters. That is where all twenty of us slept in bunk beds.

At the opposite end of the apartment, beyond the second living room, was the bathroom. It contained two showers, one toilet, three washbasins, and our cooking stove. Yes, our cooking stove was in the bathroom. Sometimes you would enter and find a man cooking eggs on the stove on the left-hand side of the room while, a few feet away on the right-hand side, another man was shitting on the toilet.

Schmidt was exhausted his first night at Frankfurt on the Oder, and despite the muttering and snoring of his many roommates, he slept as if he were dead. On Schmidt's first morning of work, the friendly warden, Oberstleutnant Shultz himself, took him on a guided tour and introduced him to guards and inmates alike.

Schmidt found his new home was like being on a barren island with no way to escape and a native population that was not always friendly. The single definitive feature of the place was the white stone wall that rose up and surrounded the outer perimeter of the premises. The wall was not terribly tall, about twenty feet in most places, but it presented a mass so dense that to Schmidt it was more discouraging than the Berlin Wall had ever been. A watchtower stood at each of the four corners of the wall. Each tower was manned twenty-four hours a day. Every evening as twilight fell, batteries of floodlights snapped on, bathing the entire exterior of the prison in bright light until morning.

The main structure inside the wall was a five-story, gray, concrete building. Spiral staircases at each end of the building wound up through the floors to the corridors in the cell areas. Steel-barred doors blocked the corridor entrance at the top of each staircase. The top three floors contained rows of one- or two-prisoner cells. Schmidt's apartment for twenty was on the second floor. On the first floor was an identical unit occupied by a *Straf-kompanie* for women prisoners. There were about fifteen of them.

Prisoners' working areas were located on the ground floor at one end of the main building. These included a forge, a paint and carpentry shop, a kitchen and laundry (operated by women), as well as a stable containing two pigs. The KFZ was across the courtyard in a low structure next to the wall.

The courtyard was like a road around the main building, about fifteen feet wide. At two separate points, there were huge gates that could be closed across the courtyard to block it into separate sections. Usually those gates were opened, and later Schmidt was allowed to run laps around the two-hundred-yard inner perimeter of the prison wall.

As the *Oberstleutnant* gave Schmidt his tour, he not only explained the various physical facilities, he also kept up a confidential running commentary on the inmates they encountered. In the carpentry shop, he pointed at a fat, bald prisoner and whispered that this man was called *der Glatte,* the Slick One, and that he was *"ein Asozialer"*— one of many "antisocials" in this prison. An antisocial crime against the state might simply be the refusal to work, but it was punishable by three years in jail. The warden told Schmidt, "Be wary of that one."

In the rear of the carpentry shop, Shultz introduced Schmidt to Peter Zimmermann, *Brigadier* (leader) of the prison carpenters. Later, the warden told Schmidt that Zimmermann had been in prison for ten years. He was a confidence man and check forger, said Shultz. Zimmermann was good-looking and had a certain charm, said the warden, and his modus operandi was to visit nightclubs in small towns and find women to spend the night with him. Then in the morning he would pretend to be asleep when his victim left for work. He would ransack her place until he found her checkbook, then he would forge a check and cash it at a bank. Zimmermann had been arrested twice already for this same crime. The first time he spent four years in prison, the second time he got six years.

The *Oberstleutnant* introduced Schmidt to another member of the carpenter-shop crew named Rainer Zidorn. "Stick close to this man," the warden said. Zidorn was a short man in his forties with an onion-shaped nose and spectacles. He looked for all the world like an absentminded professor, but he was a swindler who, as an official in the Communal Housing Administration, was caught accepting bribes for finding people apartments.

At the end of the tour, the warden took Schmidt to his own workplace in the KFZ section. Physically this consisted of a row of many garages where vehicles from the prison fleet could be repaired, painted, or washed. Here Schmidt met Otto, the *Brig-adier* of the auto-service battalion. Otto, as it turned out, was a short-tempered, slovenly fellow of about fifty. Later Schmidt learned that Otto had been a policeman once, but that he had been a bad drinker who got involved with another woman, then lost his wife and his home in the ensuing divorce. Shattered and full of resentment, Otto had then proceeded to drink himself off the police force. Ultimately he became such a public nuisance that he was sentenced to thirty months in prison for being *ein Asozialer*.

Schmidt met two other fellow workers in the KFZ that first day. One was nicknamed Skibbi, a former bus driver who, according to the warden, had caused an accident in which a couple of his passengers were killed. The other was Sosse, which means sauce. He was only twenty-one years old, said the warden, the son of an important *Genosse* (comrade) in the local government. One night, Schmidt learned, Sosse had drunk a bottle of wine by himself, had run over a pedestrian, and had fled the scene without getting out of the car. The next day he confessed to his father. The two of them went to the authorities together and were told that the pedestrian had died. There was a trial and Sosse went to prison for two years—a remarkably short term for such a serious crime.

It was a marvelously motley crew that Oberstleutnant Shultz introduced him to that first morning in Frankfurt/Oder. And as the months dragged by, Schmidt discovered that there were many more strange and unusual birds sharing this cold stone island with him.

Besides Otto, Skibbi, and Sosse in the KFZ, I also worked in the KFZ with "Klecks," which means blot or stain. That was his nickname. He was in bad shape when I met him. Klecks had been a gas station attendant in Frankfurt/Oder who, with several other attendants, got involved in an illegal currency operation. They would take Western currency from foreign customers and substitute East German money for it, which was worth much less. Then they had gone on a spending spree with the foreign money. It was only a matter of time before they were caught. Klecks got four and a half years, a long time for this crime. When I met him, he had completed three years, and he was psychologically very ill. He was pale and thin and registered sick a lot of days because he really couldn't work hard anymore.

We also had two Jehovah's Witnesses in the prison. They had refused to do the mandatory eighteen months of military service in the army and had been sentenced to two years each. One of them was named Bernd; the other was a fat man whose name now escapes me.

Then there was "Strippe," which means cable. He worked as an electrician, but he was also a spy for the *Oberstleutnant*. This was one interesting fact that Herr Shultz had failed to tell me about on the first day of introductions. Strippe was young, blond, and he always went to tell the warden what we were saying and what was going on among us.

Then there was Sergeant Priebe. Sergeant was his nickname. He had had a car accident under the influence. It didn't amount to much, some damage, no casualties. They gave him one year. He was really out of his territory in jail: Sergeant had been a builder of small rowboats in Erkner on Dämeritz Lake, near Berlin.

Then there was Henry, a small man from Schwerin who was in for petty check fraud. He told his story with great humor. He had lived upstairs in an old lady's house, and from time to time, he helped her with her chores. Once he was alone in her place and found her savings book. He sat down in an armchair and was delighted to find that there was four thousand marks in her account. Then he blinked and looked again and realized that there were more zeros and that she actually had forty thousand marks. Immediately he and a friend drove to the bank, wrote out a withdrawal slip for two thousand marks, forged the old woman's signature, and were caught two days later.

There was Mischa, who worked in the forge. He was always sniffing. There seemed to be something wrong with his nose. He also had hemorrhoids and was in such terrible pain that he couldn't sit. There were lots of jokes about that, but he really hurt. He was taking sitz baths with oak bark. In the evening he would sit in the bath and create landscapes on paper with colored pencils. He would send these to his daughter, who was only three or four years old. Mischa was a thief and a hamster [a hoarder], and that was why he was in jail. On the outside, he had been crazy about motorcyles.

He said he had a farm somewhere where he had collected about fifty dismantled motorcycles—Avo Sport, RT, MZ, all the popular makes of the GDR. He disassembled the engines and stowed the parts in a storage room in his barn. He had more than two thousand spark plugs stored there. Hoarding was illegal, of course, and no one was supposed to know he had such a surplus of hard-to-get items. Then one day the police came to his farm and searched the place. They found parts that had been reported stolen by Mischa's employer.

They put handcuffs on Mischa in his own living room in the presence of his mother. "Why?" he demanded.

"Because you are a thief and a hamster," they said. Mischa used to say, "When I get out of here, the first thing I'll do is install an electric fence around my land so nobody can trespass." He told us that his farm was so big that he had built himself a motocross circuit around his house, around his chicken coop, around his barn. He said he never let anyone race on it but himself. He said that even though he tried to be careful, he sometimes ran over one of his chickens.

There was also Dynamite Harry, another misfit and a liar. His first name was Günter. He had only three fingers on his right hand, and half the hand was gone, too. He told us that this had happened because he had built a bomb to blow something up. But that was a fairy tale he'd concocted.

The real story was that Dynamite Harry and a friend had been sitting in a pub in a village near Magdeburg near the border, drinking beers. After they had had quite a few, the friend nudged Harry and said, "Come on! Let's get the hell out of this country." They left the pub, went to the border, and climbed over the first fence they saw. There was no planning, no idea of what they might face. When they got to the main fence, Dynamite Harry saw this wire in front of him. He touched it. It was attached to the trigger of an automatic machine gun that was aimed at that spot. The bullets tore half of Harry's hand off. His friend was sprayed by bullets in the back and was badly hurt. They both passed out there at the fence. Later there was a trial and Dynamite Harry was sentenced to a few years in jail. What a fool that man was—a double fool. The funny part of it is that he had actually defected to the West once before. He had held a job in a Coca-Cola bottling plant in Hanover for years. Then one day, he decided that he wanted to go to West Berlin and he boarded the interzonal train, which goes through East Germany. At the border, of course, the police caught him as a defector, picked him off the train, and wouldn't let him out of the GDR again. So Dynamite Harry sat in jail now with half of one hand gone instead of drinking Coca-Cola on his coffee breaks in Hanover.

Despite their colorful nicknames, prisoners in Frankfurt on the Oder were officially referred to by numbers. The men in Schmidt's *Strafkompanie* were numbered between one and twenty-two. Schmidt was nine, while Rainer Zidorn was thirteen, Otto fourteen, the feckless Dynamite Harry eleven, Klecks four, Zimmermann one, etc. Each night, Schmidt lay in an upper bunk in the company of his roommates and listened to a low din of snoring, sighing, muttering, and farting. Eventually, he got to know very well which number made which sounds. Number fourteen snored like a truck engine, number eleven sighed a lot, number ten talked in his sleep. Sometimes as he lay there, he wondered if number nine would ever get out of there alive, and if he did, if he would still be sane.

Usually, he was too tired to stay awake long.

There was very little time for anything but work. A day at the jail
went like this: Wake-up call at six A.M. Breakfast between six and
six-thirty. At six-fifty, a guard came to unlock the barred door in
the apartment, and we went down the spiral stairs to our workshops
where we put on our work clothes. We worked until twelve-thirty,
then there was lunch until one-fifty, then back to work from two
until five P.M.

Eventually, he was allowed to begin to train a little.

Shultz let me have a couple of dumbbells, and I was permitted to
do weight training from five P.M. to seven P.M. in the KFZ garage.
The smell of gasoline was all around, but I was desperate to get
some feeling of strength and energy going through my system again.
I also ran laps around the prison courtyard and did some jumping.

A doctor from SC Dynamo had sent him an official schedule for
down-training from high-performance sport when he was still at
the UHA. Among other things, the physician had prescribed
running fifteen minutes in place and doing one-legged knee
bends. Schmidt was wary of these instructions.

I saw these things as just another way to bring me down. Running
in place for that long would have driven me crazy. And one-legged
knee bends were bad for knees like mine; certainly they would have
caused injury eventually. Instead I did the kind of training I enjoyed
and trusted it would do some good. After I had been there a while,
a man named Olaf, number twelve to the guards, went to work at
the KFZ and began training with me. He had been a competitor at
canoeing. I never did find out why he was in prison.

I ate dinner after training. That meal was brought to us in our
cell. It was usually very simple—bread, butter, cold cuts, milk. The
usual ration of milk was a half-liter, but I got two liters because I

paid extra from my wages. Every two weeks we had noodle soup, thin soup, and also fresh-baked pancakes dusted with sugar which were wonderful. We got little meat, but a lot of hot dogs. We also got little fruit. Altogether I lost twelve kilos [26 lbs.] down from my ideal competition weight, which is one hundred fifteen kilos [253 lbs.]. All the weight I lost in prison was pure muscle, no fat.

For our work, we received wages of about sixty to sixty-five marks (about $27) a month. We worked five days a week for sure and sometimes Saturdays and Sundays, too. Once a week on Thursday was shopping. We went to a door on the first floor that opened into a small canteen. We could order crackers, chocolate, apples, cakes, juices, soft drinks, cigarettes, and tobacco. Most of the prisoners rolled their own cigarettes. They all smoked like crazy, everywhere, except in the bedroom. There everybody observed the rules: no talking, no smoking.

The work he did was hard and uncomfortable.

In the winter it was particularly punishing. Even when there was snow and slush, I had to wash cars. When my shoes got wet, they gave me rubber boots, I had to wash five or six cars a day by hand, and when they had been driven four hundred meters, they were filthy again in the slush. I always had to do a special job on the official car and on the private car of Oberstleutnant Shultz. Both were washed twice a week. He had an official red Lada 1200, and his private car was a lemon-yellow Wartburg. They both had to shine.

Rotten as the work was in winter, it was even worse in the summer. One day they brought in a six-thousand-liter tank truck from the army, a huge rusty old tanker, dark green bearing a warning in white letters: *Feuergefährlich* [highly flammable]. I had to derust it with a small wire brush. It was like rubbing a coat of rust off an ocean liner. When the rust was finally all scrubbed off, I had to wash the tanker with scalding-hot water. Next I sprayed it with green paint after I had mixed colors myself to get a proper military green. Then I had to write *Feuergefährlich* on it with white paint. I made a stencil for that—very smart because that summer I had to do six of those damned tankers. It was sweltering, but I had to wear many layers of clothes so I got as little paint on my skin as possible. I also wore a kerchief over my mouth and a fur cap that they gave me. I always got paint spray in my eyes. I had to wash them out quickly with benzine, which stung like acid. I was afraid I might go blind.

To make it worse, the conditions in the KFZ under Otto, the terrible-tempered slob, were disgusting. Schmidt clashed with him early in his stay. "What a junkyard this place is!" he yelled at the *Brigadier*. "Is that how you kept things at home?" Otto's eyes blazed. He had lost his home, and to be reminded of that fact made him wild. He flung a hammer at Schmidt's feet. It bounced off the floor with a shower of sparks just inches from Schmidt's shoe.

The place was filthy. There were mice everywhere. One day we were having a morning snack when a mouse came out between storage shelves. Otto threw it a piece of bacon. He was nicer to the mice than to his fellow inmates. He was actually encouraging the mice to live there, and that was really disgusting. That night when I stayed to train, I put out two mousetraps with bacon, and bingo, within a short time I had caught eleven mice. No more came and I think I had nabbed the whole family.

There was a cemetery just beyond the prison wall. We could see the treetops from the courtyard, and sometimes funeral music drifted over when someone was buried. However, on some days when I was washing cars, I would almost be knocked over by a terrible stink. I asked Otto what it was, and he told me there was a crematorium in the cemetery where bodies were being burned and that the wind was probably blowing our way. "It's just a little burnt flesh. Don't let it bother you," he said.

Domestic life in the twenty-man apartment was not entirely unpleasant, but there was tension.

Every night we watched TV in the apartment, sitting in the theater rows of chairs in the living room. Sometimes I played chess. The others played skat, a simple card game, but I didn't.

In all the months I was in the apartment, I never bitched about the GDR or the sports system or anything. The only one I could talk with was Rainer Zidorn, who seemed intelligent and knew much about the world. As a rule, it was better for me to be very quiet. That was true for all of us. Everybody was afraid that if he said anything out of line, another roommate would rat on him. Any cracks about the regime or the country could add weeks, months, on your sentence, and everybody wanted out before his full term was served. This made us very nervous, for we knew we were under surveillance at all times.

THE SAME WAS TRUE OUTSIDE PRISON AS IT turned out. His parents had come under constant surveillance, too. Worse, Ernst had lost his job. His health had taken a turn for the better, but he had been left at home for the European championships in Athens and an eight-nation competition in Tokyo during the fall of 1982. In mid-November, a few days after Wolfgang entered the prison in Frankfurt on the Oder, Manfred Ewald had summoned Ernst to his office. He spoke quite coldly: "You cannot remain in your position anymore, Ernst. You have made contributions, we have been well served by you, but it is time to go now."

Ernst recalled later, "He laid on a bit of foam, a bit of snow, but I was finished."

Ewald told Ernst that he would receive his full salary for two more years, until he was sixty-five, but that he would no longer be allowed to coach. He would no longer be allowed to travel abroad. He would have an interim job until he was sixty-five: He would be in charge of selecting and buying equipment for the track-and-field team.

It was a demotion, clearly meant to be punishment for Ernst because of his son's crimes. Later, word spread among journalists and track-and-field officials in the West that the proud old coach had been demoted to an equipment caretaker. This was not the case. Ernst himself later said of his assignment, "It was not an entirely unimportant position. I worked closely with Adidas, for example, regarding shoe imports. I had to decide which items were important enough to buy with hard currency. I planned all types of equipment purchases with all of the sports clubs, buying everything—discuses, javelins, bandages, shoes, hammers. It was quite satisfying." For the record, he continued in the job until he was sixty-eight, retiring finally in 1988 when it was firmly suggested that his time had come.

Ernst's wasn't the only job lost because of Wolfgang. Bettina had worked as a secretary at SC Dynamo for four years until a couple of weeks after her brother's trial, when she was found guilty, too. Gretel wrote Wolfgang: "Last week, Bettina had a discussion at the club, and according to rules for members of the VP, she is no longer allowed to work there because you are an immediate relative of hers. She had two choices: to give notice herself or be fired. So Bettina chose the former and took the rest of her vacation. She has already found another job and we hope it will work out all right. Bettina and Wolfgang [her husband] asked me to tell you that you should not worry. We can't change it and life goes on."

Gretel Schmidt kept up a brave and hopeful front through it all. She wrote Wolfgang in December, "Everybody is all right. . . . Now, my dear Wolfgang, we wish you peace and thoughtfulness for the Christmas days. We think of you so often, but especially during this time everything is more difficult. But this time will pass also, although we will never forget it."

Their lives had taken on a nightmare quality. The Stasi kept hounding Ernst and Gretel. They were followed occasionally both on foot and in their car, and eventually they became certain that their apartment was bugged.

It happened this way: Earlier in the fall, the apartment below theirs had become vacant. A tailor named Beyer had used it as his workplace for many years, but he had retired. Not long after Beyer vacated, someone else began to use it. A young man wearing a black coat arrived each day with a small suitcase, entered the apartment, spent a few minutes there, then left and did not return again until the next day. It dawned immediately on Ernst and Gretel that this reeked of Stasi.

Ernst inquired at a local police precinct and was told that, yes, indeed, State Security was using the empty apartment. The official reason, he was told, was that there had been sex crimes committed in the neighborhood recently—some women attacked—and the Stasi had staked out that apartment in order to protect the local womanhood. Neither Ernst nor Gretel had heard anything about sex crimes.

In an attempt to document their suspicions, Gretel went to visit Beyer the tailor in his apartment nearby. At first, she was elaborately circumspect. She told him that her washing machine had overflowed into his old apartment and that it had to be opened to check the damage and did he have a key?

"Well, Mrs. Schmidt," he said, "that is not so easy. At first I have to call a phone number and tell them I wish to go into that apartment. After I do that, there will be some gentlemen coming to this place here, and then they will accompany me back to my old apartment."

She decided to attack point-blank. "What are they doing in that apartment?"

He said, "Women have been molested in the neighborhood, sex crimes were committed."

She told him, "You know, Herr Beyer, that is not true. The whole thing is directed against us. There is a recorder in there."

He was stunned. "But that can't be true! If I had known that, I would never have let them in."

Shortly after that visit, Herr Beyer did return to his old apartment with a strange man. Gretel waited until they were inside, then she knocked loudly on the door. The tailor opened it, and she said she wanted to come in and discuss the washing-machine overflow she had told him about a few days earlier. He invited her in without hesitation. When she entered, the other man was nowhere in sight. Beyer said nothing, but motioned with his hand that the man was in another room. Together, they examined the bathroom and the kitchen for damage. There was, of course, none to be seen. Gretel left and went outside to a street corner. She saw Beyer leave first and a short while later, the stranger. She followed him. Two blocks away, he got into his car with his small black suitcase.

Finally Ernst confronted the mystery head-on. One afternoon in mid-November of '82, he returned to the apartment after driving a group of Soviet coaches to the airport following a series of joint training sessions. "As I entered the hallway, I saw light burning in the tailor's empty apartment through a transom of milky glass above the door. I decided this was it. I ran upstairs, deposited my briefcase, and was about to descend when I heard someone lock the tailor's apartment door, and then footsteps hurrying along the hallway and out of the building. I ran downstairs and sprinted out onto the sidewalk. I saw a man walking rapidly away. I shouted at him to come back. He did. He was a young man, as they all are who do this dirty work for the Stasi, and he was wearing the telltale black coat that they all wear."

Ernst towered over the young man. He demanded to know precisely what the young pup was doing in that apartment. The young man stammered that he had taken it over from the tailor to use as a studio. Ernst ordered the young man to return to the apartment door. "Show me what you are doing in this studio! Are you carrying in loot in the dead of night or what? Unlock the door please."

"But why?" the young man asked.

Gretel had followed Ernst downstairs and she said sharply, "You know it is customary in this country that when someone moves into an apartment, he registers in the house book. With you, several months have already passed. The house book is in our apartment. Why don't you register?"

He shrugged. She then demanded to know why he always parked his car several blocks away. She asked him exactly what it was that he carried in the suitcase when he came to the apartment. She asked him what it was he took away in the same suitcase when he left.

It was obvious to the young Stasi that she had been watching him closely. His face turned quite pale, and then he opened the apartment.

It was dark inside, the curtains were drawn. After a stroll around the place, the Schmidts realized that there was nothing suspicious in sight. Neither of them felt that they had grounds to conduct a thorough search at that point. Ernst then demanded the young man's ID, but he refused to show it, saying he was not allowed to. Ernst recalled, "I was very angry and I almost decided to grab the young lout by the collar and drag him upstairs and call the police. But then, I hesitated. I let him go. I was really not one hundred percent sure that what we suspected about a recording device was true."

The Schmidts did not know how to confront the situation because they could not prove either the bug or the recorder was there. For the next three months they lived like fugitives in their own home. Ernst recalled, "We did not invite visitors. We went for long walks in the evenings because it was the only way we could speak freely. We sometimes visited Bettina's apartment— although we could not be certain she didn't have a bug, too. We visited friends. We only came home to say a few words, to eat, to sleep."

At last, the Schmidts grew exhausted by the tension. They went together to the local precinct and complained. This time an inspector met with them and gave them an entirely different story about why the Stasi were occupying that apartment: Swastikas and the word *Solidarisch* had been smeared with paint on several buildings in the neighborhood, he said. The Stasi were in the apartment, watching and waiting until the moment came when they could apprehend the vandals.

Ernst was exasperated. He yelled at the inspector, "You must think we pull up our pants with pliers! You know and we know that what you are doing is only directed against the family Schmidt! There are no swastikas and there is no *Solidarisch!* There is a tape recorder that is listening to everything we say and that is all the truth!"

The inspector did not retreat. He said, "No, it is as I say. We will be there another couple of weeks until this matter of the swastikas and *Solidarisch* has been cleared up. We'll let you know when we move out."

Gretel snapped, "Don't bother telling us anything! You didn't let us know when you moved in, you needn't tell us when you move out!"

The Schmidts were allowed to visit Wolfgang once a month in Frankfurt on the Oder. There was always a watchdog present, and they assumed that listening devices recorded every word they spoke. Ordinarily they went out of their way to avoid anything provocative, discussing only the blandest of subjects, such as job opportunities Wolfgang might have if he ever got out of jail. But after a couple of months of living with the bug, Ernst lost his patience and spoke about it to his son.

"I told Wolfgang that we were bugged and I told him right in front of this hound who was listening," he recalled. "I said that we knew that a bug had been installed in our apartment with a recording device in the apartment below us. I said this loudly and clearly in front of the watchdog and the hidden microphones so that it would definitely get back to our supposed old friend Mielke at the Ministry for State Security. I told Wolfgang, 'This is the ultimate impudence!' "

After that outburst, Ernst confronted Manfred Ewald at the DTSB. The little man scoffed, "Come on, Ernst, you are seeing ghosts."

Ernst said, "I am seeing no ghosts. It is a fact, and I want you to know about it." Then he added sarcastically, "And please give my regards to comrade Mielke and tell him that this is a damned dirty trick he is doing to us."

Ernst's attempt to stand up to the authorities caused nothing to change. The bug remained in the apartment, the young man in the black overcoat continued to drop in regularly, and the recorder probably taped every sound for more than six years.

3

Meanwhile life dragged on in prison. The deadening interrogations had begun again with Schmidt's old nemesis, Wiedemann.

Once a month, he arrived from Berlin to talk to me. He was my permanent educator, so to speak, my brainwasher and my own personal interrogator. I rather looked forward to Wiedemann's visits because they meant I got to eat two lunches—one with him and one when I got back to my cell. When I ate with Wiedemann, the food was quite good. Always a big steak and a big dish of ice cream.

Except for the food, I didn't look forward to seeing Wiedemann. He was the same arrogant big shot he had been at the UHA. I always looked at his nails to see whether he was still biting them. He was. But he came on like the Lord of Alexanderplatz.

"What do you think now?" he would always ask. "What do you think you want to do with yourself? Hm? Do you still insist on going over there? What do you want to do with yourself when you get out of jail? Life will have to go on somehow for Wolfgang Schmidt. Would you perhaps like to open a café? Or would you like to own a car wash? What do you want to do?"

I said, as I always had before, "Well, my favorite idea for the future would be to become a world-class competitor in the discus again."

But he shook his head and said, as he always had before, "That's not possible anymore. Not anymore. There are no more sports for a man who violated the law, a man who wanted to betray the GDR."

After several meetings with Wiedemann, I was completely frustrated. In March of 1983 I consulted some of my fellow prisoners—including my onion-nosed adviser, Rainer Zidorn. I asked him how I could get out of the GDR. He said, "You should put in a formal application for an exit visa. It could work."

The next time Wiedemann came to visit was a day in April 1983—April sixth to be exact—and I told him, "I would like to apply for an exit visa to leave the GDR. I don't want to live here anymore."

He looked surprised, but he said nothing and gave me a piece of paper and his ballpoint pen. With his pen, I wrote, "Re: Application for exit visa to leave the GDR and move to the Federal Republic of Germany. Reason: In my life there have been occurrences since 1980 that are in direct contradiction to what society demands of me and that make life in the GDR impossible for me."

Now it was on the record for all of them to see. I wish I had known how much trouble it would cause me.

Wolfgang had told Ernst and Gretel about it when they visited on April 8, and they were distressed. Ernst pondered the situation for a couple of weeks, then wrote a long letter to Wolfgang— the only one he sent while his son was in custody. It was a wrenching document—part harsh reprimand, part heartbreaking cry of grief and love for a missing son:

"Dear Wolfgang: With my head filled with worries I completely forgot today on Sunday, 4/24, our 30th wedding anniversary. Really an unforgivable matter for, as I look back, my work, which I could accomplish without worries and with much love and commitment, was only possible because we had order and mother looked after the house and also after our beautiful garden in excellent fashion, as she does even as I write this letter. It took me a long time to digest what I was told about the last visit [of Wiedemann]. Of course, you are in a desperate and hardly hopeful situation. During a visit a long time ago, you told us we should keep a clear head and not lose our nerve . . .

"The methods that were employed to remove you from performance sport were terrible. But it was also obvious that you fell into every trap and that you contributed to [your own demise]. . . . It is especially tragic for you that all this happened at a time when you were at the pinnacle of your competitiveness, but it was not a pleasant matter for our sports organization either. Of course, you will take years before your anger at the measures taken subsides or diminishes, where other duties will give you pleasure again, and everything becomes past and possibly even forgotten.

"[But] an application for an exit visa is not a solution on which you can build [a future]. An athlete who was so much in the public eye will not be given that permission. Think about it. With an application for an exit visa, you will live your life without job prospects, you will live at the edge of subsistence, and hopelessness may even drive you . . . to choose suicide. . . .

"All this is leaving its mark on me as well because there were other solutions that would have been possible [but] they would have required your coming to your senses. . . . The most important thing, after all, is to get out of this humiliating, freedom-restricting detention. I offer you my help to the extent that I can still give it to you, and I tell you again, I was and am interested in your becoming a useful human being who considers the . . . duty to work a matter of course. I cannot agree with your decision since it goes against my conviction, and I must disassociate myself from it.

"If a basis for [the decision] is your belief that you can continue to practice your sport, you must consider that you are going to be 30. If you still hope to prove that you are the best, you are chasing an impossible ambition that is not worth pursuing. Sport is a beautiful element for young people, but it is only possible for a limited period of time.

"Consider also other possible repercussions that I may be facing [because of this decision]. . . . It was to be expected that because of the charges brought against you, I had to give up my position as national coach. They simply do not go together, this high position and one's own son in jail. Surely, you must have seen this, too. After 38 years of self-sacrificing activity, I was looking forward to a more quiet autumn of my life, and all this happened five minutes before I reached retirement age. The duties I have been given are no less important, and I especially appreciate no training camps and weekends free for recreation and work in the garden. I could really put up with this and (if it were not for the problem with you) could live peacefully and happily. But I am troubled again because you have again acted rashly and did not think it through to the end. . . . Sport is not your future anymore and cannot become your future again. It should not be difficult to recognize that clearly.

"What happened [to you] in 1981 and 1982 did not cause the world of sport to collapse. And now you are in your third year away from that [world], and furthermore, you are in jail. Philosophy tells us that man's existence determines his convictions. I understand that you stand in contradiction to socialist convictions, but there was a time when [socialist conviction] was already well developed [in you]. Now other influences have caused you to lose your clear attitude. You are drifting like a ship with engine trouble and you hope for a landing, which could easily turn into a crash landing. You should give priority to the family and its unity. See to it that you get out as soon as possible, and be smart when considering your present—and your future—fates.

"We all send our regards and hope to see you again in good health.

"Your father."

This letter angered Wolfgang when he first received it. Nevertheless, by the time he responded in writing on May 8, he sounded reasonable and considerate of the old man's feelings.

"Dear Daddy: Many thanks for your letter. You will understand that I did not immediately answer, but first thought about everything again thoroughly. Your letter tells me about your and mother's worries about my and our family's future. About the same time, there was another talk with the *Oberstleutnant* [Wiedemann] that also dealt with my future. I am only mentioning this so that you can see that you are not the only one who is trying to change my mind. I believe that you have my best interest at heart. Still, I have to disappoint you. My decision to leave the GDR remains unchanged. I cannot answer all your questions and problems in a letter. But please believe me my decision is not a thoughtless one. I simply cannot imagine a life without high-performance sports. You and mother brought me up to love sports, and I gave everything for it. Even though you, and certainly some others, think that I want to betray the GDR, I have to tell you that my only incentive for all of this is to perform again at my sport and for that I have to accept these hard times. . . .

"Believe me, Daddy, I am very sorry that you had difficulties because of my actions. I also hope that you can understand me a little bit even though you cannot accept my decision. Well, Daddy, I don't have anything else to say to the problems you have with all this. . . .

"I am treated correctly, and apart from a few little aches at the knee and back, I am well, considering the circumstances. We will be able to discuss all this during your visit, which I look forward to.

"Greetings.

"Your Wolfgang."

His parents had different views on his adamant desire to leave East Germany. They assumed mail was read, both coming and going, at the prison. Ernst saw the dark side: "I worried about his expressing these thoughts because the Stasi had the power to destroy a man psychologically." Gretel was more optimistic: "I was happy when he stood by his decision to leave. I always hoped it would work, that they would let him leave, that they would finally throw him free. There were many who had been released from prison to the West. I hoped that, sooner or later, he would be one of them."

NO OFFICIAL WORD ON WOLFGANG SCHMIDT—
from teammates, the DTSB, or the East German press—had gotten to the West since he was arrested. Obviously, his sudden
disappearance from international competition did not go unnoticed. When he missed the European and World Cup competitions
in the fall of 1981, the questions began. Mac Wilkins recalled:
"We knew there was something wrong then, but the change of
his status over the winter of '82 hadn't got back to us. We didn't
know he'd received *Sportverbot* in March, and of course, we didn't
know he had been arrested in the summer. I missed him even
though, at that time, we had never actually seen that much of
each other. Our relationship was unique. There would be times
when I was training in California, working out in the mountains
or driving, just appreciating being in California, sunny and warm.
Wolfgang would be with me in my imagination. He was an
invisible partner, and sometimes I'd explain things as if he were
with me. Then when I lived up in the mountains with Al Feuerbach, his East German counterpart was Udo Beyer, and we'd talk
about those guys, how they didn't have the freedom to be creative,

the freedom to come out here and enjoy this beautiful country and do nothing but train all day."

In September 1982, Wilkins wrote a letter to Schmidt expressing concern over his whereabouts. He heard nothing from Wolfgang, but Gretel Schmidt responded in a letter postmarked December 19, 1982, from West Berlin:

"We have been very worried about Wolfgang since July 2, because from that day on he has been in jail. This started when he was not allowed to compete in the Europa Cup and World Cup since he had shown undisciplined behavior and had placed second at the GDR championships. The real reason was, however, that Wolfgang had contact with athletes from capitalist countries, which is forbidden! He was very angry, but he trained throughout the whole winter very hard and wanted to prove in 1982 that he was still one of the best in the world. But then they were looking for things and flaws so that they could establish proof of unsportsmanlike behavior and lack of discipline, and in March he was banned from national and international sport. . . . He spoke his mind and made comments that proved to be his undoing. . . . They did not want him to travel abroad anymore since they feared he would not return. That is the real reason for everything! But they will never say so or admit it. Instead they arrested Wolfgang and sentenced him to one year and six months imprisonment on suspicion of escape from the GDR! I wanted you to know what really happened to Wolfgang. But I would also like to ask you not to say publicly that I wrote to you. Everything would become very difficult for us. . . .

"Yours, G. Schmidt.

"P.S. we hope that Wolfgang will survive everything well."

No word had ever appeared in the East German press about the disappearance of the world-record holder. In January 1983, after he had been in custody for six months, Verschoth called Volker Kluge, an old friend and respected journalist in East Berlin. He had often acted as press liaison for the GDR's national team, and Verschoth believed he had always been truthful. When she asked Kluge about Schmidt, he replied, "He is with the police again. But not as an officer, of course. He is a strange bird, very undisciplined."

Meanwhile, surreptitious efforts were going on in the West to free him even as he was scrubbing cars in the KFZ. It was all very touchy, but two cousins of Gretel Schmidt's living in Hamburg—Marlene Heinz and her brother Peter Walter—had been writing a series of confidential letters to members of the West German Bundestag in Bonn. On January 17, 1983, Marlene Heinz sent a typical letter to Friedel Schirmer at the Bundestag. First, she listed the harmless "crimes" Schmidt had committed— dating a Canadian woman, owning a flare pistol, shaking his fist during the Moscow Olympics. Then she made her plea: "We know Wolfgang's mentality very well and know that living on in the GDR will destroy him. He is a man who loves freedom, who could never adapt to a regime, especially since he has experienced the free life in the West." She suggested that it would be in West Germany's interest to arrange for Schmidt's release. "We believe that besides the human side, there are also his athletic possibilities to consider. Wolfgang is of interest to the Federal Republic of Germany because—given that he is the world-record holder with excellent technique and given the good performances that can still be expected of him—he would be a great asset to the FRG." Though she received sympathetic responses to such letters, nothing was done.

Another man who refused to give up on Schmidt was Klaus Blume, a longtime sportswriter for *Die Welt* in Bonn. In the early summer of 1983, he went into East Berlin to cover a meet, as he had often done in the past. As always, he was met at the border by a Stasi watchdog who stayed at his elbow throughout his sojourn in the East. At the stadium, Blume had spoken with the East German journalist Klaus Huhn, who said menacingly, "I know why you have come. You are not here for the meet, you are here because of Wolfgang Schmidt." Blume only shrugged, but a short time later he slipped away from his Stasi guard and managed to rendezvous with another East German journalist who told him everything about Schmidt's arrest, trial, and imprisonment.

Blume spread the word among friends and colleagues in the West and organized a petition calling for Schmidt's freedom. Hundeds of people read about this in *Die Welt* and started their own petitions. "We sent them all to Honecker," said Blume, "because he was the only one who could make anything happen."

Then on May 29, 1983, everyone in the small world of track and field suddenly focused on Wolfgang Schmidt once again. A Russian discus thrower, Yury Dumchev, broke Schmidt's world record on that day, the record he had had for four years, nine months, twenty days. Once again, people were shocked to remember that this great athlete had simply disappeared at the peak of his career.

His mother wrote Wolfgang a consoling letter: "Now your world record has been broken, don't take it hard. There will always be better ones! But how unfair it is, in my opinion, that you had to take that without being able to fight for it."

Schmidt's own reaction to losing the record was focused entirely on how it might affect his chances to gain freedom.

Of course, I was disappointed that I lost my record, but it was more important to me that I had applied for the exit visa while I was still officially the world-record holder. At that time, I thought "world-record holder" on the form might move them to be more agreeable.

Newspapers of the GDR did publish stories about Dumchev's new record, but nowhere did they mention the name of the man whose record had been surpassed. In their eyes, Wolfgang Schmidt was not only gone, he had never existed.

The Western pursuit for information about him grew more feverish after that. For obvious reasons, it reached something of a climax in Los Angeles on June 23, 1983, two days before a dual meet between the US and the GDR, sponsored by the *Los Angeles Times*. At a press luncheon held at Julie's restaurant before the meet, athletes such as the star sprinters Marlies Göhr and Marita Koch and shot-putter Udo Beyer were available for questions. At first, the atmosphere was warm enough, but then Mal Florence, then the track-and-field writer for the *Los Angeles Times,* suddenly demanded, "Whatever happened to Wolfgang Schmidt?" Florence recalled later, "It was like dropping a bomb in the restaurant."

The East German team leader was Georg Wieczisk from the track federation and he replied, "Schmidt has not been a member of our national team for two or two and a half years."

Florence: "Well, why was he dropped from the national team?"

Wieczisk: "That's a question for our national federation."

Florence: "Was it something he did that led to his dismissal?"

Wieczisk: "I can't give you any more than my answer. The national federation decided he can't be a member of our team."

Florence: "Do you know where he's living?"

Wieczisk: "It's a country of seventeen million people. We don't know where everyone is living."

Florence: "We've heard rumors that he might defect. Is that true?"

Wieczisk: "There are so many rumors. I can't give you more information than I have."

The next day, Florence ran the interview with Wieczisk under the headline "East German Discus Star Is Missing."

American competitors at the meet, including Dwight Stones and John Powell, tried to get members of the East German team to talk about Schmidt. No luck. "They all go *shshshhh,*" said Powell.

Dwight Stones told a gathering of journalists: "You can't press those people for answers. They know exactly where he is. We know where he is, too. Wolfgang made a big mistake. He speaks some English and has been extremely friendly with people on our team. If there was ever a guy on that team who would potentially no longer be on it, it would be Wolfgang. He was never sly about what he was doing."

Steve Futterman, a reporter for National Public Radio, managed an interview with Udo Beyer. To a question about Schmidt, Beyer replied, "No comment."

Futterman: "But have you seen him?"
Beyer: "Yeah."
Futterman: "Is he okay?"
Beyer: "It's okay."

SCHMIDT WAS DECIDEDLY NOT OKAY WHEN BEYER uttered those words. Even as his name made news in California, he was in deep trouble in prison. His father had been right; filing a formal written application for an exit visa was a serious mistake. Since July of 1982, Schmidt had orally confessed many times to Wiedemann and other Stasi interrogators that he wished to leave the GDR. They had threatened him and insulted him, but they had never mistreated him physically. For some reason, the written word ignited their wrath. With brutal efficiency, they went to work to break him.

There had been no reaction from the authorities for about eight weeks. Then, one morning in June before eight A.M., my beloved *Brigadier*, Otto, suddenly ordered me to go out of the workshop and do some work outside the front door. Ordinarily it was against prison rules to be outside the shop before eight o'clock, the starting hour for work, but since Otto was the boss, I followed his orders.

Suddenly Oberstleutnant Shultz himself appeared and said

roughly, "Schmidt! Come, come! Go, go! Off you go. *Ruck zuck* [in a flash]! Solitary!"

And that was that. They hurried me off to a tiny solitary cell, three meters square, glass-brick window, plank bed. No toilet, just a pail in the corner. No washbasin, just a bowl. A small table, a chair.

Two days after they threw me into solitary, there was to be the dual meet between the GDR and the US in Los Angeles. It was televised into the GDR. It was my chance to see my old American friends compete. I had looked forward to it for weeks. I had scarcely dared think about it for fear I would jinx it and it would not happen. Of course, it didn't happen. In solitary they would not even let me have a newspaper, and they refused to tell me the results.

They left me there alone for ten days. When I woke up in the morning, I always felt absolutely whacked. My back was in terrible pain from sleeping on the hard plank bed.

I fell into a state of somnolence, like being in hibernation, and I dozed all the time I could during the day. I had what they call hypersomnia. But even though I was alone and silent, there was always noise to disturb me. My cell was at the beginning of a long corridor, and there was a steel, barred door a few feet away leading from the spiral staircase. Whenever someone opened that door and slammed it shut, it made a clashing, explosive sound that reverberated into my cell.

After ten days, they moved me to a regular single cell with a toilet, washbasin, and a normal bed. I stayed there two days. Then two guards arrived and said, "Come along." They took me into the office of Shultz. He sat like a big block of wood behind his desk and said, "Well, Schmidt. Where are we going from here? You don't do this and you don't do that around here. You are one big problem prisoner." He accused me of failing to finish certain jobs, of not wanting to work on weekends. It was true, I didn't want to work weekends because I wanted a little time to recover my strength. He was very irritated. "Where are you going from here?" he asked. "What is next?"

I decided it was time for me to speak up; I had been quiet for so long. I said, "You know what? You disappoint me. I would have expected more from you as a Communist and a comrade. You are just a small speck of light as big as this"—and I held my thumb and forefinger about one-sixteenth of an inch apart.

This really angered him. His neck swelled and his eyes grew small and he said, "Well, well, well, Schmidt. So you had your say and now you will see what it's gotten you into."

I wanted to insult him. I wanted to tell him that he was not the most powerful man on earth. I didn't care about any repercussions because in my situation things couldn't get worse.

He summoned the two guards and had them take me to a cell in the hallway near his office. They left me there half an hour, then the guards returned. One who was blond and looked very strong barked like a dog, "Come along!" The other was small, fat, and ugly.

I followed without resistance. Then, to my horror, we arrived at the door of the same solitary cell where I had just spent ten terrible days. This terrified me. They opened the door and the blond one said, "Get in there!" I refused to go. I stared at the plank bed. I couldn't face one more hour in there. I twisted against the guards. I said, "No!" They took a couple of steps back and unfastened their truncheons from their belts. The fat one grabbed an alarm wire with one hand. Then suddenly they began to beat me with their clubs.

They hit me over the back, the shoulders. Both of them were swinging their clubs like lunatics. Their eyes were popping and they were grunting and panting as they pounded. Both of them hit me together, harder and harder. I could maybe have beaten them, but what good would it have done? Finally I gave up. It was useless to resist. Where could I run even if I did overpower them? There were dozens of guards. I was alone.

I jumped into the cell and they slammed the door behind me. I lay on the bed. The next day there were deep-blue marks on my shoulders.

This time, my sentence in isolation was also for ten days. Counting everything, that meant I was put away for twenty-three days. I had gotten pretty desperate in all that time, but I never thought seriously of suicide. Instead I played an idiotic mind game with myself. I kept telling myself, "I'm only an actor in a film and I am making a film about being in prison, and the shooting schedule is dragging out longer than it should. But it can't be helped. It just has to be that way."

During those twenty-three days in solitary, I also relived all my memories. I went through every hour I could remember of my visits abroad, my conversations with old friends such as Mac and John and Ricky, my good times in Helsinki and Montreal and Cologne and Stockholm. Thank God, there were so many good times.

Sometime after the seventh day of my second ten-day sentence in solitary, Wiedemann came from Berlin to see me. He did not come to my stinking cell. He summoned me to an office on the ground floor. The first question he asked was, "Have you gone crazy? What is the matter with you?" Then he asked, "Where do we go from here? Do you want to stay two more years?"

I said nothing, and he said coaxingly, "Are you sure you don't want to withdraw your application for an exit visa?"

I said, "I won't withdraw the application."

He was a little harsher. "You'll see what this will get you. Things will only get worse. Are you sure you don't want to withdraw the application? Would you really rather serve an extra two years in here? Is that your choice, Wolfgang?"

That scared me, but I managed to keep my mouth shut and they put me back in solitary to finish the ten days.

When they let him out, he was not the man he had been before his ordeal began.

I was a wreck when I got back to the apartment. I had lost another six kilos [13 lbs.]. My roommates raved about how much weight I had lost, how hollow my cheeks were. But they were not happy to see me back and did not offer any sympathy.

You see, they were never my friends. From the start, most of them disliked me because I was famous, because I had seen the world, and because I had led a much more pleasant life than any of them. They were jealous of me, and when I got into trouble, they were delighted. Most of them were gloating that the authorities had finally punished one of my privileged class—a decorated athlete who had always lived better than they.

Rainer Zidorn was more clever than the others. He was very good at drawing out people to make them tell him everything. He liked to use the information he got from other prisoners to figure out how State Security might act in different situations.

Now that I was back with the others, I followed my usual routine with the cars, spraying tankers and washing cars. However, even though things seemed normal on the surface, I sensed that something was wrong, that I was in jeopardy again. I noticed that everybody seemed extremely irritable toward me, the guards as well as my fellow prisoners. I caught people watching me when I wasn't looking, as if I had been singled out as a victim of some prank or practical joke that they wanted to witness when it happened.

Finally Rainer told me what was going on. He had connections and he knew. He said the word was out that they wanted to put me in solitary again. They intended to break me for good. They wanted to force me to rescind my application to leave the GDR or they would finish me off. Rainer admitted that formal applications for exit visas had sometimes caused them to deport prisoners to the West. But he said this was out of the question for me because I was too well-known.

"They want to muck around with you again, Wolfgang," said Rainer. "They'll never let you leave the country. They'll put you in solitary again and again."

Though Rainer had been the one whose advice I had followed in filing for an exit visa in the first place, he said he had to switch full circle. He said that I had no choice but to withdraw the application in order to get out of jail as soon as possible.

"Your health is at stake, Wolfgang, maybe your life," he said.

With Rainer, one never quite knew what his motive was. Maybe he had arranged to get some favor from Oberstleutnant Shultz for convincing me to cancel my application. One never knew with anyone in that prison. But I realized that I was fighting a hopeless battle. If they weren't going to kick me out of the country, then the application was pointless.

And I knew very well that if I was put back into solitary, I would suffer too much damage to my health—mental even more than physical. I knew I couldn't survive any siege for long. They were going to finish me off unless I gave in.

I made it known to Oberstleutnant Shultz that I urgently wished to speak to Oberstleutnant Wiedemann. A few days passed, and he arrived. I told him, "I am withdrawing my application for an exit visa, and I renounce my goal to compete in sports in the Federal Republic of Germany." I didn't mean this, of course, but I knew I had to play their games by their rules.

Like the actor he was, Wiedemann asked incredulously, "What! You want to withdraw your application now? But why? You'll have to explain that to me very carefully."

I said again, "I am giving up my goal to compete in the West."

Wiedemann asked me to put this decision in writing, and I did: "Herewith I withdraw my application for an exit visa. It is my wish to work in the GDR as a coach in the throwing events or as the caretaker of a fitness club."

Wiedemann insisted that I add the words "My decision is voluntary." I did that, too.

None of what I wrote was true, but that was all it took—telling them a couple of lies they wanted to hear. In five weeks, I was out.

H E LEFT FRANKFURT/ODER ON OCTOBER 14, 1983,
exactly 469 days since the summer afternoon he was arrested. His
sentence had been shortened by two and a half months.

He was not informed officially of his early release until the
very moment two guards appeared to escort him from the KFZ.
By then, Schmidt had already heard a rumor of his impending
freedom through the grapevine operated by Rainer Zidorn. The
little man with the onion nose had passed the word to Schmidt
the day before he was released.

I worked that morning as if nothing were going to happen. I cleaned
everything in my work area. Then two guards came to me and said,
"Number nine! Pack your belongings!" They took me to the apartment and I quickly grabbed my belongings.

My own clothes were returned to me. They hung even looser
than they had when I arrived. They also returned my watch, still
ticking, and they paid me the last bit of my wages and gave me the
small amount of money I had saved. They also gave me a certifi-

cate—a small piece of paper—indicating that I had served eleven months.

Then Shultz was there to see me off, like the principal at a school graduation. He was all smiles and insisted that a guard take a photograph of me. When he shook my hand the final time, there were tears in his eyes. It was the first time I had seen him show any feelings. This was the man who had slung me into solitary twice and was fully prepared to destroy me with another sentence there. I should have wrung his neck instead of shaking his hand, but I let it happen. I was taking no chances on upsetting anyone.

The ironies that day were cruel. Schmidt had lain for days on a board, gaunt and alone. Now he was treated as if he had been a revered houseguest. He had been reduced to hallucinating that he was a movie star in order to keep his sanity. Now he was treated as if he really were a movie star.

Oberstleutnant Wiedemann himself was waiting to drive me to Berlin in a Lada with a Stasi *Null Acht Fünfzehn* as a chauffeur. I climbed into the backseat. We were like a couple of big-shot buddies together, my official brainwasher and me. When I bade goodbye to the guards, I inadvertently said, *"Auf Wiedersehen,"* meaning "See you again." Immediately Wiedemann nudged me and said slyly, "Better not, Wolfgang."

But all that—the teary-eyed warden, my ride with Wiedemann— that was nothing compared to the next treatment they gave me. As we drove into Berlin, I wasn't thinking much about the procedures ahead. I guess I assumed we'd go to some office somewhere, some bureaucratic little room, maybe even back to the villa on the lake in Motzen where I might be interrogated a little more before they let me go. But no, they took me directly to the SC Dynamo Sporthotel in Berlin!

I was led in through a back entrance and taken to a reception room. There, waiting to greet me, were the last two men on earth that a former jailbird would ever expect: Manfred Ewald, president of DTSB, and Major General Heinz Pommer, who was not only a vice president of SC Dynamo but was also a major general of the Stasi. Four hours ago, I was about to spend the day washing filthy prison cars, and now I was being received like an honored dignitary by the highest official in GDR sport and a major general.

At first I was shocked. I thought, what a reception! But it didn't take long and I caught on to why they were doing this. That was when Manfred Ewald and General Pommer mentioned that my name had been making headlines in the Western press and that Ricky Bruch had been speaking out for me. When Ewald talked about that, I almost burst out laughing because I realized how embarrassed they were, how embarrassing my case was for the whole sports organization. They wanted to be left in peace, and they wanted me to stay in the GDR, and they were prepared to offer me anything if I wanted to stay. Ewald even promised me that I could practice my sport again. They wanted my name to be out of the public eye.

They inquired eagerly after my health and were anxious to know what plans I had for the future. Ewald's belly protruded a little and he had narrow shoulders with a very big head. He was built with the proportions of a newborn baby, but there was nothing innocent about him.

He said, "What would you like to do now, Wolfgang? What kind of job would you like to have?"

I replied quickly, "I would like to compete in sports again."

Sweet as sugar, Ewald said, "Oh, please, do go ahead and try. We are behind you."

Then Pommer told me that my car would be returned to me. It had been presented from the state in the first place for excellence at sports, and now it was being presented again for excellence in surviving a jail term. This was funny, but I didn't laugh. They said work had been proceeding on my house while I was in prison. The interior was just about finished. It had nice wood paneling, built-in furniture in the living room, they told me. Of course, they had also installed a bug, but they failed to inform me of that.

Ewald told me, again very sweetly, that I should finish my studies at the College for Physical Culture in Leipzig and that they were ready for me to begin classes. He said, "We would like to see you lead a successful life in the GDR, and we will do everything to make that possible."

Pommer then chimed in that there had been some articles in the Western press about me, and that Ricky Bruch had had his fingers in it. "That drug addict!" Pommer shouted. "Spreading lies and slander."

I was delighted to hear this and had a hard time suppressing laughter.

After ranting about Ricky, Pommer made an appointment with me two days later to introduce me to my new job. I told him I had hoped to take a couple of weeks off, but he shook his head. It was better if I started right away. I had no choice. That's how your rights are violated in the GDR even when you're not in prison.

After the discussion at the Sporthotel, I was driven to my parents' summer house. Frankly, I would have preferred going directly to the West at that moment.

The atmosphere at home was a little oppressive. My father said, "Well, there you are again." They had been expecting me because Ewald had invited them to his home and informed them I would be coming home. He had been as friendly to them as he was to me.

Then I drove with my parents to my house. They had done a lot of work in the house during the year and three months I had been gone, and the house had been furnished, of course, as Mielke had promised. Seeing the place at last in a finished state made me sad and depressed rather than happy. That dark feeling never left as long as I lived there. Often, later, I would look at the furniture and feel sick to my stomach. I was thinking how dearly I had paid for it. The tab had been fifteen months in prison, three weeks in solitary, and the end of my sports career. I would have liked to take an ax then and demolish the place. Sure, the house was pretty. It was worth at least a hundred thousand marks [$50,000], but I had no interest or liking for it then.

They could have given me anything, and I would still not want to live in their rotten Stasi state anymore. I wanted out of this secret-police cage more than ever.

PART 4

ONCE FREED FROM PRISON, SCHMIDT WAS BY NO means free to pursue life as he wished. Despite Manfred Ewald's sugary encouragement that he should "by all means" embark on a high-performance sports career again, Schmidt had already been exterminated as an athlete in the minds of the sports authorities. Two days after his formal reception from Ewald and Major General Pommer, Schmidt began work on his new and unwanted career as a coach. He met with Pommer and several high-ranking officers wearing the uniform of the Wachregiment, the National Guard, which is actually an arm of the Stasi. The military men drove with him to Adlershof, a section of East Berlin so close to the West Berlin border that Schmidt could see The Wall. Here he was assigned to the Felix Czirzinski unit of the Wachregiment.

There were several barracks for the unit, and I was put to work as a coach for soldiers of the National Guard. Their usual duty was to stand guard at public events and make certain that various big shots in attendance were well protected. They put up the barriers before large parades, such as the May Day parade and the one on Rosa Luxemburg–Karl Liebknecht Day on January fifteenth.

At the Adlershof barracks I was coaching a group of eight soldiers, primarily in throwing events—shot put, discus, and javelin throw. They were talented, too. But the reason they had given me a job with the National Guard was so they had me under tight control at all times. To my surprise, I liked the work. It put me back in contact with my sport, and the young soldiers, all between nineteen and twenty-one years old, were good guys. The best thing was that I could now train myself. I participated with these kids and it was great fun. The only trouble was that Adlershof was so far from my home. Every day I had to drive about thirty-five miles to get there from north of Berlin, where I lived, to south of Berlin. Then I had to drive thirty-five miles back—more than seventy miles per day. They paid me well, though—two thousand marks [$1,000] per month.

Even though he had been exiled to this sporting limbo, the establishment treated Schmidt as if his crime had never occurred. Everyone seemed eager to restore him as quickly as possible to the lifestyle he had previously enjoyed as a bona fide hero of the state. The two thousand marks salary for coaching a few soldiers was six hundred marks ($300) more than he had earned as a star athlete (not counting prize money) and nearly twice as much as an average worker earned. On the very first day he was free, they had returned his Lada 1600, newly washed and polished. After a few weeks, he was able to move into his house in the countryside.

The address was Emile-Zola-Strasse 30. The neighborhood was quiet and modest, consisting mainly of small bungalows and cottages built on lots with trees and shrubs everywhere. His was a neat, gray, one-story structure with bright-white trim on the windows, a backyard with a large cherry tree in the middle, a walnut tree, and several small, newly planted pear and apple trees along the sides, as well as a vegetable garden. Tall black fir trees lined one side of the driveway, and there were flower beds here and there, planted by Wolfgang's mother. The interior had been finished in a style that even party members in good standing rarely ever enjoyed. The walls were covered with a capitalist-executive-suite-style wood paneling, with built-in bookcases, and large built-in closets in the bedroom. Everything had been done with precise care to meet exactly his desires.

An enemy of the state only days before, Schmidt was living in the style of a champion in every way except that he was not allowed to compete as a champion. The death sentence still stood.

Nevertheless, he could not help but hope. After a time, he arranged a meeting with Pommer and asked the big question: Could he ever compete again?

Pommer spoke like a king on a throne: "A Wolfgang Schmidt does not have the right anymore to represent the GDR abroad."

And that was that. They would never change. In truth, if they had ever let me go abroad to compete, I would have stayed there.

Discouraged though he was, Schmidt felt obliged to pursue the question with Ewald himself.

I confronted him at the DTSB. It was the spring of 1984, about five months after I had left prison, and a short time before the Warsaw Pact countries had announced their boycott of the 1984 Olympics in Los Angeles. I discussed my job and my studies, which were to begin at the German College for Physical Culture in Leipzig, and I asked him again whether I could pursue my sport again.

He talked to me as if I were stupid. "Well, why do you think you want to get back into sports again? It makes no sense. You've got your job and your studies. You still think you could have time to get back into sports? How do you expect to manage all that?"

It was insulting. Lots of other athletes managed all those things quite easily. I could have, too. But I had my answer and I was resigned to it for a while.

Ernst was perhaps more of a realist about the situation than Wolfgang. To him, it was hopeless: "I was certain they would never let him back into sport because they would have lost face if they did. And of course, because of what he had gone through, they could expect that he would defect as soon as he could during his next competition abroad. I told him he should concentrate on his job, get married, have a family, because that should bring him happiness whether he was allowed to do performance sport again or not."

But Schmidt was acting as if he were still a national hero in good standing. He had grown tired of coaching the National Guard, and he didn't hesitate to complain to the highest sports authority in the GDR:

I went to Ewald and told him that I didn't like the long drive back and forth and that I also wanted to coach athletes who had a chance of making it in performance sport. I didn't tell him that I also disliked working in a military atmosphere. You didn't see any women there, only men. It was definitely not an atmosphere to my liking. A little too much like prison, perhaps.

By September of 1984, Schmidt was transferred to a job coaching children. Ironically enough, at times he trained them at the Sport Forum at SC Dynamo Berlin where he had spent so many years of his own youth and young manhood.

I had twenty children, about thirteen years old. And I knew from the beginning that none would ever develop to be on the national team. The worst thing was that some of them wouldn't make it because they had relatives in the West. They were politically tainted. Most of the others who did not have relatives in the West were not talented enough to make it. This was a group from which the best had already been selected and promoted to advanced training. There was one who really had the potential to become world class, and he worked hard, too. But because he had a grandmother in West Berlin, there was no chance they would allow him to advance to the point where he might leave the country for international competition.

Schmidt's yearning to live free beyond The Wall was with him always.

I was staying in my house alone and sometimes I awoke in the morning feeling so happy and so alive. And I would begin to get up and realize that I felt so good only because I had been dreaming that I was in the West. When it struck me that the dream wasn't true, I'd be in a sour mood all day. That happened pretty often.

His obsession haunted him in his waking hours, too. In his free time—of which there was a lot—he and a friend, Mario Knezević, a bodybuilder who sometimes trained with him, spent hours walking in the vicinity of The Wall. They scrutinized its intimidating surface, gauging what supernatural acts of strength and agility were required to get over the top. As they discussed strategies and techniques, some of their ideas sounded like the make-believe of little boys, and others fell only a little short of pure hallucination.

I would gaze at The Wall and say to Mario, "I'd like to just sprout wings and fly over that thing."

And he would say, "If we had a pole for vaulting, would that carry us far enough?"

And I would say, "Think about the man shot from a cannon in the circus. That would do it, wouldn't it?"

There were border guards with submachine guns. They drove in trucks along The Wall. There were watchtowers. There was barbed wire. But we figured there had to be ways of getting past all that to the other side. For instance, at the Jannowitz Bridge where the River Spree flowed beneath it. I'd say, "With a diving suit we could swim underwater and get to the other side."

And he would say, "Don't you think there is barbed wire stretched across under the water?"

I had been told that there was indeed barbed wire underwater, but I had also been told of places where there probably was no barbed wire.

I was always thinking about possibilities for finding a hole. Mario wanted to get out, too, but he was uneasy about hanging around near The Wall. People had been arrested just for walking there.

But I couldn't stay away. My mind was churning nonstop, every day, about ways of breaching The Wall.

When I watched the LA games on TV, I saw the rocket man who flew into the Coliseum with a rocket on his back during the opening ceremony. I said to myself, "I should have such a gadget. I would zoom across too fast for the guards to see me, too fast for them to have time to shoot."

I also thought of using a helicopter, one with a red cross on it. I didn't think they would shoot down the Red Cross. But of course, one couldn't be sure.

Perhaps logically enough, Schmidt's obsession with freedom ran deeper and hurt more when he was outside prison than it had when he was confined inside the Chinese boxes at Frankfurt on the Oder—the locked cell inside the stone building inside the stone wall. Now there was only the one Wall, but the very nearness of freedom seemed to make him crazier than when it had been unthinkably far off.

In the summer of 1984, Schmidt discovered that he was still considered a suspicious character by the Stasi. He and three friends—Mario Knezević, Wolfgang Blume, an ex-boxer and physiotherapist whom Schmidt had known since 1973, and Rainer Krüger, who worked as a TV mechanic at the Hotel Metropol—had decided to drive to Bulgaria. It was to be Schmidt's first vacation since he had been thrown into prison two years before.

They had planned to drive by way of Czechoslovakia, Hungary, and Rumania. The others got the visas they needed with no trouble, but the authorities refused to give Schmidt a visa to visit Rumania. He knew why.

It was then fairly easy to escape from Rumania into Yugoslavia, much easier than getting across The Wall. The Danube is the border at one point, and many people had already escaped by swimming the Danube. My friends had their visas, so it was decided that they would drop me at Budapest and I would take a plane to Varna, Bulgaria, where they would pick me up after they had driven through Rumania. However, when I landed in Varna, three policemen were waiting for me. They asked if I was Wolfgang Schmidt and demanded my passport. I gave it to them and they checked to be sure I was who I said I was. Just minor hassling, I thought.

Then, when I was in the car with my friends, we noticed that we were being followed. Our driver, Wolfgang Blume, decided to see exactly what was going on. He made a quick right turn into a village, then a left, and suddenly we could see that there were several cars—three of four—following our exact route. They were all unmarked, and the men inside were not in uniform. They were from the Bulgarian KGB, of course. And as we well knew, they were there to watch me.

We drove to Kavatcite, our campsite destination, and slept that night in a bungalow we had reserved. We had not gone to the campsite office to register that night, figuring we'd do it first thing in the morning. Again, the police arrived. They stood outside our bungalow and ordered us to the registration office. We got there and our visas were all stamped "Void" and we were told to get out of Bulgaria immediately. All four of us. The other three could drive back home, they said, but I had to fly immediately back to Berlin. They also charged us a fine, about two hundred marks, and not only that, I had to pay seven hundred marks for my plane ticket.

When I got back, I expected a whole gang of police to meet me, but no one was there. I was furious. I went right to SC Dynamo and demanded an audience with Major General Pommer. I shouted at him, "What a dirty trick, to ruin our vacation! Am I never going to be free to live a normal life?" He was disturbed, he said, and he told me to write a report. I did, and believe it or not, they refunded the seven hundred marks I had paid for the plane ticket and told me not to tell my friends. But they had gotten what they wanted: They had hassled me, messed up my vacation, and reminded me once again that I was an outcast and a criminal.

Of course, Schmidt had never given any indication to the authorities that he had reformed his maverick ways. He had not abandoned his friendships in the West. He was writing letters frequently to Mac Wilkins in California, to Alwin Wagner in West Germany, and to Ricky Bruch in Sweden. These letters or cards were carried into West Berlin by some friend and mailed from there. Always, Schmidt wrote that he was unhappy, that he was obsessed with escape. When he heard that Bruch had thrown a new Swedish record, Schmidt sent him a telegram of congratulations. Later, Schmidt received a postcard signed by Bruch and John Powell. The message was a single sentence: "We are thinking of you."

Lots of People in the West Were Thinking of him.

Peter Walter and Marlene Heinz, Gretel's cousins in Hamburg, had never stopped beseeching Western authorities to do something in his behalf, and at times, their hopes had soared. "In 1984," Frau Heinz recalled, "we were told by West German government officials that Wolfgang would be in Hamburg in six weeks. We expected him to knock on the door at any time. But no Wolfgang. In early 1985, we were told again that he'd be here in two weeks. Again no Wolfgang. In March we heard from the Bavarian Staatskanzlei [State Chancellery] that Ministerpräsident Franz-Josef Strauss had done everything in his power on behalf of Wolfgang. Nothing had happened. In April, we were informed by the government in Bonn that they had tried hard, but it was not possible to achieve Wolfgang's move to West Germany."

It seemed that the East Germans were treating Schmidt as if he were a spy who knew too many state secrets to be allowed out of the country. Frau Heinz recalled, "His father had been instrumental in many developments of the sports program, and we came to believe that that was the reason they didn't want Wolfgang to leave. He would be a *Geheimnisträger*—one who bears secrets. This was especially true where sports medicine and drugs were concerned. Wolfgang knew all these things. They believed that he would tell all in the West."

Other friends besides the relatives in Hamburg were working on other, more dramatic schemes to spring him free. One grim day in February 1985, as Schmidt arrived at the SC Dynamo gym for his 5 P.M. coaching session with his children, he was suddenly confronted by his old friend and rival, the Swede Ricky Bruch.

I drove up to the gate at the club and who should be standing near the gatekeeper? At first I wasn't sure who was standing there, but then I realized it was Ricky wearing a black, long-haired wig. We embraced quickly, and immediately I led him to my car and we drove away. I was so excited to see this crazy guy in the East that I simply left the children to train on their own.

Bruch and Schmidt had first met in 1976 at a meet in Halle between competitors from the GDR, Norway, Sweden, and Bulgaria. Bruch was, at that time, still among the best discus throwers in the world. He had once set the world record in 1972. Now, in 1985, he was very much a has-been. He was thirty-nine years old, and though he professed always to be on the verge of making a comeback, something always prevented it—such as being suspended from the team after slapping a Swedish federation official.

Ricky had been in West Berlin for a film festival where a quasi-documentary he had produced and starred in was being shown. He had gotten a day visa, good until midnight, to visit Schmidt in the East. His film was entitled *The Soul Is Bigger than the World* and in it Bruch portrayed himself as an athlete who had unjustly been left off his country's Olympic team in 1984 solely because of age. The climax of the film came when Bruch produced a grand throw of 233'9½" a couple of months after the '84 games. This would have won him the gold medal in Los Angeles. In the film, Bruch told Schmidt, he phoned John Powell (who also played himself) and shouted, "Who is the best thrower in the world now?"

Powell shouted back, "Wolfgang Schmidt!"

Bruch was shocked. "Wolfgang Schmidt! He just sent me a telegram that says, 'Ricky, you are the greatest!'"

Bruch told Wolfgang there was another scene in the film in which he was describing aloud to himself the rescue operation he imagined he would use to spring Schmidt free. He said, "Yeah, that's how it'll work. Let's assume Wolfgang lives in this house here. [The screen shows a house.] His father lives next door, we know that. Heavily under surveillance. So here I come. [Bruch arrives in a car.] My friend, the driver, stays in the car, and I go inside to visit Wolfgang. I stay for ten minutes and leave with Wolfgang. We take a walk. I see that the guard follows. I stop him to ask for a match or some guidance. [Bruch is talking to a guard while the actor playing Wolfgang walks on and quickly climbs into the car as it moves slowly past him. The car disappears at high speed while Bruch continues talking to the unsuspecting guard.]"

This visit to Schmidt didn't result in any melodramatic rescue attempt, but they talked eagerly about making a break in the future.

The two of us drove from SC Dynamo to a quiet place in the country. Possibly I went a little crazy, seeing this friend from the West after all the time I had spent crated up inside prison cells. I pleaded with him, "Please, Ricky, Ricky! Get me out of here! It is killing me, making me kaput! I am so unhappy and so damned helpless!"

Ricky said calmly, "I'll get you out. I'll help you." We talked of nothing but escape for two hours.

Schmidt drove Ricky Bruch back to the Hotel Metropol, a bustling Western-style hotel in the center of East Berlin. They agreed

that Bruch would come back to the Metropol in a week and that
they would meet to further discuss escape plans on either Friday
or Saturday at precisely seven P.M.

Schmidt was very excited about the prospects of escape, but
Ricky Bruch was not the world's most reliable coconspirator.

I went to the Metropol both nights the next week. I waited a full
hour each time. Ricky did not show up, either on Friday or on
Saturday. I was depressed. I thought maybe Ricky had pulled out
and left me on my own. I should have known better. He was too
good a friend for that.

One night that spring, Schmidt had driven from SC Dynamo
Berlin to his house. It was about ten P.M. and the neighborhood
was dark as he turned into his driveway and pulled up to the
garage door. Suddenly, a car rolled up narrow little Emile-Zola-
Strasse and stopped in front of the house. No one got out. It sat
there with the motor running.

I was startled and I walked toward it. I was very suspicious. I saw
that it was an old Saab, quite small. I had no idea who it might be.
I walked over and said, "Who is this?"

The voice came back, "Who do you think this is?" It was Ricky,
and as usual, he was agitated. With him was a handball player who
was driving because Ricky had no driver's license. Ricky told me
they had driven from Sweden and he wanted me to climb into the
backseat of the car right then and leave the GDR.

I looked in the car. The backseat was covered with a pile of
wigs. Ricky is a pretty messy person. His idea was that I would lie
on the floor, cover myself with wigs, and then we would drive out
of the country on the transit autobahn. This is the highway used by
cars and trucks to cross East Germany on their way to West Germany
and other countries. They are not allowed to leave the autobahn.
As a rule, transit vehicles are not put through heavy inspections at

control points. The Saab had not been searched on the way in. However, Ricky and the handball player had broken the law by leaving the autobahn a few miles from my house.

The whole scheme seemed a little loose, but I took it seriously for a few minutes. Why not make a run for it? What did I have to lose? My life wasn't worth much anyway, the way things were working out. But then I looked at that tiny backseat and those crazy wigs and I thought it was just all too impossible. Such a small place to hide—and under a pile of wigs? I said no. Ricky shrugged and said, "So, okay, we'll do it another time."

We went into my living room and talked about plans for a future escape. Ricky suggested that we could do it on the transit road. He said that I could hide in the woods at some point, and he would stop quickly while I climbed into the backseat. I reminded him that stopping on the transit road was not allowed and that armed guards and police cars were everywhere.

Ricky shrugged and said, "Okay," and then began to talk about how I might get away by swimming from shore to a seaplane waiting on the Baltic Sea. Or how I might swim underwater with diving gear and a cartridge in my hand that would propel me along. He also talked about using a helicopter that would lift me out of Hungary and carry me across the border to Austria. All crazy ideas.

The handball player never said a word. He was the chauffeur and he looked scared.

Ricky and I talked for a long time, but we didn't decide anything concrete. They finally drove off into the night.

Later I learned that if I had hidden under the wigs in the Saab, I would have made it across the border. They were not searched and they went right through.

In August, Schmidt and his friend Wolfgang Blume, the ex-boxer, flew to Budapest for a track meet, hoping that perhaps Bruch would be there with some new plan for an escape. Bruch wasn't there.

But there were others—many others—who were serious about helping Schmidt to escape. By this time, Verschoth had begun working on a story for *Sports Illustrated* about Schmidt's plight. She had first learned details of his situation from her old friend Klaus Blume of *Die Welt*, in the spring of 1985. She then convinced her editors that the story was worth pursuing for the magazine.

She had begun her reporting by telephoning Bruch at his home in Malmö, Sweden. He told her briefly about his visits to East Germany and about contacts he had made with Amnesty International on Schmidt's behalf. He agreed to meet Verschoth for dinner on July 11, 1985, at the Hotel St. Jörgen in Malmö. She arrived on schedule and spent two days in Malmö without seeing Ricky Bruch at all. She interviewed his mother. The woman knew nothing of her son's whereabouts. However, she invited Verschoth to her house and proudly showed her a huge display of her son's trophies as well as a larger-than-life size painting of Ricky wearing a buckskin suit with fringes.

Fortunately, there were sources for Verschoth's story other than the wayward Swede. At a dual meet between the GDR and Great Britain in Birmingham, England, early in July of '85, Verschoth interviewed a reputable East German coach, Wolfgang Meier, who was coaching the great sprinter Marita Koch and later married her when she retired. Meier offered this opinion of Schmidt: "He was so stupid. He was going around saying, 'I am a Californian.' You don't do that in the GDR." She interviewed the journalist Klaus Blume again and gleaned all the information he had, including the groundless rumor—probably Stasi-planted—that Schmidt had been seen waving his flare pistol in an East Berlin pub and proclaiming, "I am going to shoot my way into the West."

Klaus Blume put Verschoth in touch with Peter Walter and Marlene Heinz in Hamburg. Frau Heinz gave her this account of Schmidt's state of mind in the summer of '85: "He has become a very angry man. He can't accept what they have done to him. Even his sister Bettina says, 'You can't talk to him anymore. You can't have a conversation. There is nothing to talk about except his problem.' His mother says, 'As long as he is still here, he won't have peace.' There is a close relationship between Wolfgang and his mother. His mother stands between father and son as a buffer. His father tells him, 'It's high time for you to accept the situation. You have a better life here than most!' But for Wolfgang, there is nothing but out! *Out! Out!* We have twenty-six family members in the GDR. Only Wolfgang wants out. He is used to getting whatever he wants. He is spoiled."

Then, late in the summer, it was arranged through a coded phone call from Peter Walter to Schmidt in East Berlin that on September 14, 1985, Verschoth could meet the subject of her inquiries in the lobby of the Western-style Palasthotel on Karl-Liebknecht-Strasse in the heart of East Berlin.

Peter had simply said there was a journalist who wanted to interview me. I didn't want an interview, I wanted help. But I was happy to be meeting somebody who might bring some ideas about how to get me out. I expected a lot from this meeting because she was a stranger who was interested in my fate.

They passed each other in the hotel lobby and Schmidt whispered, "Meet me outside at the white Lada." They drove the short distance through the city to Mont Klamotte, the tree-covered hill made from postwar rubble. They went into the woods and sat on a bench. Dusk was falling and it grew quite cool. Every time a bird stirred in the trees behind them, they turned nervously. Schmidt implored Verschoth to help him, speaking softly and hurriedly as if he were afraid he would be caught before he finished.

"When Ricky Bruch visited me, it was one of the most beautiful days of my life," he said. "But I can't afford to be seen with you or they'll put me back in jail. What are you trying to do? Write an article about me? You'll only get me arrested again."

Verschoth said that it was necessary to write about him in the West, to keep his name before the public, to let the world know how badly he had been treated. She said she had brought a camera to take a picture of him for *Sports Illustrated*.

He was alarmed at this. "No! You can't take my picture. You cannot write that you met me. You cannot say that I want out! But I must get out! *Out!* They're killing me here. Please do something. Can you find one of those gangs to smuggle me out? It costs money, I know. But Ricky has money, doesn't he? From his movie?"

Words were bursting out in bunches. Verschoth calmly told him that Ricky was broke, that he was not competing at this time, that he could do nothing to help. Schmidt abruptly changed the subject.

"You could hire a helicopter with a red cross on it that could carry me across."

Verschoth said, "They'll shoot you down."

"They don't shoot down the Red Cross. I want out. Just out, *out!* Are you going to leave me here until I'm fifty years old?"

He rushed on, veering from one disconnected subject to the next, first complaining that he was only given children to coach, then telling her excitedly how he had lost twelve pounds in solitary confinement but that he had gained back ten pounds now, then relating the story of an East German soccer player, Lutz Eigendorf, who had defected to the West and then was killed in a mysterious car accident a few years after he had left the GDR.

"What would prevent them from having a truck run into me?" Schmidt whispered. "It would be the perfect solution. They'd be rid of me."

A moment later, a young man in a black leather jacket ambled by on a path below them. Schmidt froze. He said nothing until the passerby was out of sight, then whispered, "When I see one of those jackets, I'm always careful. The Stasi have listening devices that enable them to hear a conversation from four hundred meters away. He can hear what we are saying right now." By the time he drove Verschoth back to the Palasthotel, it was dark. He had now become unnaturally calm, silent, and resigned. She promised to do anything she could to help him.

Back in New York a week later, she reported the conversation to her editors at *Sports Illustrated*. She asked them if it would be possible for the magazine to put up money—perhaps as much as

$40,000—so that a professional escape gang might arrange to spring Schmidt from the GDR. The managing editor, Mark Mulvoy, was somewhat interested, envisioning a series of articles in the magazine and perhaps a book later. "All that for forty thousand dollars," he said. He told Verschoth that he would discuss the idea with the corporate editor of Time, Inc. That was September 19. On October 14, Mulvoy summoned Verschoth and told her that she should not overtly involve either herself or the magazine in any escape attempt by Schmidt. It was a criminal act under East German law, and Time, Inc. could not formally support illegal activities by any of its employees. The managing editor said that once Schmidt was in the West, *Sports Illustrated* might be interested in buying his story.

Verschoth said, "I have a mission and I can't stop now." Mulvoy said, "I know you have a mission."

Verschoth next contacted the late Horst Dassler, the powerful president of the Adidas Shoe Company in Herzogenaurach, West Germany, in hopes that he would either sponsor or help find someone else to finance Schmidt's defection. Dassler was sympathetic, but he pointed out that Adidas supplied shoes and sportswear to all of the countries in Eastern Europe, and he said, "If I got involved, I would have a lot of trouble."

Dassler's refusal to help was a blow, but by that time Verschoth had found a likely angel in New York to underwrite the great escape. Bud Greenspan of Cappy Productions was a talented, highly respected, and successful sport-film producer who had produced several official Olympic films. When Dassler said no, Greenspan promised Verschoth that he would put up $25,000 himself for the rescue mission. He wanted to make a film about Schmidt.

With money in hand, Verschoth plunged deeper into the world of Wolfgang Schmidt. What had begun as an impersonal, but compelling journalistic assignment had turned into something very different. She now found herself deeply committed to do everything she could to help free a man she had come to like and admire very much.

ON DECEMBER 3, 1985, KLAUS BLUME OF *DIE WELT*
introduced Verschoth to another West German journalist from
Frankfurt who had contacts that might be of use in breaking
Schmidt free.

The Frankfurt journalist had been involved in an abortive attempt in 1979 to smuggle three East German relatives from Hungary into Austria. They had tried to escape by simply climbing
over one of the barbed wire fences along the border. Someone
touched an alarm and they had all been caught. The East Germans
were sent home and put in prison there, while the Frankfurt man
was sentenced to eight months in a Hungarian jail at Vac, not
far from Budapest. While he was in prison, the journalist had
made friends with a Swiss and a Dutchman who were serving
time, too.

The Dutchman was in jail for smuggling antiques out of Hungary. The Swiss was serving five months for something a little
more altruistic—aiding an illegal border crossing. He had been
caught escorting a young East German woman across the
Hungarian-Yugoslav border with a phony passport that he had

altered in Zurich. He had been caught because the woman's boyfriend, an Austrian, had phoned her repeatedly at the Intercontinental Hotel from Vienna the day before the escape, incessantly inquiring whether she had met her rescuer yet. Since international calls were routinely monitored at all the big Hungarian hotels, border security men had been alerted to the escape attempt and were waiting for the woman and the Swiss when they arrived.

The Swiss was a restorer of antiques by trade, and he earned extra money by the delicate art of changing passport photos and applying ersatz stamps for escapees from the East. Before the snafu that had put him in jail, he had successfully smuggled two other East Germans and a Hungarian to freedom.

On January 15, 1986, Verschoth and Peter Walter, Gretel Schmidt's cousin, met in Düsseldorf with the Dutchman, the Swiss, and the Frankfurt journalist. (Some people involved in this caper preferred not to be identified by name since they committed punishable crimes, such as altering passports, in their efforts to free Wolfgang Schmidt.) The group hatched a plot that called for Schmidt to apply for a tourist visa to Budapest for the Easter holiday. Once that was approved, the Dutchman would find a volunteer closely resembling Schmidt who would travel to Budapest, give Schmidt his passport, and then report its "loss" after Schmidt had successfully used it to cross the border.

One problem with this plan was that the Hungarian police routinely interrogated people with "lost" passports as if they were criminals, keeping them in custody for as much as three weeks while they were cruelly grilled. If the owner of a "lost" passport broke down and confessed he had aided in an illegal escape, he faced months, maybe years, in jail. For such a high risk, the Dutchman estimated that they would have to pay their volunteer passport-loser a lump sum of at least $10,000 plus $100 for every day spent in jail.

Despite its drawbacks, the conspirators decided to pursue this plan. On January 29, Peter Walter informed them that Schmidt had indeed gotten permission to visit Budapest from March 28 to April 1. He would travel with an East Berlin tourist group via a charter plane.

Early in February, the Dutchman introduced the group to the Wolfgang Schmidt look-alike who would "lose" his passport in Budapest. He was a nervous, boyish-looking fellow, twenty-five years old, standing about 5'11" tall. To make matters worse, the young man had a girlfriend in Budapest. This was unimportant, except for the fact that, in the event of his arrest, she could also be picked up and used as a hostage to force her boyfriend to confess his crime.

The Swiss had never been keen on this plan, and now he set out to convince his colleagues that it was both foolish and dangerous to try. He said that he could just as easily alter a real passport for Schmidt's use. He had done it before, and though it was complicated, it was less dangerous.

His plan worked like this: The Swiss would obtain for a fee the passport of a cooperative citizen from a Western European country. He would then exchange the citizen's photograph for Schmidt's. He would then forge the proper Hungarian border stamp in the passport to make it seem that it had been stamped when the bearer entered Hungary from Austria at an earlier date. The passport would then be carried into Hungary by someone with a legal passport, then be given to Schmidt, who would then simply board an Austria-bound train and show the passport at the border as if he were a bona fide tourist returning from a short visit to Hungary.

The major problem with this scheme was the fact that Hungarian authorities changed their entrance stamp from time to time. When the Swiss had successfully worked this ploy before—seven years before—the changes in the stamp had occurred quite infrequently. They were doing it more often now. Therefore, someone had to make the trip from Austria to Hungary at a time close to the actual date of the escape in order to have a proper, timely stamp for the Swiss to duplicate in Schmidt's phony passport. The border stamp was an intricate and complex mix of numbers and tiny changeable symbols, and it always took time for the Swiss to do a precise duplication.

With $2,000 from Bud Greenspan's contribution, the Swiss "rented" a passport. On February 24, an Austrian friend went to

Budapest by train from Vienna in order to get the proper border stamp in his passport. The Swiss then went to work duplicating the stamp in the "rented" passport. Verschoth was to bring it into Budapest on March 30, deliver it to Schmidt, and accompany him back to Vienna on the train.

From time to time during this period, Verschoth had been asked by her editors if she was making any progress on her "mission." Assuming that they had no objection to her helping Schmidt as long as the magazine was not directly involved, she had kept them informed generally, and now, at the end of February, she told them of the new rescue plan in detail. To her great surprise, she was told that Time, Inc. lawyers and editorial executives wanted her to cease all contact with Wolfgang Schmidt. She was told to inform her colleagues that she was no longer a part of the plot, and that she should not go to Budapest to assist in Schmidt's Easter escape.

On March 1, Verschoth flew to Hamburg so she could personally explain her situation to Schmidt's relatives and her fellow conspirators. She carried with her a valise full of Western clothes supplied by Mac Wilkins. They were to be given to Schmidt to replace his East German clothing when he took the train out of Budapest. Because Verschoth could not be there on March 30, and because the Swiss could no longer get into Hungary due to his status as an ex-convict there, someone else had to be found to deliver the passport. The Swiss suggested two friends of his living in Vienna, an Austrian citizen and his Hungarian wife. The conspiracy now began to use code names in its dealings by phone. Schmidt was Amadeus. Verschoth was Annegret. The couple in Vienna became Klaus and Rosi.

Verschoth returned to New York and the plot continued afoot. On March 25, three days before Schmidt was to leave East Berlin, she talked by phone with Klaus in Vienna. He was optimistic: "Everything is okay. There is no need to be concerned about anything."

He was quite wrong.

The Swiss had delivered the passport with its forged stamps to Vienna on March 27. Rosi had just returned that day from visiting her parents in Budapest, and her passport had been stamped both coming and going. They compared the stamps in the two passports and to their great chagrin, found that they had been changed—not the numbers and not the design, but the color of the ink.

There was no point in contacting Schmidt in East Berlin. If he canceled his trip at the last moment, it would be suspicious. The next day, he arrived in Budapest, assuming that freedom was just around the corner.

The trip to Budapest had easily been arranged with a travel agency that specialized in groups. They got the visa and everything, no problem. I had asked Wolfgang Blume to travel with me and we stayed together at the hotel. In the evening, at the hour I had to leave to meet the people from Vienna, I told my old friend, "Wolfgang, I have to do something tonight that I can only do alone."

He looked sad. I had not told him anything about the plan, but he wanted desperately to leave the East, too, and I am sure he knew what I was up to. I told him as gently as I could, "It is possible that I won't return. It would be best if you knew nothing about the circumstances."

He touched my arm. "Man, please let me come with you."

I said, "I'm sorry, old friend, I cannot."

Klaus and Rosi had driven to Budapest from Vienna that day. The plan was to meet Schmidt at the famous restaurant the Mathias Cellar. This was a cavernous, kitschy place filled with singing tourists and strolling violinists. Tables were packed with Englishmen bellowing drinking songs and Japanese taking pictures with flashbulbs. Schmidt arrived first and took a table. Rosi, a spunky woman who was pregnant at the time, arrived alone to give Schmidt the bad news.

I waited for her for what seemed like a long time. I was quite afraid. At last she came and sat down at my table. We ordered wine. She told me they had changed the stamp at the border and that I couldn't leave as planned. She explained to me that we would have to wait until I could get another visa to Budapest—which was, perhaps, a long time. I must admit, I felt very mixed about this—partly relieved, mostly disappointed. We went for a walk when we left the restaurant. She explained to me the plan that would be in effect the next time. She said that in the morning, she and Klaus and I would make a tour of my escape route so I would know next time where everything was. I asked her if it might be possible to take my friend Wolfgang Blume with me next time. She was dubious, and later we decided it would be difficult enough to get one man out, let alone two.

When I left Rosi and returned to the hotel, Blume was standing on the street outside, looking as melancholy as if he had lost his best friend. When he saw me, he rushed up and embraced me and cried, "Oh, how happy I am that you came back!"

I was not entirely happy to be back, of course, but I couldn't tell him anything.

The next morning, Klaus and Rosi took Schmidt to the Budapest railroad station and showed him exactly what they would do to prepare for his next attempt. They would bring the suitcase full of Western clothes—some of them Wilkins's—and put it in a luggage locker at the station. Inside the bag would be a wallet containing the Swiss passport with Schmidt's photograph, a visa, and—God willing—the proper border stamps, as well as Western currency, phony photographs of loved ones, and a round-trip train ticket from Zurich to Budapest and back with the Zurich-Budapest portion used. They had seen to it that the locker was next to a men's room with a shower where Schmidt could change into a Western suit, shirt, tie, and shoes. He was to leave his clothing from East Berlin in the luggage locker, then board train No. 466, which would leave Budapest at four-fifteen P.M. and arrive in Vienna at eight-fifteen P.M. A seat would be reserved in first class in the name of the owner of the passport he was carrying. On this morning, they guided Schmidt to the luggage locker, the men's room, and the platform the train would leave from. He seemed uneasy at first. They suggested that perhaps the next time, he should take a tranquilizer before the escape began so he would not appear so nervous. He said he did not like to use such drugs, but he grew more calm as the tour proceeded. When he returned to East Berlin, he was feeling quite confident now that he was familiar with so many details.

It was almost four months before Schmidt was able to get another exit visa to Budapest. At the sports club, his boss asked, "What? Again Budapest?" Schmidt replied, "I have really come to like that city."

The date was July 15, and this time he believed the great escape was certain to succeed.

When I left from Schönefeld Airport, I said good-bye to everything. I was thinking, Now I'm on my way, now the plan will work, I know it will. I was so optimistic and I wasn't at all unhappy to be leaving my home, my family, my life, in the GDR. I was sure I wouldn't be homesick. I had packed all my valuables and stored them in a safe place that my parents would find. My mother knew all about my plan, but we had kept it from my father. I was taking only the most essential things to Budapest. I was going to leave my suitcase behind in the hotel room. Everything was ready—and especially I was ready.

The preparations by his fellow conspirators had gone smoothly. Verschoth had arrived, having decided to keep an eye on the operation. Klaus and Rosi had gone to Budapest early in July to collect the proper border stamp. They had sent this to the Swiss in Zurich, who had used Greenspan's money to rent another passport and gotten a Hungarian visa for it. The stamp was ready to be applied, but this time, they had decided to wait until the last possible moment to ascertain the color of the ink and the exact order of the coded numbers. On July 15, Verschoth took a train from Zurich to Vienna and gave the ticket to Rosi, who went on to Budapest on the same train so the first half of the Zurich-Budapest round-trip was used. Verschoth flew back to Switzerland. Klaus drove to Budapest to meet Rosi. They were to telephone Verschoth and the Swiss in Zurich on July 16 with a coded message telling which color and which numbers to use. By that time, Schmidt was already in Budapest, waiting to be sprung.

At nine P.M. on the given day, a shocked Rosi phoned Verschoth; "It is impossible. They have substituted half-moons for triangles in the design. Everything is upside down. We cannot use the stamp at all."

There was no way to forge another stamp in the short time— July 16 to July 19—that Schmidt could stay in Budapest. The rescue had to be aborted again. Rosi said to Verschoth, "It is important that you come. Amadeus needs cheering up."

Verschoth flew to Budapest on the evening of July 17 and was met at the airport by Klaus and Rosi. In the backseat of their car sat Schmidt, looking stricken. Verschoth embraced him, and they all drove to a small, dark park near the Hotel Forum where she was staying. They tried to cheer him up. Then Klaus and Rosi left, and Verschoth and Schmidt sat on a bench and talked for hours. He had caught a cold and was so hoarse that he could barely speak, but he rambled on and on about how desperately he wanted to leave East Germany. He told her of a dream he often had that he could fly across The Wall. He told her that the jeans he was wearing had been bought ten years earlier in Montreal during the Olympics, that he had bought thirteen pairs at the time and this was the last of them. He told her that maybe they should abandon the forged passports and simply rent a helicopter to fly him out across the Elbe River where it forms the border between East and West Germany. He told her, "When I left Berlin, my mother said, 'It won't work. You'll be back.' Now I'll have to apply for a visa again. Again Budapest? What will they say about that?"

They met again the next day in a park on the Danube. Verschoth took pictures of him because they had run out of passport photos. It was sunny and hot and sticky. They walked on the promenade above the great river. His voice was a gravelly whisper, but he continued to talk almost nonstop. He was worried about what would happen to his house after he defected: "I have three rooms, with a small child's room and an entrance hall. There is a garden. When I come home, I work in the garden. I mow the lawn. What will happen to it?"

He was worried about whether he should apply for a permanent exit visa again: "The last time I did that, they put me in solitary and I had to sleep on a bench as hard as these in the park. If I put in for an exit visa, they'll fire me from my coaching job. They'll make me an enemy of the state again. They'll take my salary, my house. I won't have money to live on."

They went to the Hotel Forum for lunch. He drank hot lemon juice for his sore throat, then ordered a mixed grill and a beer. They ate and talked, and at three P.M., Verschoth left for the airport. She promised that she would visit him on August 15 when she would be covering a track meet in West Berlin.

She was as good as her word. The day was dark and rainy, and the track meet was held under swampy conditions. When it was over, about ten-thirty P.M., Verschoth drove in a downpour through Checkpoint Charlie and on to the Palasthotel where she was to meet Schmidt at midnight at the end of a driveway leading to the hotel. She went from the lobby into the rain at the appointed hour with an umbrella and was startled to see a man follow her out and stand watching her as she hurried down the driveway. Schmidt was not there, and frightened, she began to walk toward the lights of Karl-Liebknecht-Strasse. Now she saw another man, a big man, walking toward her in the dark. She hesitated, then realized it was Schmidt. He reached out his huge arms and embraced her. Then he took her to his car. This time he was driving a silver Volkswagen Golf, which a friendly Stasi from SC Dynamo had arranged for him to buy to replace the Lada 1600, which had begun to deteriorate.

He said, "I'm going to take you on a sight-seeing tour." He

drove her through East Berlin's gleaming streets to Stahlheimer Strasse, showed her his boyhood apartment building, then gave her a complete zig-by-zag replay of the route the Stasi had chased him over on that fateful day of July 2, 1982. At the corner of Indira-Gandhi-Strasse and Bizet-Strasse, he got out of the car and pointed to the spot where the arrest had occurred. Then he drove to a large parking lot, pulled into a tight space between two cars, and turned off his headlights.

"I have to talk to you about my future," he said. He spoke for two hours, explaining how worried he was that he might get to the West and then have no way of supporting himself, let alone a chance to pursue a full-time career as a discus thrower.

"What can I live on?" asked Schmidt. "If I leave now, I have no profession to fall back on. I only have one more year of studies left here, and then I'll get my diploma as a sports educator. Perhaps if I stay to finish my studies, I'll have a way of making a living, at least a piece of paper to show I am qualified."

They talked until three A.M. before they parted, but Schmidt was back at the Palasthotel by ten A.M. to pick her up for a drive to his home in Hohen Neuendorf, about fifteen miles beyond the city limits. It was a clean, sunny day after the rain, and even the streets of East Berlin looked fresh and pretty. They drove through green rolling countryside, passing through an old village here and there.

Just before they reached the house, Schmidt confided to Verschoth that, despite all his doubt, he had decided to make another run for freedom through Budapest. "It is as if a mighty voice from above has told me, 'You must go.'" he said.

Schmidt's mother arrived from the nearby summer house she and Ernst had owned for so many years. Schmidt had invited her to sit in on this planning session with Verschoth. By contrast, his father had been told nothing at all about any of Wolfgang's potential escapes. It wasn't that they didn't trust him. They were afraid he would rant on and on about keeping the family together. They didn't need that.

Schmidt told his mother that he wanted to escape as soon as he could, that the Budapest route was the best way to do it, and that he would apply for another vacation visa to Budapest from September 13 through 17. They discussed the scheme, the timing, the details, the dangers. After a time, the discussion turned to more mundane matters. What might happen to his house if he defected? Did the state own it or did he?

Gretel said, "You will probably lose it. When Ernst and I were married in 1953, my aunt Berta told me, 'Don't ever buy anything. Don't get a home in the East. Go to the West where you can keep what you have.' That was good advice."

Schmidt protested, "I paid for the house myself, didn't I? And all of this furniture was given to me by the sports club. It is all my property."

His mother said, "Well, just think of so many who had simply to leave everything behind when they went West. They suffered and maybe you will have to, too."

Schmidt shrugged, "So be it. The time I spent in prison made a man of me."

Gretel patted her son's huge hand. "Sometimes you are still a child."

Then she turned to Verschoth and said, "Do you think it will work this time?" Her face flushed and her eyes filled with tears. "Don't you think it will be too dangerous?" Her voice broke and she wept.

Gently, Wolfgang told her that he had to try it. Gretel nodded. She embraced Verschoth tightly before she left.

Now Schmidt told Verschoth that he was going to bring a girlfriend, a nineteen-year-old waitress from Zwickau, with him to Budapest. "It will make it seem less suspicious," he said. "I know I can't tell her anything and I will have to leave her behind at the hotel. That'll be rotten of me, but it will be better for her to know nothing when she returns to Berlin without me."

Verschoth flew back to Switzerland that afternoon. Now she and the Swiss had to come up with yet another passport. The first they had gotten from a man who sold exotic fish and needed cash to bolster his business. The second they obtained through a tattoo artist who had a friend who needed money. They had paid $2,000 to each of the donors. Thanks to Bud Greenspan, money was not a problem. But finding someone to take the money in return for his passport was not so easy—especially finding the very, very large someone who matched Schmidt's proportions. Unlike American passports, which list only gender and date of birth, European passports also include the owner's height and weight. This time, Verschoth came up with the idea of looking for an athlete who specialized in events similar to Schmidt's.

On August 26, she traveled to Stuttgart for the European track-and-field championships. Through binoculars from the press box, she scrutinized competitors for a clone of Schmidt. She settled on two men, one a decathlete, the other a shot-putter. After studying them up close, she decided the shot-putter was the better choice. After his competition was over on August 30, she found him in the Athletes' Village and told him that she wished to discuss an extremely confidential matter with him.

She said she was trying to help an East German athlete defect, a discus thrower who had been banned from the team and had served time in prison. The shot-putter brightened: "Of course, I know who you are talking about. How is he? I was always one of his fans."

She replied, "He must get out. He is very unhappy." She explained that she needed a passport and asked the shot-putter if he knew of any retired athletes close to Schmidt's size who might be willing to help.

The shot-putter said, "I can't think of anybody right now." He paused, then blurted, "Ah, but I will gladly give you my passport."

Verschoth gazed at the young man. Tears filled her eyes. His sudden act of generosity overwhelmed her, and she couldn't speak for a moment. Then she said, "But you don't know who I am. You have never seen me before and I have nothing to prove you should even trust me."

He hesitated for a moment, studying her, then said, "Stay here. I will bring my passport back in twenty minutes." He refused to take any money.

Back in Zurich the Swiss went to work changing the photographs, and Verschoth, wishing to make absolutely sure the plan would work, traveled by train to Budapest to collect the all-important border stamps and to use up one-half of the round-trip ticket. The date was September 8, five days before Schmidt was to arrive in Budapest. Verschoth stayed overnight, then bought a new one-way ticket the next day and passed through the rigorous document checks at the border. She noted each detail so she could tell Schmidt precisely what to expect.

Back in Zurich that night, she and the Swiss were elated to see that the stamp was the same one he had already copied, only the color of the ink had changed. It all seemed to be working so smoothly. But as Verschoth and the Swiss raised glasses of bourbon to toast what seemed to be imminent success, the phone in his apartment rang. It was Peter Walter calling from Hamburg with an urgent message from "Amadeus": "The birthday party has to be postponed. The weather is too bad."

Walter said that no one knew what had happened. It was too dangerous to try to get more information from East Berlin by phone. He urged Verschoth to go to the city and visit Bettina. The next day, September 10, Verschoth reached Schmidt's sister by phone and said, "This is 'Annegret.' May I come to your party tomorrow?"

Bettina responded quite cheerfully, "Oh, hello. Yes, please come at six P.M." She gave her address.

Verschoth flew to West Berlin, crossed Checkpoint Charlie, found Bettina's apartment, and learned that Schmidt apparently had no serious problems. His vacation in Budapest had been delayed because he had been summoned by a professor to the German College for Physical Culture in Leipzig to make up work on a late term paper. Wolfgang would try to make the trip to Budapest at another time.

There seemed no reason not to believe this. Verschoth returned to the West that night, phoned Peter Walter to tell him what she had learned, and then called the shot-putter to ask if they could keep his passport a bit longer. He agreed without hesitation.

On September 17, Verschoth had to leave Europe for Seoul and a two-week assignment for *Sports Illustrated* covering the Asian Games. On September 22, she received a distressed call in

Seoul from the Swiss. Marlene Heinz's husband had phoned him, explaining that he was making the call because his wife was too distraught to talk.

The message was that Schmidt had been picked up that day by the Stasi. They had interrogated him for four hours. His mother and father had been summoned, too. The Stasi knew every detail about his plan to escape.

IT WAS NOT UNTIL JANUARY 3, 1989, THAT ERNST Schmidt actually found the bug behind the wood paneling at the house at Emile-Zola-Strasse 30. By that time, Wolfgang had been out of East Germany for over a year. Ernst had retired. He and Gretel had been living in Wolfgang's house full-time for a year.

They had suspected ever since the Stasi arranged to finish the house that they might have installed an apparatus to keep an ear on Wolfgang. Ernst had kept looking and finally found the bug while he was making a systematic examination of electrical outlets. There it was, in the outlet next to the dining table. It was a cheap-looking little device, with an antenna wire snaking up the inner wall to the roof. Across Emile-Zola-Strasse, in a small clearing, was an abandoned gardener's shed. It was there, they figured, that the recording machine had been concealed, picking up every sound in the house for the four years Wolfgang lived there after his release from prison.

Ernst, the feisty old socialist, was even more enraged by this invasion of privacy than he had been by the one in the apartment on Stahlheimer Strasse. He was a retired country squire now who spent his days puttering with power tools and gardening. What right—or what reason—did they have to listen to every cough and hiccup that went on in *his* life? He waited six weeks before deciding what he should do.

He finally took his objections straight to the top. He called the office of Egon Krenz, the head of Internal Security for police and for sport, who later served briefly as chief of state after the Honecker regime fell in November of 1989. Ernst demanded an audience with Krenz. He got one with Krenz's personal assistant, one H. G. Schubert, who courteously took a letter addressed to Krenz along with a photograph Ernst had taken of the bug. Ernst told Schubert that he assumed that Rudi Mittig, deputy in charge of intelligence, would certainly know all about the bug. That was March 2. On March 16, Ernst and Gretel were received by Mittig himself in the guesthouse of the Council of Ministers. They sat with Mittig at a table set with Meissen porcelain and fine silver and ate cake and fruit and sipped coffee. Mittig brought out the photograph of the bug during the repast and told Ernst, "This is very primitive. We wouldn't use anything like this."

Ernst replied, "It's been there since 1983. You didn't have anything better then."

Mittig pulled a long face, then shook his head. "I can only guess that it must be something planted by Western espionage."

Ernst could only laugh. The meeting lasted more than two hours, but Mittig never admitted any complicity in the planting of the bug. Later, after The Wall had come down, Ernst marched in a protest parade in front of Stasi headquarters carrying a hand-made sign with a crude cartoon drawing he had made of the bug with the words: "Bug Behind Wood Paneling." He told onlookers as he marched, "They listened to us day and night."

And on February 22, 1990, Ernst received a letter from the military prosecuting attorney of the GDR in answer to his earlier letters of protest over the bug. The prosecuting attorney wrote: "I have to inform you that the electronic device you found in your house was definitely the receiver for an acoustic room-surveillance installation that was placed and operated by the former Department for State Security. According to our investigations, this unconstitutional acoustic surveillance of your house was conducted upon the personal order of the former minister Erich Mielke in connection with the criminal proceedings against your son, Wolfgang."

Mielke had been charged with high treason, the attorney told Ernst, and he added, "Your reports and your testimony will be added to the evidence in the preliminary proceedings against Erich Mielke."

Of course, the device had already done its dirty work. It had been planted in the wall between the living room and bedroom, and the August morning that Schmidt, Verschoth, and Gretel had so thoroughly discussed the details of Schmidt's escape through Budapest, it had been transmitting every word direct to the Stasi listening post across the road.

The secret police had responded to revelations from the bug on September 17.

I was at work early in the morning in an office I used at the SC Dynamo training center. Suddenly a man entered the room without knocking and showed his ID card—Department for State Security. "Would you please follow me?" he said.

He drove me to the Sporthotel, and there waiting for me in a hotel room was Wiedemann.

He shook hands quite warmly and said in a friendly voice, "We haven't seen each other for a long time. How are you doing?" I replied just fine, thank you very much, and he asked other things about my house and my work and the children I was coaching. I spoke as lightly as I could, but as the small talk went on and on, I became increasingly tense. After all, I was planning to escape soon. What the hell did he want?

Then, suddenly, he made it clear what he wanted. "Why don't you stop planning to leave the GDR?" he demanded.

I tried to sound calm. "Who wants to leave the GDR?" I said. "I have a good life here."

He ignored that. "What journalists are you in contact with in nonsocialist countries? Or to give you a hint, what journalists are you in contact with from the USA?"

I said, "I don't know what you are talking about."

He said only, "Anita . . ." He paused as if he were waiting for me to supply the last name. I said nothing.

We talked quite a while about whether or not I had contacts with the West and whether or not I was trying to escape. Then Wiedemann looked at his watch. He said, "I'm sorry, I have to go to the bathroom." He stayed in there for a while and it suddenly hit me: There was a tape recorder in there picking up everything we were discussing and he had gone in to change the tape.

When he came out, he said, "You know, Wolfgang, if you want to leave, you can only do so by applying for an exit visa. Officially. We want to protect you from leaving the GDR illegally, you see?"

I said nothing, and he went on in his haughty way, "We are trying to protect you from breaking the law. We do not want you to leave us illegally. Least of all do we want you to leave us in a spectacular escape with help from America."

He let that sit there in the air. And then the door opened and a second Stasi came into the room. Behind him were my parents.

Ernst and Gretel had been interrogated in another room while Wiedemann worked on Wolfgang. Both claimed total ignorance of any scheme to free their son. Of course, his mother knew about the Budapest plan from the discussion with Schmidt and Verschoth. His father was completely in the dark.

They sat there in the room with me, listening to Wiedemann. They said as little as possible, and the Stasi pig repeated again that it was against my own interests to try to escape illegally, that I should apply for an official exit visa if I was so determined to leave.

After the big shot was done, we were allowed to leave. We raved to each other how the Stasi had done it to us again; put us in separate rooms and questioned us so it would be my parents' word against mine. They were as bad as the Nazis.

The escape attempt from Budapest was now scrapped for good, but Schmidt was frightened at the idea of applying for a formal exit visa. He went through a couple of weeks of painful internal debate with himself and angry external debate with his father. The two of them had long fought with passion over the merits and demerits of socialism, but the battle over Wolfgang's departure threatened to doom their relationship forever.

He wanted to keep the family together, and I couldn't understand this. He must have been blind. But of course, he was blind! Wasn't he the one who had always approved of The Wall? Wasn't he the one who stood guard while the bastards put up The Wall? Wasn't he the one who did whatever the party said?

Even after I got out of jail, he hadn't changed. He'd say, "You should be happy, you still have a better life than most people here."

Instead of discussing with me what I should do to get out to the West, he fought the idea all the way. He should have realized that there was no way I could come to a happy end staying in the East. He should have helped, he should have said, "My boy, you must go about it like this. . . . Here is the best way to get to the West, here is the best way to manage your life once you are there."

But he gave me no such help. Oh, I know that he wanted to keep the family together. That was a healthy, normal attitude. But it didn't help me or make me happy. For me, there was no future in the GDR.

He was so tough about everything. When I talked about writing formally to the Department of the Interior, he told me, "If you apply for an exit visa, you don't have to show your face in our home anymore!"

He talked as if it were my fault my life was so shitty. *"Jeder ist seines Glückes Schmied"*—everyone is the architect of his own fortune. I had to listen to those goddamned slogans while there I was, trapped in this barbed-wire cage of a country!

I felt that he defended that whole bunch of assholes, and I could have hit him in the mouth!

Ah, forgive my vocabulary about all this, but the pigs pumped me so full of hatred I couldn't talk any other way. I never used words such as *pigs, asshole, shit,* filthy language like that before the pigs got ahold of me. They were so despicable. And of course, it was they who caused the terrible battles between my father and me. They caused all that pain we both felt. *They* were the enemy, not my father, not me!

Schmidt finally decided that he had no choice but to apply for an exit visa through official channels. That very same action had resulted in great pain in prison, but Wiedemann made it seem as if it was the only hope he had of reaching freedom. Wolfgang asked him point-blank, "Aren't you going to lock me up again when I put my application in writing?" Wiedemann said, "No, the application will go its winding way."

My application had to be filed with the Department of the Interior. I went to my lawyer, Starkulla, and asked him how it was done. I figured since the lawyers all worked with the Stasi anyway, I might as well do it right from the start. He gave me some hints about how to write the letter.

On October 21, 1986, I wrote to the Department of the Interior:

"With this letter I submit my application for emigration from the GDR to the Federal Republic of Germany.

"Reason: I was in prison from July 1982 through October 1983. My expectations have not been met and my hopes that had been raised were not fulfilled.

"I ask you to let me go. Wolfgang Schmidt."

And as Wiedemann had promised, the visa application began its winding way through the bureaucracy.

At first, those guys at the Department of the Interior gave me a lot of soft soap, asking me so nicely, "Won't you tell us why you want to leave? Are you quite sure you want to go? Exactly what has been so bad for you?"

I told them, "You should get in touch with Oberstleutnant Wiedemann and ask him to show you my whole file, what led to my arrest and what happened after I was arrested. That will explain to you very nicely why I want to leave."

Of course, the Stasi released nothing. So I told the whole story in a nutshell. After that, I began to receive notices to appear for certain hearings. "We ask you to appear on December 4, 1986, at 1 P.M. at the District Council of Oranienburg, Department of the Interior, Room 27A"—notices such as that.

The man who usually saw me was named Hollatz. He was in charge of my case. He was a small man with a beard, calm and friendly. He couldn't help that he was in his position, it was only a job. He made me write and rewrite my résumé, explaining my background and my reasons for requesting an exit visa, three different times. There was always something he didn't like. Such as, he didn't like that I wrote I had been the subject of a shameful political trial. That, I had to take out.

I did everything I could to expedite my application. I went to the Council of State and submitted a petition. Along with it, I submitted the original résumé I had written telling of my real reasons for wishing to leave the GDR—*Sportverbot*, prison, the shameful trial. I wanted people on the Council of State to know all of these things. I wrote a letter to Erich Honecker, explaining my case at length. Neither the Council of State nor Honecker answered me. I wrote to Franz-Josef Strauss in Bavaria. He didn't answer either.

The whole thing was a fight, a hell of a fight. They never let me forget that they didn't trust me. Sometimes when I would leave the Department of the Interior after a hearing or a meeting, several cars pulled in behind me as I drove away and followed me through the city. Just to harass me, to keep me on edge.

His mother and father, too, were on edge. They had been called for interrogation and were asked if they agreed with Wolfgang's decision to apply for an exit visa. Gretel had replied, "We tried everything else, everything. We have no choice but to accept his decision." The interrogator asked Ernst if he thought his son could ever again compete at the same level as before. Ernst said sadly, "What do you expect after so many years? Maybe he can still throw a few meters, but never like before."

Weeks passed, then months. Every once in a while he would receive a notice—"We ask you to appear on Monday, January 12, 1987, at 1 P.M. at the District Council of Oranienburg, Department of Interior, Room 27A"—and he would appear for whatever purpose they wished. He continued coaching children at SC Dynamo and spent a great deal of his spare time with Wolfgang Blume, who was now the doorman at a discotheque called the Yucca Bar, not far from, the Schmidt family's apartment.

With his official visa application in the works, Schmidt had given no further thought to plans to escape. Then in June '87, Ricky Bruch appeared one more time with one more melodramatic scheme. Earlier, the Swede had phoned Verschoth in New York and asked for $12,000 to finance an escape plan he had hatched. He would not tell any details over the phone. Verschoth called Peter Walter in Hamburg to see what he knew of Bruch's scheme, and Walter told her that under no circumstances should anyone give Bruch any money because he was far too harebrained. Soon after that, the Swede turned up at Emile-Zola-Strasse 30.

This time, I was asleep in my bedroom on a bright sunny morning. The sun was shining into my bedroom, my window was wide open. Suddenly, I sensed that a huge shadow had moved in front of the sun. Startled, I opened my eyes, and there was Ricky standing at the window, grinning. Whenever I saw that crazy guy, my spirits went up, and I leaped out of bed and shouted, "Come inside, old friend! Hurry up! What is the news!"

We sat in the living room and shouted with joy and talked at the top of our voices. Of course, now we know that the Stasi got it all on tape, but we were babes in the woods then, and what an earful they got!

Ricky had another chauffeur with him, this time a rally driver, a Formula III race-car driver. On this day, he was behind the wheel of a souped-up Volkswagen. While I made breakfast for all of us, Ricky announced the details of his latest plot. That night at seven o'clock, I was to meet them at a restaurant at Stolpe in Mecklenburg, close to the border where the transit autobahn leads to Hamburg. I was to leave my car there and hide in the trunk of their Volkswagen, and they would drive me across the border.

I hesitated. The exit visa had been in the works for more than six months already. I didn't know when it might come through. I was very frustrated. I agreed to try it.

Late that afternoon I drove the hundred and thirty miles from Berlin to Stolpe, and when I arrived at seven P.M., they were waiting for me. It was quite dark already because a thunderstorm was approaching. The atmosphere was full of bad vibrations. I was losing interest in the whole project.

Ricky opened the trunk where I was supposed to hide. We studied the situation. Suddenly, the rally driver declared that the trunk was too dangerous. He said that he might have to crash the barriers at the border in order to get me through. He said that he was afraid that they would fire at the car from behind as we raced away and that bullets would penetrate the trunk door and kill me. He suggested the backseat would be safer. I got into the backseat and tried to lie on the floor. There was no way I could fit in there. I was more skeptical every moment. Finally, we decided to abandon it all as too risky.

I drove back to Berlin and they drove on to the border. When they got there, Ricky told me later, six men with machine guns were waiting. They searched the car from top to bottom. Obviously, they knew what we had planned to do.

On July 14, Wiedemann summoned Schmidt for an audience at the Sporthotel. His first question was the usual "How are you doing?"

Schmidt had no idea what the meeting was about and replied cautiously, "How do you think I'm doing?"

Wiedemann ignored the question and said, "Would you like something to drink, some juice?"

Schmidt said, "No, thank you."

The Stasi pretended to be offended. "You don't want to take anything from me anymore, is that it?"

"No, I'm just not thirsty."

Wiedemann shrugged, then said, "You are perhaps wondering why I've asked you here." Without pausing for a reply, he said in a calm, even voice, "I wish to tell you about your application for emigration."

He paused tantalizingly. Schmidt's heart thumped quickly and he feared Wiedemann was going to tell him that it had been canceled.

The Stasi went on quietly, "It has been approved."

Schmidt felt a wave of elation rush through his body, but he refused to show the Stasi any emotion. He stood stiffly, listening as Wiedemann went on, "We would prefer that you keep quiet about it and tell no one. There are still some required visits to certain officials, and the exact date of emigration hasn't yet been determined. You should remain calm. It will take some time, but it has been approved."

Schmidt managed to keep a straight face.

I had won! This was simply the greatest victory in my life! I had defeated the pigs! Nothing that had ever happened in my life was such a thrill, such a triumph! But I held it in in front of that arrogant bastard. I would give him no satisfaction if I could help it.

I nodded very calmly, very gently.

The approval did not mean that the bureaucratic process was over, not by any means. But it was an amazing turn of events. What had happened? Well, some powerful pressure had been exercised in the highest political circles of the GDR.

Months earlier, in December '86, Verschoth had contacted one of Europe's most powerful men, Berthold Beitz, chairman of the board of Krupp, for decades one of Germany's mightiest industrial corporations. Beitz had been a member of the IOC for fourteen years and a vice president for four years. Verschoth had gotten to know him well during her coverage of that body for *Sports Illustrated*. Through Krupp and the IOC, Beitz had made many high-level connections in East Germany. When Verschoth told him Schmidt's story, Beitz responded with enthusiasm. "I'll be traveling to the GDR sometime in January," he said. "I know the top guy quite well. Send me some background information."

Because of illness, Beitz didn't make his trip to the GDR until early April. When he returned, he told Verschoth that he had made inquiries about Schmidt with "the number two man" below Honecker in the government. "It is difficult," Beitz told her. "Call me again after Easter." Verschoth kept phoning him at regular intervals. On May 20, he told her that he had no answer yet about Schmidt's future, but that she should leave it to him and not bring anyone else in to try. "If anybody can help, it's me," he said. "Nobody knows these people like I do."

What Beitz did after that, Verschoth never knew. But when she saw him next, on July 14, it was at an IOC meeting in Lausanne. She walked up to him and said, "Have you anything new to report?" He said in a confidential tone, "It's all negative. Honecker said to me, 'Don't mention him.' " Then, Beitz winked, and as he walked away, he gave Verschoth a jaunty thumbs-up sign.

That happened on exactly the same day, July 14, that Wiedemann informed Schmidt that his exit visa had been approved.

Two days later on July 16, Wiedemann summoned Schmidt and his parents to the Sporthotel again. "First," the Stasi said quite cheerfully, "I can repeat, Wolfgang, that the application has been approved and is moving well and that none of you is to talk about it with anyone else. That is understood?"

The Schmidts nodded, and Wiedemann went on briskly, "Next, you must write a letter to SC Dynamc giving notice that you will be leaving your coaching job. Understood?"

They nodded. "And next"—he paused rather dramatically—

"next, you must surrender all of the decorations that you have received from the state for your previous success in sport. That includes the Fatherland's Order of Merit, of course. These are to be surrendered tomorrow at ten A.M. promptly to Comrade Wunderlich of the Central Administration Office of SC Dynamo Berlin. Understood?"

Schmidt agreed eagerly.

I would have given them anything to guarantee that I could leave that shithouse country. My house, my car, anything.

From that day in July forward, I began to train harder. I had always trained three, four days a week—with my National Guard charges, with my children—but I began to train more often and harder in order to build up my body, to get a head start for competition. Yes, I was thirty-three now, but for me, it was always an unquestioned fact: If they let me go, I would compete again. The first reason was that I loved my sport. Secondly, it was the best way for me to make a living. Through competitions, I could put money away, save a little here and there. Sure, I could have made it as a coach or a physical education teacher in the West, but I wanted to travel again, go to California, meet my friends again, compete with them. To me, that was the most beautiful life I could imagine.

The bureaucratic process continued to be painfully slow. Paper piled up. Schmidt made endless visits to an endless assortment of identically banal offices. The summer passed, fall arrived.

Late in September he left yet another useless meeting with yet another faceless bureaucrat at the Department of the Interior. He was alarmed to look in his rearview mirror to find a caravan of four Stasi cars following him. Why? Was it simply more harassment? He recalled that he had made a call to a friend in West Berlin from his home phone one week earlier to find out whether his phone was bugged. It looked as if it was.

They still tried to know everything about me. It was frightening. How was I to know what innocent act they might consider a crime that would cause them to cancel my permission to emigrate? I didn't try to outrun the cars. I drove slowly, legally, and eventually they left me alone. I was tense, always double-checking my behavior to be certain I offended no one.

Wiedemann summoned me again on October 27. I was afraid something had gone awry. But no. This time he only wanted me to sign a declaration promising that I would speak to no Western journalists once I left the GDR. I signed without a moment's hesitation.

Wiedemann looked at me. His beady eyes were bright as always, but he seemed tired all of a sudden. I could see that his fingernails were typically gnawed. He said to me with a sigh, "You will be departing soon. The one thing we don't want, Wolfgang, is a confrontation with you."

Good God, could I believe my ears? The all-powerful Stasi, the secret kings of East Germany, were telling me, Wolfgang Schmidt, that they wanted to avoid a confrontation with me! They were surrendering. To me!

The following day, at the Department of the Interior, Schmidt was told that his date of emigration had now officially been set for November 2, 1987.

SCHMIDT WAS TRAVELING WITH TWO SUITCASES
and a gym bag when he left the GDR, a man bent on starting a
new life with a minimum of baggage from the old.

My mother had asked me about taking china, linens, some things
I had bought on my trips West. Also my trophies. None of that
interested me. I wanted only to have a normal life in the West. To
me, a normal life meant one thing: training. So, the most important
things I packed were my weight-lifting belt, my throwing shoes, my
good competition discuses, and my training gear. I took my jeans
and my best T-shirts.

The night before he left, Schmidt celebrated, but he was tense.

I was only thinking, "Let's get out of this socialist cesspool." We
had a farewell party at the Hotel Stadt Berlin with my parents,

Bettina, and Aunt Christel, who lived in the same apartment house as my parents. It was a family party. Then I went to the Opern-Café, the disco I liked best then, and met my friends. Mario, his girlfriend, Heike, and other friends were there.

I was wired tight. I stayed up forever. I didn't sleep even three hours.

I was scheduled on a train that left about nine A.M., but first I had to take care of a problem. The state required that before I left, I had to return my ID card and pick up a certificate of discharge from my East German citizenship. I had to drive from my house to the office in Oranienburg, seven miles. I didn't oversleep that time. I got that business done, and then Wolfgang Blume drove me to the railroad station. Mario and Heike were there. And of course, my parents.

I felt I was existing in another dimension from everyone else at the station. My father was a bit soft. And my mother, well, we had no idea when we would see each other again. My parents were upset, but my friends envied me. I was just anxious, very anxious to get going, and my mind was locked on one thing and one thing only: I must start my daily training—now! That was all I could think of: Now I can begin to train *every* day. *Every* day! My sport would be everything again! The *only* thing! *Every* day!

He was rising from the dead to live again as an athlete. He was already thirty-three and more than six of his best competitive years were gone. There was no guarantee that he could reach even average levels of competition among the young and aggressive discus throwers who had grown up while he was gone.

His father watched with a sense of despair as Schmidt climbed into the train. "I thought to myself, Now he has been away from the sport for so long, away from high-level conditioning. He'll not be able to come back. He is probably finished. And I knew that was exactly what they believed at State Security, too. This was what they had wanted—to prevent him from ever competing again, and least of all for another country."

The train left at nine A.M. and Schmidt found himself in a car full of aged and retired people. In those days, men over sixty-five and women over sixty were allowed to travel regularly to the West. Schmidt attracted attention—not because of his fame as an athlete (that had waned and vanished in the passing years) but because of his youth.

An old man mistook him for a West German returning from a visit. "You are going back home then?" he asked.

Schmidt said quietly, "No, I am leaving home. Forever."

The old man looked at him with surprise, then shook his head slowly and said, "Well, well. You will need luck. It isn't easy to start over."

The train clattered noisily out of the station and headed west to the border at Marienborn, one hundred miles away.

I was just sitting there with all these old retired people. I was at a window, looking out. Suddenly I felt very hungry. The woman next to me unwrapped some sandwiches, and as if she had read my thoughts, she offered me one. I was grateful, and it seemed no time at all until we were at Marienborn. I was anxious about the border police. I figured they would go through my luggage, and I was smuggling one hundred and forty west marks out. Also I had brought some of my training records with me, some very recent, some from years before, and perhaps if they had found them, they'd have taken them away.

But the border police were friendly. One woman officer knew who I was and said, "Ah, you are leaving?" I said, "Yes!" emphatically. They were acting as if it were a nice, normal little thing to leave that rotten police state, as if I had simply decided I'd take a nice little vacation one day, instead of having to spend so many years clawing for space.

And then, without further restraint or restriction, Wolfgang Schmidt and the trainload of old people rolled west across the border.

It was a no-man's-land, acres of open ground crisscrossed with barbed wire. We rode through, and then we were in the West. It was that easy. Immediately, the train seemed to be traveling more quietly on the tracks. The houses were more colorful, the cars were bigger. The West German ticket inspector proved to be unfriendly, however, very grouchy as if he were thinking, These damned backward Easterners!

The train went from East Berlin to Marienborn and then to Hanover. In Hanover, I got off to transfer to the intercity train to Hamburg where my relatives were to meet me. I had to wait, alone with my suitcases, for half an hour on the platform. People were standing all around me. There were lots of people, it was crowded. But they were all somehow different. How would I put it? They were easier, more relaxed, unusually tranquil. I felt as if I had suddenly arrived at another planet.

When I got to Hamburg, it was getting dark. The train crossed a bridge over the Alster River and the lights were like necklaces, so many more lights than in the East. Then we rolled into the station.

I stepped down out of the train and my relatives were there. And oh, the welcome. It was all the warmer because for some reason they had expected me on an earlier train and had begun to wonder if, once more, the reports of my freedom were wrong. Peter [Walter] jumped up at me like a small boy and Marlene [Heinz] and her husband, Horst, and their daughter, my cousin Brigitta, all were full of tears.

I went a little soft then, too, and we drove in their BMW to Horst and Marlene's home and we toasted with champagne. It was a welcome that made me very happy, though inside I felt raw and excited. We telephoned my parents and then I slept like a child after an exhausting birthday party.

The next morning, Schmidt rose to the marvelously alien world of freedom. He went to a photo shop, had a passport picture made, then went directly to City Hall at Hamburg-Altona where he applied for a West German passport. Wonder of wonders, it was presented to him the very next day. He could leave the country anytime he wanted! He hurried immediately to the US embassy, applied for a visa to America, and had it stamped on the spot. Now he could travel whenever he wished to his own personal Valhalla—California, here I come!

Along with his own private freedom, Schmidt was also suddenly exposed to quite another kind of freedom—the freedom of the press to be insatiably, aggressively, maddeningly curious about people it deemed to be celebrities. From the first day, television news crews from ZDF, the West German TV network, and other broadcast outlets were on his trail. He was interviewed in Mainz on *Sport Studio,* a popular TV program, with his old friend and rival Alwin Wagner. There were radio interviews, newspaper stories, headlines, and photographs everywhere. Since Schmidt's arrival, Peter Walter had initiated negotiations with major publications to sell the rights to his story. He had contacted Horst Cronauer, a writer and editor for the tabloid *Bild,* and Klaus Blume of *Die Welt,* as well as editors of *Der Spiegel,* the country's largest weekly newsmagazine. (Verschoth had also contacted *Sports Illustrated,* but the editors were no longer interested in the story.)

After intense debate, Schmidt and the family had decided that the best deal was to sell exclusive rights to *Bild,* which had the biggest readership in West Germany. For a week, Schmidt went every day to the *Bild* offices and spent hours with Cronauer and a second writer, who wrote under the pseudonym Florian Zander. Initially, these intensive interviews were an emotional ordeal for Schmidt.

I was sick to my stomach during the first days, all that excitement and nervousness. I only drank tea and I lost some weight. The big problem was that I couldn't make myself trust the *Bild* people. In the East, I had always been told that you had to avoid all Western journalists like the plague. They were described as liars, the most deceitful of men. It took me a while to shed those beliefs, but once the stories began running in the paper, I knew I could trust the *Bild* writers. They were printing honest and truthful information about my life and about what had happened to me. I relaxed and my stomach problems went away. I ate mountains.

Bild ran a five-part series titled *Ein Held von drüben*—"A Hero From the Other Side." The stories attracted a large readership, and Schmidt soon began receiving letters from old friends of his and his father's who had defected to the West years before. He continued to appear on TV, and people began to recognize him on the street.

With the *Bild* money, he opened a checking account at a bank, a phenomenon that Peter, Horst, and Marlene had to explain at length because such things were utterly unknown in the East. His relatives also introduced him to yet another mystery of the Western world—the credit card.

Schmidt refused to let anything—publicity, fame, or his newfound wealth—steer him off his intended course. He began training the day after he arrived.

In the beginning, I ran to the bakery to buy fresh rolls, then home again. And after eating the rolls for breakfast, I ran in the park and then did some weight training. One day the weather was nice and warm for November, and I actually threw a discus in a stadium. I had the feeling that I was in pretty good shape. I needed to gain some more weight, but it wasn't bad. In the GDR, I had only trained a couple of times a week. Now when I began to train daily, my bones were hurting and I had sore muscles.

The next important thing on his agenda was to affiliate with a major sports club in the Federal Republic. This required negotiation, too. Some offered him more than others to join—such as guaranteed employment with a sponsoring corporation or perhaps a monthly stipend for food or perhaps a free apartment. They came after him in droves. Obviously they believed that the champion had not lost his prowess after so much time in limbo.

There were clubs after me from Hamburg, from Leverkusen, two from Frankfurt, one from Mainz, two from Stuttgart, one from Wolfs-burg—eight in all. And I listened to all of them. I spent one week traveling with Alwin Wagner, my expert on negotiating with sports clubs. He drove me all over West Germany on the autobahns—and so fast we went! Alwin took time to help because he wanted me to be integrated into the West in the best possible way. I learned a lot from Alwin.

The possibility for corporate employment as part of club membership particularly appealed to Schmidt. In Frankfurt, a club offered work with Hoechst, a big chemical company. In Leverkusen, the club offered work at Bayer, also a chemical firm, where he could have worked with a maintenance crew on electrical installations. In Stuttgart, both clubs offered him a job with Mercedes, but only one—the Kickers—also came up with a rent-free apartment (albeit a tiny one-bedroom basement unit), as well as a monthly food allowance. The training facilities were also good, so Schmidt said yes to the Kickers.

He moved to Stuttgart. His contract with Mercedes as a physical education teacher paid him a salary of two thousand marks [$1,000] a month and freed him from his job whenever he needed time to train. He also negotiated contracts with Adidas shoes and later with HLS, a leasing firm in Stuttgart. For a man born and bred to socialism, he was doing remarkably well in the hustling world of capitalism.

He trained diligently in Stuttgart for two months. Then he was ready to fly to the source of his dreams: California.

On February 1, 1988, he left Europe. Except for a one-hour stopover in Houston once in the late 1970s, it was his first visit to the US. The plane flew nonstop from Hamburg to New York City where Verschoth met him. They had barely embraced when he asked her if she had been able to arrange a place he could train every day. Yes, she had indeed arranged a workout schedule at the New York Athletic Club for weight lifting, and she had even found a gym at Manhattan College where he could put the shot for a few hours. While he was in New York, she bought him a dinner that included the biggest lobster he had ever laid eyes on and took him to the Millrose Games at Madison Square Garden. Nevertheless, Schmidt saw the glamorous Big Apple as just another place to unpack his gym bag for a few short workouts before he went to California.

Yes, New York was fascinating, and the five days I spent there were beautiful. But I was always thinking of training, only training. I had steeled myself before I left Stuttgart to stay away from temptations in the West. I had promised myself: Training, training, training— that is why you are in the West, Wolfgang, and that is all you should let into your life when you're there. I really didn't have much time, you see.

Mac Wilkins and Al Feuerbach met him at the San Francisco airport. Wolfgang instantly found everything about the sprawl of suburban California to be utterly intriguing. It was as if he had been born in the East Bay instead of East Berlin.

The dimensions of the San Francisco airport moved me—everything seemed so big, the gates, longer corridors, all so much larger than I had seen. And then the roads. I had flown several thousand miles, from Hamburg to New York to San Francisco, but the fifty miles we rode in Mac's car to San Jose on Interstate 280 were more exciting than any I had traveled. All the green freeway signs showing the way to Oakland and Los Angeles and how many miles it was. The lanes of fast-moving heavy traffic. The shopping centers. There were malls in Western Europe, but nothing like these in California I asked Mac to take me to downtown San Jose, but there is no downtown San Jose, of course, only malls. The first night Mac took me home and I slept on a waterbed!

Malls and waterbeds were only the beginning. Soon after his arrival, Schmidt did the most California thing of all: he bought a car.

Mac was always driving me around and I realized it was a burden for him. So I decided I needed a car to be free and independent. Mike Weeks [a former discus thrower] and I went looking. We went to a small used-car lot. I picked out this 1974 Cougar. It was a big machine that appealed to me. But I looked at the price on the sign. "Twelve thousand dollars," I said. "Oh, that's way too much."

I turned away from it to look for something else, but Mike said, "No, no, Wolfgang, it's only twelve hundred dollars."

I said, "It can't be. Twelve hundred is too cheap."

He insisted that I look again at the sign, and yes, it was twelve hundred dollars. A saleswoman came by and we took the Cougar for a drive. The steering was a little funny, loose, but I told her I liked the car and I said, "Okay, I take it, but I will only pay one thousand dollars."

She said okay, and I took the car. Sure, some things needed fixing and over the years I spent another fifteen hundred dollars on new tires and other things, but I always keep it in San Jose when I return to Europe.

Schmidt moved into a small house in San Jose with several other throwers, paying three hundred dollars a month for a room. He stayed for three months that first trip. He competed in a few meets around the US, and again, he was quick to adapt to the ways of a capitalistic society.

I had asked John Powell to take me with him to a couple of competitions in Florida. He thought about it, then called the organizers, who told him to bring me along. After the first meet, John gave me a check for five hundred dollars, and after the second meet, he gave me another check for five hundred dollars. I was amazed. I asked him how all this worked; he explained that we were paid appearance money by the organizers because our presence—our fame—was valuable and helped attract spectators. I was struck with the marvelous logic of the system.

Schmidt gained weight and polished his technique in the California throwers' paradise. When he returned to Stuttgart in early May, he was in splendid condition. He planned to compete in a number of meets in Europe that summer. By far the most important was a dual meet between West Germany and East Germany scheduled for June 19 and 20 in Düsseldorf. It had already attracted a lot of media coverage—largely because of a controversy over whether or not Schmidt would be allowed to compete for West Germany.

The East Germans—led by Manfred Ewald—had, of course, fought against his appearance in the meet, saying they would cancel the whole affair if Schmidt was allowed to throw.

Ernst Schmidt followed the controversy in the GDR and he recalled, "Wolfgang was clearly one of the best in the Federal Republic, but here was Ewald trying to dictate which athletes the FRG had on its team. Ewald had been enraged by the newspaper articles that appeared revealing the cruelties Wolfgang suffered by being in jail for fifteen months. He was trying to get back by blowing this situation all out of proportion."

To Schmidt's disgust, the president of the West German track-and-field federation, Eberhard Munzert, had promised the president of the East German track-and-field federation, Georg Wieczisk, that Schmidt would not compete.

When Munzert informed me of this, I told him that it was my right to compete. I knew that Munzert and other officials at the federation were not entirely delighted about my being on their team. I was a problem and they didn't like problems.

But of course, the media was fascinated with the injustice of it all—those pigs in the GDR trying to control my life after I had sprung free from their cage. I insisted on my rights. I told my story in the papers and on TV, and in the end it was the West German secretary of the interior, Friedrich Zimmermann, an important man in the Kohl government, who decided that I would be allowed to compete.

Because of Zimmermann's decision, Munzert resigned his presidency a couple of months later.

In the years he had been in limbo, a new crop of young discus throwers had risen around the world. In Düsseldorf, Schmidt was to compete for the first time against the brightest star of them all. He happened to be an East German: Jürgen Schult, then twenty-eight years old, a grim young man, cast perfectly in the mold of the stoic, obedient socialist soldier that the East German regime liked so well.

Until 1986, Schult had been more or less a journeyman performer. He had never thrown as far as 70 meters in competition. Then on June 6, 1986, he had suddenly broken the world record with a herculean throw of 74.08 meters—243'½". Many thought the record was a fluke. Mac Wilkins recalled, "His next-best throw in competition that year was 214 feet. We thought he might have been terrifically lucky, that maybe he was a one-night sensation. He was seventh in the European championships in 1986, but then in 1987 he won the world championship, and in 1988, he won the Olympic gold medal. When he set the record, he was really not that good, but since then he showed that he definitely deserved to be the world-record holder."

Wolfgang had been training under proper conditions in the West for only seven months when he went up against Schult in Düsseldorf. No one expected him to defeat Schult, and he didn't. Schult threw 67.40 meters—221'1½". The West German champion, Rolf Danneberg, threw 66.54 meters, 218'4". Schmidt finished third with 63.32 meters—207'9".

We were on the victory stand, the three of us, and I held out my hand to Jürgen Schult and said, "Congratulations." He wouldn't accept my handshake. He kept his hands at his sides. He glared at me. He looked down at the ground. He was very uncomfortable. He said nothing. I laughed and kept offering him my hand. There was no response at all.

I suppose he was not allowed to shake my hand, but at least he could have said to me, "Sorry, I can't" or at least a simple "*Danke schön*." But he didn't. I must say that he seemed to enjoy playing the role of the hard socialist hero who defeated an enemy of the state.

After the meet in Düsseldorf where the GDR easily defeated the FRG 250.5 points to 151.5, Schmidt was more sharply aware than ever of the great difference between athletes in the West and those in the East.

The system in the West was shocking in comparison. In the GDR, I just had to arrive at ten A.M. and all would be prepared for me. In the West, I have to organize everything myself. I have to motivate myself, I have to drive myself. If I don't go to a workout, no one cares, nobody is waiting to chew my ear about it. The Americans have no system at all. No money from the government, no structure of sports clubs, no doctors who specialize in sports. It is a little better in West Germany, but essentially I am my own engine.

Yet even without the Miracle Machine, Schmidt was performing with increasing power and consistency. In the summer of '88, he broke the eleven-year-old West German discus record with a throw of 68.22 meters—223'10"—and he competed in 30 international meets, winning 17 of them and only once finishing worse than third.

The Olympic Games lay ahead, scheduled from September 17 to October 2 in Seoul. Eight long, awful years had passed since his last Olympic appearance in Moscow. He could not have competed in Los Angeles in 1984 even if he had been in good standing because of the Eastern Bloc boycott.

I have to admit that I gloated a little in 1984. I knew all the East German athletes were hurting because they couldn't go, but since I couldn't go anyway, I basked in their bad luck. The boycott was so stupid. Just like kindergarten: One kid slaps another kid and that kid slaps him back.

But there were no boycotts to spoil the 1988 games, and Schmidt yearned to compete. He was not allowed.

There were two rules in his way. The first was an IOC regulation that required any competitor who switched countries to reside in his new country for at least one year before the Games in order to be eligible for its Olympic team. Schmidt's residence in West Germany would fall six weeks short of one year when the Seoul games began—a fact that he firmly believed was the main reason the GDR had delayed so long in allowing him to leave for the West. He was also blocked from competing by a rule of the IAAF requiring that an athlete had to reside in his new country for *three* years before he was eligible for international championships. The IAAF allowed the three-year waiting period to be waived if the federation of the country the athlete departed was willing to file an affidavit stating that it had no objection to his competing for another nation. The sports despots of the GDR had no intention of giving Wolfgang Schmidt permission to compete for anyone.

So he was a man without an Olympic team.

I kept complaining about the rules, the unfairness of keeping me out of the games. In order to keep the matter in the public eye, I kept protesting. But to be honest, I was so happy to be in the West that I wasn't really that upset. Furthermore, I probably had no chance to win a medal in Seoul.

But he persuaded *Bild* to pay for half an airline ticket and he paid for the other half and he went to Seoul anyway. To old friends—including Verschoth, who was covering the games, and Wilkins, who was competing—Schmidt seemed to be in a constant state of agitation. Sometimes, he ranted loudly through dinner, raising his voice so that nearby diners were disturbed by his shouting. At one point he ran into Juan Antonio Samaranch, the imperious president of the IOC. A brisk conversation ensued.

Schmidt said, "I am Wolfgang Schmidt."

Samaranch said, "Yes, I know who you are." He paused, then cocked an eyebrow and said, "What are you doing here anyway?"

Schmidt shrugged. "I am sitting in the stadium watching the discus competition. What else can I do?"

A photographer from *Bild* shot a picture of the Olympic outcast standing next to the Olympic potentate and the encounter was over.

Schmidt stayed in an apartment arranged by his benefactor, Bud Greenspan, who was producing the official Olympic film. His roommate for a time was Brian Boitano, the American who had won the gold medal for figure skating at the 1988 Winter Olympics in Calgary.

I knew who he was, but he didn't know me. We got along just fine—two different worlds, two different sports.

Schmidt managed to obtain tickets to a number of events, including the most painful of all—the discus throw.

Of course, I kept my fingers crossed for Mac, but I doubted he could win it [he finished fifth]. I might have pulled against that Red ass

Schult if there had been any suspense in the competition. But his first throw was already so far [68.82 meters or 225'9½"] that I knew nobody would beat him. Sure, I was troubled at all times as I watched. Sure, I believed that I should have been there on the field, throwing.

How might he have fared in that competition? Wilkins said, "Wolfgang definitely could have made the finals in Seoul. The thing about him is that he is a perfect throwing machine. Nothing clutters his mind except his athletic priorities. He had had enough training to be in very good condition—not his best, but very good. I think he could have finished in the top five. He could even have been fourth. He would have been right there."

Once the strange and painful journey to Seoul was over, Schmidt again returned to intensive training in Stuttgart. He also took up with a beautiful Swedish cosmetician named Pia Nilsson, whom he had met in Malmö, Sweden, through Ricky Bruch. Eventually, Pia moved into his apartment. Life was pretty good. Schmidt was making an adequate income from his various jobs and endorsements—the Mercedes connection being the most valuable both in terms of present income and future potential as a full-time employee. He was more relaxed and better focused than he had been at any time since the Stasi arrested him.

In 1989 he won the overall Grand Prix circuit in the discus (a series of competitions sponsored by Mobil Oil). He competed in 30 meets, won 22, finished second in seven and third in one. He also produced the best throw in the world for the year, a splendid effort of 70.92 meters, or 232'8", less than a foot short of the world-record throw he had made an eon ago in 1978. He finished ranked number two in the world. Unfortunately, number one was the crude young man from East Germany. Jürgen Schult was a goad to Wolfgang Schmidt, but he also appealed to Schmidt's sense of humor.

The East German had entered only three of the 1989 Grand Prix meets, one of them in East Berlin, because the GDR authorities were still reluctant to let their stars compete frequently in the West. He turned up to compete against Schmidt in Edinburgh, and in Monaco, where the final Grand Prix competition was held in September. He defeated Wolfgang both times and tried to ignore him completely at the victory ceremonies both times.

At Monaco, Schmidt tried to shake hands again to no avail. He laughed at Schult and said, "You are such a Red ass." The East German later claimed Schmidt had called him "a Communist swine," but Schmidt insisted that, no, the term was definitely "Red ass" although he admitted that "Communist swine" was a pretty good substitute and maybe he would use it next time. Later, after The Wall had fallen, Schult told *Deutsches Sportecho*, an East Berlin sports newspaper, "In all, we competed three times. He pestered me every time. He called me a 'Communist swine.' I stick to that and I am done with him. However, I must say that when I didn't shake hands with him in Düsseldorf, that was not my decision. That was the decision of Professor Röder from the DTSB and Walter Gröger of the Central Committee of the Communist Party. If it had been left to me, I would have accepted Wolfgang's congratulations."

The presence of Schult as a foe in the political arena as well as an opponent in the discus ring perhaps added some fuel to Schmidt's competitive fire for a while. But in the time since The Wall came down, the fierce animosity between them has eased somewhat. They have actually shaken hands from time to time.

Schmidt was performing measurably better against Schult in the summer of 1990, winning five decisions. Only once Schult turned the tables and defeated Wolfgang in the European championships in Split, Yugoslavia. Schmidt had been the favorite and had certainly seemed superior to the East German early in the competition. He had gotten into the finals with a single qualifying throw on August 31 of 64.84 meters (212'9"), the best of the day—and the best of the meet as it turned out. Schult made the final with a throw of 62.50 meters (205'1"), which was only the seventh-best qualifying mark.

The next day the final was nip and tuck. Schult threw 63.70 meters (209') in his fifth of six attempts. Schmidt came up last of the eight finalists for his fifth throw and flung the discus 64.10 meters (210'4"). That put him second by fourteen inches to the surprise leader, Erik De Bruin of the Netherlands, and sixteen ahead of Schult. On his last-round attempt Schult produced a powerful last-ditch throw of 64.58 meters (211'10½") to go into first place. Neither De Bruin nor Schmidt could do better on their sixth and final attempts, so Schult got the gold, De Bruin the silver, and Schmidt the bronze.

Schmidt was furious at the result. He kept repeating, "Schult! For God's sake, of all people! Schult!" At the medal ceremony, he stood on the victory stand below the winner and was forced to listen to the East German anthem. He turned to look up at Schult and snarled, "It makes me sick to have to listen to that thing one more time." Schult smirked and said, *"C'est la vie."*

No matter what happened in the future, that was the last time Schmidt—or anyone else—would hear the anthem of the GDR at a track meet. Indeed, it was Schmidt's and Schult's last appearance as members of opposing German teams. With reunification an accomplished fact on October 3, 1990, they officially became teammates—if not bosom buddies—on a single combined German team that came into official existence on November 24.

Even though slightly more than a year had passed since The Wall had fallen, the idea of East and West German athletes competing together still seemed outrageous and unreal. But it could not be denied. What had been for four decades the natural order of things in the world had simply vanished overnight. Throughout Eastern Europe, loyal supporters of socialism had been forced to face for the first time the full extent of the corruption and deception practiced by their leaders. Ernst Schmidt was no exception. Shocked and angry, he tore up his party card in January 1990: "I came to the conclusion that socialism was an unusable experiment and a hindrance to the development of any country that had subscribed to this ideology." The aging "activist of the first hour" spoke with consuming bitterness.

In retrospect, Ernst saw the revolution of 1989 as an inevitable outgrowth of the oppressive ways of the regime he had once revered: "The worsening economic situation, the travel restrictions, the way we were treated like children by the state—all that had become insufferable for everyone in the GDR—except for those who belonged to the Stasi."

And what of the vast and costly sports system to which he devoted his life? Was this, too, another insufferable element of socialist policy? Ernst said, "It was given incredible financial support because it was supposedly the showpiece of 'real socialism.' But all of this was an enormous financial burden on the people. No country in the world could have afforded it, and this poor country least of all. But sport in the GDR played a leading role in the world during those years, and the great number of medals won were a result of this system. My life's work has been justified by the great success we had. Perhaps we could have been as successful with fewer people, spending fewer marks, but we will never know. It is over."

Indeed it was. The citizens of what had been East Germany, faced with economic chaos and an unpromising short-term future, had no interest at all in putting up their meager marks to pamper athletes anymore. And certainly their new countrymen in the West had no such desire. In its best days, the GDR's system devoured 1.1 billion government marks—about $700 million—every year. By contrast, the government contribution to the sports budget in West Germany was one-twentieth of that. Citizens of the GDR had supported an army of 592 full-time coaches for track and field. West German tax money paid for exactly 17. The fuel for the Miracle Machine had dried up forever—both cash and talent. The nineteen *Kinder- und Jugendsportschulen* with their 3,500 elite young athletes and the twenty-four sports clubs that formed the foundation of the mighty system would either be greatly reduced in number or dismantled for good. The huge state-operated steroids-dispensing system was out of business, and the vast network of sports doctors had vanished. No one could afford to pay for it anymore.

Looking back, the people of East Germany seemed to feel no

sense of loss. Their attitude was one of resentment and disdain toward their formerly adored superstars. Even a onetime darling such as Katarina Witt, the great figure skater, drew their wrath. An article in March 1990 in the West German magazine *Sports* reported, "Her fans say that through her performances and her charm, she enhanced a washed-out regime; she allowed herself to be bought through privileges; she remained silent for too long. After all, she called Honecker 'Erich' and he called her 'Kati.' Since the change, the cold wind of the revolution is blowing into Witt's face."

Nevertheless, even without the largess the GDR lavished on its athletes, some people thought that joining two German Olympic teams into one just might produce another athletic blitzkrieg—perhaps one that was even more powerful than the one East Germany had built. At the Seoul Olympics, these people pointed out, the East Germans won 102 medals and the West Germans won 40. If they had been united, the reasoning goes, the medal totals would have been Germany 142, the USSR 132, and the US 94. It is a provocative theory, but it could not have happened that way. Each of the two Germanys in Seoul competed with the full complement of athletes in each event, meaning they had twice the number of competitors they will be allowed to field in future Olympics.

Undoubtedly the combined teams of Germany will be very strong for a while. In the 1992 Olympics, Germans could well surpass the previously all-powerful Soviets, who have their own problems paying for an expensive state-supported sports system. Nevertheless, it is safe to say that there will not be another machine—German or any other nationality—like the East German machine for a long time to come, if ever. The ruthless efficiency and absolute obedience required to make such a system work will not function in a democracy. Only a totalitarian police state could drive and maintain such a juggernaut.

Despite this ugly truth, even a man as badly used by the system as Wolfgang Schmidt could admire it for its pure, cold mechanics.

It's a pity in a way that it had to go. It was a perfect machine that supplied such good products. Just as Mercedes produces beautiful cars, the sports machine produced beautiful athletes—although many were without brains.

But what of those beautiful athletes? What might become of them?

They have been embedded in that system for a long time. They are still bound up with old socialist habits. Some will adjust, but I don't know whether they can stay at the top.

I was in the GDR at Christmas '89—the first time I could go back because The Wall was down and the Stasis were no longer in charge. They all came running again, the teammates and the people who had avoided me when I was in trouble. I told my parents, "Listen, I don't want to have anything to do with them. I now live somewhere else. I have other problems. They are just curious. And who was on my side before? I know of no one who stood up."

Mother understood this, but Father was saying, "Come on, come on, let up on them."

Udo Beyer was the first to call. I didn't want to take the phone, but I finally talked to him. He had been retired, but now he said he wanted to compete again. He said he had started to train again. He asked me about competing in the West and especially how they conducted doping control. Well, I could understand that he wanted to benefit from my experience.

But look, I remember what has happened. In Düsseldorf during the dual meet, Udo didn't look at me. Now he was stealing my time, trying to take my knowledge, digging around in my experiences. They would all like to do that. But I don't care what happens to them. Chapter East is finished for me. I am not looking back.

At the European championships in Split last summer, members

of the team from the GDR were not looking back either. Quite the contrary. They performed as if there were only tomorrow ahead—and they were awesome. Heike Drechsler, the great long jumper and sprinter, won a gold and a silver in Split. She gave credit to the dismantled Miracle Machine because "it made me what I am." But, she said, "My greatest motivation now is to produce a high-level performance because my financial future on the all-German team will be at stake." What was at stake in Split was *Sporthilfe,* meaning the money paid to top-ranked German athletes—not by the government, but by commercial sponsors of the unified team. How athletes finished in Split would dictate how much they would be paid under the West German system that would prevail in the future. Ulf Timmermann, the gold medalist in the shotput in Seoul and winner of the gold in Split, had no doubts about how priorities would be set up in the years ahead: "The issue is no longer political prestige. This is the beginning where you have to establish your worth on the market."

Performing for the last time in their familiar light-blue uniforms with the hammer and circle emblem on the chest, members of the team showed no regrets, no grief that their country's monumental string of successes was at an end. No East German wept on the victory stand, save for one distraught javelin thrower who had finished third when she should have won the competition. True to their tough character, the last track team to compete under the colors of the GDR went out and absolutely demolished the competition. East Germans won twelve gold, twelve silver, and ten bronze, a total of thirty-four medals. Great Britain had a surprising nine golds, five silvers, four bronzes (eighteen in all), and the fading superpower, the USSR, had six gold, nine silver, seven bronze (twenty-two in all).

West Germany was sixth in the national standings with just three golds, two silvers, and two bronzes (seven). Demoralized members of the FRG team—particularly the women—were shattered by the certain knowledge that they were about to be shoved aside by the powerhouse from the East.

Yet the best and the brightest of those who had been molded

and trained in the East German sports machine had little hope that the phenomenal success they achieved in Split could continue for more than a couple of years. Drechsler said, "Top athletes who continue to perform won't have any problems, but the up-and-coming youngsters will have trouble because there will be no financial support for them. Germany will have a good team in 1992, but I fear for the worst after that. Much is being destroyed, and no efforts are being made to save what was good in GDR sport." A leading coach of East German sprinters, Thomas Springstein, put it even more darkly: "The political change meant that we had to change our way of thinking. We had to become independent and we did, and now we have succeeded better than ever—for the moment. But there are factors that will disturb athletic development. Coaches will lose their jobs. Money will be scarce. Young talents will not find support as it was in the GDR. Everything will be like it has been in the Federal Republic—no selection system for youngsters, few full-time coaches. Perhaps we can conceal this lack of support until 1996. But after that the all-German track team will become mediocre, like the West German team is now, and I am very sad about that."

The curtain had fallen on an unforgettable era in world sport. There were no athletic blitzkriegs to come, only talented individuals competing against each other.

Wolfgang Schmidt remained absolutely determined to be the best of anyone he happened to be competing against. In the first meet after the defeat in Split, he returned to top form, hurling the discus 65.90 meters (216'2½") in Koblenz to demolish Jürgen Schult, who was fourth. When the 1990 season came to an end several weeks later, Schmidt had competed in twenty-three meets and he had won no fewer than *twenty* of them, finishing second once and third twice. *Track & Field News,* the world authority in the sport, ranked him number one for the year among all discus throwers.

This was phenomenal for an athlete of thirty-six who had been sentenced to death as a competitor more than eight years before. But Schmidt was just as cocky and casual about this triumph as he had been during his maverick years in the GDR.

No, I was not surprised to be number one. I was the best. I was the most consistent. Okay, I had a bad day at Split, but otherwise I was the king. This is what I expected when I kept telling Wiedemann that I had no choice but to continue in performance sport. This is what I meant to have happen when they let me out at last. No, I am not surprised.

But how did he do it? Mac Wilkins, said: "Wolfgang drives himself just as hard as he did twelve years ago. He simply will not recognize his age. Why does he keep on? First of all, he does it because he *can* do it. To be ranked number one in the world at the age of thirty-six is very impressive. He loves his sport and he does well financially because of it. Those are the main reasons for his exceptional drive. Certainly, Schult motivates Wolfgang, too, but not as much as the other factors. It is by no means an outrageous idea that Wolfgang could beat Schult and win the gold at the Olympics in Barcelona. There's nothing on earth he wants more than that."

Schmidt badly wanted to win a gold medal, all right, and he might well do it in Barcelona. But here was a man who had already won a far greater victory than the Olympics could offer. He had survived the worst a cruel and paranoid regime could do to break his spirit and ruin his physique. He had never flagged in his determination to compete in high-level sport again. He had never stopped fighting for his right to leave the GDR. And in the end, when he had at last been thrown free by men who were convinced they had destroyed him as a world-class discus thrower, he quite literally resurrected himself and became the best in the world again.

No gold medal could match what Wolfgang Schmidt had already won. But he was bound to continue.

It is hard, but this is how I live. I have to think about making money, about security in the future. I have to stay in the sport and I have to compete to be secure. Maybe I won't be the big champion every year, but I'm still good enough so I can earn the money.

Barcelona is a long, hard way. I wish I were ten years younger, but I have to try as long as it is possible. There is pain in my knees and pain in my back. But I am one who likes to have success. I'm not a loser type. When I compete, I mean to win.